Milton Shaw

Joseph W. Shaw

# Joseph T. Shaw
## The Man Behind

## Milton Shaw

BLACK MASK
2019

This story of the life of Joseph Thompson Shaw is dedicated to Joe and Sandy, and our families. It is the legend of a remarkable man, a legacy that is deeply cherished.

Milton Shaw
24 May 2004

# Table of Contents

# Introduction

IT WAS January 1952, Nan and I had finished packing the car in readiness for our impending trip to the West Coast. Our destination was to be Camp Pendleton, California. This post was the staging area for Marines being funneled into the First Marine Division, a combat organization that was in its second year of fighting in that three year "forgotten" war in Korea. Nan and I had been married the previous June, and Nan was now pregnant with our first child. Our decision was to stay together as long as we could before I shipped out from San Diego with the eighteenth replacement draft.

It was now time to say goodbye to my mother and father. As my father and I embraced, I looked into his face and the thought flashed through my mind that we would never see each other again in this life. Because of the relatively high attrition rate of Marine second lieutenants, I sensed that I would precede my father in death. I was correct in my assessment that one of us would perish before we had the opportunity to be together again, but I was wrong as to who would precede whom in death. On August 1, 1952, my father died of a coronary thrombosis. He was seventy-eight years old.

Although there was a vast disparity in our ages, my father was fifty-three when I was born. I never knew my father as an old man, rather, as a very close friend. No single individual has had a more profound impact on my life than my father. We were father and son, but more than that, we were best friends. Both my mother and my wife Nan have been two major influences as to who I am and where life's paths have taken me; however, the significance of my father's influence on my life was during those formative years when I was a young person struggling to find myself and establish my identity.

When the Red Cross representative informed me of my father's death, among the many thoughts passing through my heart and mind was the realization that Dad and I had been together for only twenty-five years. Yes, I was grateful for that time together, but I regretted the fact that even though we knew and understood each other from a personal point-of-view I was only aware of bits and pieces of his professional life. My father never talked about his accomplishments; his interest and energies were always focused on me, my growth, my needs.

Another mitigating factor in my lack of knowledge of this facet of my father's life was that at age seventeen, as World War II was winding down, I enlisted in the Marine Corps. This step was the start of a journey that kept me away from home, except for periodical leave and liberty visits, for the next twelve years. One benefit from this absence was that my father and I corresponded by letter. Especially important is the fact that, for the five-month period I spent in Korea prior to his death, the weekly letters have been saved. As I reread these letters after not having seen them for forty-nine years, as expected, they contained no information about my father's work-life even though at age seventy-eight he was still commuting to work in New York City on a daily basis. What the contents did reflect were observations of our respective environments, and my father's continued words of advice and guidance.

My father left with us what he referred to as a "rambling" auto-biography that was probably written in the late 1920s or early 1930s. It reads as follows:

I was born in Gorham, Maine, May 8, 1874, of the eighth generation on American soil of the descendants of Roger Shaw who sailed over here sixteen years after the *Mayflower* docked. It happens that one member of this line took part in each war of the country, and while I cannot claim a great part in sending Wilhelm to Doorn, at least I had the honor of maintaining the family tradition in the World War. The direct lineage on my mother's side goes back to the family of Thomas a Becket, an uncle of Thomas of Canterbury. And, since, we are told, Gilbert married a Saracen princess, I have often wondered if a drop of the Saracen blood, persisting through the centuries, has been responsible for the very devil of a conflict I have constantly experienced between a desire for the sea and roaming adventure and the Yankee instinct to attend to business. I have wondered also if it gave me preference in reading for romance and adventure over philosophy and psychology and my willingness, indeed, to draw my philosophy from adventure and romance.

I commenced my attendance at school at the rather early age of three-and-a half, walking a mile or so for that rather dubious pleasure, and kept at it for seventeen years or so, graduating at Bowdoin where I majored in every form of athletics in the college curriculum. It has been said that we of Anglo-Saxon derivation possess a hereditary instinct for the bow and arrow. I know at least that my choice of all weapons has been a sword. As a boy a stick felt natural in my grasp; striking and guarding a matter almost of intuition. This may explain why I was able to win the national championship in sabers, after a little more than a year of instruction in that weapon, and the president's medal for the championship in all three weapons, foil, épée and saber.

Analogous to my tendency for roaming, my preference for an occupation has always been for that of writing. This too was subjected to the same conflict with business. If I prepared for anything in college, where I was editor of the college periodical, it was for the writing game. On graduation I went immediately to a New York metropolitan daily and from that to a semi-trade weekly of which I became editor. A tempting business opportunity presented itself and I was associated with other business enterprises until the war broke out. During that earlier period I found opportunity to write short stories, a more or less technical history of one of the country's industries and a book of impressions of Spain.

Before my own chance came, I specialized in training pre-draft men and in bayonet instruction with some of the national army units. Commissioned as Captain I went over in 1918. On the Armistice I was offered the post of athletic director of the Ninth Corps, in the Army of Occupation. It was so tempting I refused it and went instead to Czechoslovakia as chief of a Hoover Mission. My experience there was of a Graustark variety with practically unlimited power with respect to anything I wanted. My technique was very simple. In a country impoverished of the necessities of life by four years of war and plunder, I employed the slogan of the starving child and used the mighty weapons of the army commissariat. Racial editors, who had been forever fighting each other with drawn knives and no quarter asked or given, met at my board and for the first time in four years tasted white bread, butter, bacon and cream. Under the influence of their first cigarettes in that period they shook hands in the common cause. They and the hungry child did the business. An entirely new and all-embracing organization was put over that included the president, all members of the political government and the heads of every religious order. The food for the purpose was 'somewhere on the ocean.' A hundred odd tons were requisitioned elsewhere and within five weeks their own organization was feeding daily 400,000 children.

"I remained in the country nearly five years and had the unique opportunity of observing and studying the birth and first infantile steps of a republic. Tempting business opportunities obtruded on every hand. A recurrence of an illness contracted in the war sent me to the mountains and gave opportunity for meditation. Business and the mere acquisition of wealth had lost their flavor. I turned seriously to writing. I brought back two unforgettable souvenirs. The lesser is a sculptured marble group of a Slovakian peasant mother and two children, the gift of the Republic. The first and paramount is—Mrs. Shaw.

My training in writing in the past few years has been most intensive. I became editor of *Black Mask* in 1926. In creating a new form of detective fiction, in developing a magazine of quality in its field, and incidentally in trebling the output, the opportunity for study has been a rare one of which I have sought to avail myself. Reading has always been a passion with me, vying with the appeal of the out-of-doors. As a boy I absorbed everything within two covers upon which I could lay my hands. By fourteen I had read all of Scott's, a mass of miscellaneous works of American and English authors and a fair share of classics. What I especially liked I read with memory—and often some for which I did not care.

My dislikes run to cant and loafing of mind or body. My hobby is for the primitive—a tent, a campfire, a pipe, with perhaps a canoe at hand—or the tiller or wheel of a boat on the open sea. My philosophy is summed up mainly by a word of four letters meaning work.

In the ensuing years since my father's death I have become far more aware of the diversity of his professional accomplishments. With this increasing awareness comes an increased feeling of responsibility to document these achievements, to memorialize the impact his life had on many others in addition to his family. This is his legacy.

One of the great challenges of this endeavor will be to reconstruct documentation from my father's personal files that was apparently allowed to slip out of the family's possession by my mother who, in my absence, benevolently donated them to various groups and organizations. I am also plagued with that universal thought: If only I had asked more questions of my mother and father pertaining to the history of our family.

So, Dad, in spite of the many gaps that have not been closed, thank you for the fullness and richness of life that you have made possible for those of us who were left behind. When we next meet again, you know the questions I will be asking.

Captain Joseph T. Shaw in Prague.

# 1
# From the Highlands of Scotland

ONE'S LINEAGE and the environment to which one is exposed seem to be the major determining factors as to who an individual is and what that individual becomes. My father's forefathers on both his mother's and father's side came from England. On or about 1632, Roger Shaw arrived in Massachusetts, settled in Cambridge and then, very shortly thereafter, re-established himself in Hampton, New Hampshire. Following in the footsteps of their first progenitor in this country, the next four generations built homesteads in and around Hampton. Ebenezer Shaw, fourth generation, initially established residence in Hampton, but then moved to Standish, Maine, thus initiating what is called the Standish Branch of the Roger Shaw lineage. Three generations later my grandfather was born in Standish but chose to move to Gorham, Maine, where my father was born and lived until such time as he started wandering. My father represented the eighth generation of the Roger Shaw family in this country.

The ancestors on my grandmother's side of the family came to the Colonies from England in the mid-to-late 1630s, and settled in the Newberry-Essex area of Massachusetts. Nellie Morse was a seventh generation American, also born in Gorham, where she met and married my grandfather Milton Shaw. Thus the confluence of two American families took place.

Tracing the lineage of these two families back to England is informative. From my grandfather Milton, the seventh generation Shaw in this country, the Shaw surname comes to a dead-end with Ralph Shaw, Roger Shaw's father. What has yet to be established is the linkage between Ralph Shaw and his ancestors who came from the Scottish Highlands. On the other hand, tracing my grandfather Milton's ancestry using surnames other than Shaw, ten generations who lived on English soil can be identified extending back to John Sulyard who was born about 1304, in Of Eye, Suffolk. With respect to my grandmother Nellie Kimball Morse, her roots can be traced back to seven generations in America and two on English soil to the period around 1600.

Returning again to the descendants from the Scottish Highlands to the Ralph Shaw family, it is not too presumptuous to state that most all Shaws had their roots in Scotland. First of all, "shaw" is a Scottish word meaning a coppice that is further defined as a thicket, grove or growth of small trees. This definition would seem to identify land areas in the lowlands of Scotland; however, the tract of land that had been designated by the inhabitants of Scotland as "The Shaw" was in the Highlands. Excerpts from the fine book written by Harriett F. Farewell, *Shaw Records, a Memorial of Roger Shaw, 1594–1661* are revealing.[1] She states that the tradition among the Shaws of America, which had been handed down from their respective ancestors and who were immigrants to this country during the earlier Colonial period of its existence, is that Scotland was the mother country from which this hardy race first sprang. It is from Scotland that many of her sons fled during the troublesome period of Charles I of England, Scotland and Ireland. The arrogant, stiff-necked King undertook to substitute and establish the Church of England (Episcopalian) in Scotland where the Presbyterian order had been so firmly rooted, and was, indeed, established by law of the Scottish Parliament years before and confirmed by James V. Furthermore, it was Charles

---

1    Harriette F. Farwell, *Shaw Records, A Memorial of Roger Shaw, 1594–1661* (Bethel, Maine: E.C. Bowler, 1904).

who, in addition to attempting to foist his religion on Scotland, exacted many other concessions from both Scotland and England too unreasonable to be borne, which resulted in his overthrow and the usurping of the government by Cromwell. "The tradition has also been religiously kept in each of the various ancestral lines of American Shaws, that these immigrants were from the 'Highlands of Scotland' originally, although some were known to have been residents of England long previous to their coming to America." [2]

Clan Shaw is not a sept or branch of any other clan. It has a close historical relationship with Clan MacIntosh in many ways, including the fact that the Shaws were the early chiefs of Clan MacIntosh prior to using Shaw as the family last name and the name of the clan. Nonetheless, Clan Shaw was not a part of Clan MacIntosh but, rather, one of the clans that banded together in a confederation of clans known as Clan Chattan. Genealogists assent to the tradition that the "Shaws" are descended from one of the sons of MacDuff, third earl of Fife. Surnames were not in common use until the latter part of the tenth century; the son of MacDuff received his surname in either 1056 or 1057 as a result of aid given to Malcolm III, the rightful heir to the Scottish throne, in overthrowing MacBeth. It is a reasonable conclusion that the name of Shaw originated with this son of MacDuff; further, that the early Shaws of England were, in reality, MacDuff descendants who had originated in England either before or after the partial dispersion of Clan Shaw of Scotland. [3]

Before exploring the families descended from Roger Shaw, some of the traits or inherited characteristics brought to this country by those of Scottish descent and particularly those who came from the Highlands can be identified. These traits were

---

2    *Ibid.*, pp, 13–14.

3    *Ibid.*, p. 14.

created in the crucible of conflict with both the environment and those with whom wars were waged. Examining clan mottos they aptly describe many of these traits. For example, "Qui Vincet Patitur" (He who endures Conquers) or "Fide et Fortitudine" (by Faithfulness and Fortitude or Bravery). These mottos are very declarative of the expectations the Scots have for themselves. Kenneth MacLeish expresses the many characteristics he sees and senses in the Scottish Highlanders. The clans were tribes, blood related, living in their own territories, growing and making what they needed, and raiding each other for fun and profit. The gaunt mountains, haunting glens and serene lochs of its Highland domain produce a people proud of their heritage, fiercely independent, and joyful in their love of music and poetry. The intertwining of loch and land proclaim the Highland spirit, a spirit of independence born of solitude. Their love of music is embodied in the stirring skirl of their bagpipes that once led clan against clan and inspired British troops in every corner of the world. Also unique to these people is the traditional absence of class sub-divisions of Highland society. The Highlander thinks himself as good as the next man, and he is usually right. In sum, the Scottish Highlanders can lay claim to many sterling qualities that have given them staying power over the centuries. Integrity, a directness when dealing with others, trustworthiness, courage in battle, extreme loyalty, and an abiding faith in Jesus Christ define the Highlander.[4] These qualities serve as the base that produces the fierce pride and indomitable spirit that are their hallmarks, the very traits that have been carried down through the ages to the Shaw descendants in this country.

---

4    Kenneth MacLeish, "The Highlands, Stronghold of Scottish Gaeldom," *National Geographic,* Vol. 133, No. 3, March 1968, pp. 398–435.

Hana Muskova and Joe Shaw, Štrbské Pleso, Slovakia.

# 2
# To the Shores
# of New England

FROM THE preceding pages, expectations from those of Scottish blood can be identified. But what about those Scots who came to the new world by way of England, or whose background had been English over the course of one or more centuries, what factors or forces dictated who they were and why they chose to come to America? Freedom from religious persecution would seem to be the most dominant force. It was around 1536 that King Henry VIII started to take away the power of the Roman Catholic Church and to replace it with the Church of England. Although this was a momentous step forward by virtue of removing control of the Church in England from external sources, for many members of the Church of England this was only a first step.

For centuries the Roman Catholic Church dominated the affairs of Great Britain as well as the great majority of countries in Western Europe. By removing the influence and power of the Catholic Church in England, the Church of England (the Anglican Church) came more under the control of the King and his officials. To consider relinquishing control to individual churches was a concept that was unthinkable at that time, not only by the monarchy but also by those appointed to positions of responsibility within the Church. Smoldering beneath the surface was the potential controversy as to which mode of operation should dictate the affairs of the Church. Should it be the "parish system" wherein taxes would support the Church but at the expense of forfeiting internal control to the governmental political body in power at that time; or should it be "voluntaryism" wherein control was exercised by the individual congregations whose members would develop their own articles of governance thus freeing themselves from any external control? Ultimately, the New World became the battlefield for the resolution of this dichotomy, a resolution that did not occur until the late 1700s.

The great majority of the members of the Church of England submitted to the concept of centralized control that was built around a very rigid hierarchical structure; however, there was a radical element of believers within the Church, one of a class of Protestants who arose in the sixteenth century, who were called Puritans, so-named because they sought to purify the Church from within through the actual restructuring of the Church's internal operation. Among the changes that the radicals felt were essential involved the abolishment of the priesthood, the removal of the bishops from office, and the allowance of any member of the Church to preach; in effect, the changes demanded reforms in doctrine and worship, as well as greater strictness in religious discipline.

Other members of the Church of England felt that these changes could not come from within; therefore, they elected to separate themselves from the Church thus acquiring the name "Separatists." When the Separatists established their own congregations, English officials under King James I persecuted them to the extent that many Separatists fled the country to escape their wrath. One such group elected to flee to Leiden, Holland in 1608. Twelve years later, fearing a potential war between Holland and Spain, longing to rejoin English-speaking people, but desiring to maintain their own form of worship, the new land of America appealed to them. Thirty-five members of this group returned to England and joined a group of English merchant adventurers whose trip to America was underwritten by a company called the London Company. After two false starts with two vessels, only the *Mayflower* left Plymouth Harbor, England, bound for the New World carrying 101 passengers in addition to its crew. Although most of the passengers were Separatists, a goodly number were also merchants lured by the promise of religious freedom as well as the promise of land. Thrown off course by stormy weather, in December of 1620, the *Mayflower* landed on Cape Cod rather than off the coast of what is now New Jersey where they had wanted to go and where they had permission to go. Exploring the land they settled in Plymouth, and, subsequently, gained permission to remain in Plymouth.

In the early 1600s English companies were being formed to finance colonies in new lands that had recently been discovered. Shares in these companies were bought by members of the nobility and gentry, and by rich merchants. King James gave land in America to two companies, the Virginia Company of London and the Virginia Company of Plymouth (in those days all the land along the eastern seaboard was called Virginia). Both companies, each governed by its own council in England, were under a royal council that represented the King. The Pilgrims settled the third English colony in the New World, preceded by an ill-fated colony that attempted to settle at Sagadahoc, on the Kennebec River (now Maine), but was deserted within a year; and the Jamestown Colony, settled in 1607, becoming a permanent settlement only after overcoming critical challenges in the first few years.

In the meantime, in England, opposition was building against the Puritans from Anglican Church officials, the traditional members of the Church, and the King. In 1628 a group of Puritans bought the right to settle on the land between the Charles and Merrimac rivers, an area that now embraces parts of Massachusetts, New Hampshire and Maine. Shortly thereafter about forty people, all Puritans, were brought over from England and settled a colony in Salem. The Massachusetts Bay Colony had secured a liberal charter from King Charles I, and, instead of keeping it in

London as the members of the Virginia Company had, they took their charter and brought it with them to America. The stage was now set for the second significant wave of immigrants to come to the New World from England. In 1630 about two thousand Puritans came to Boston. The Massachusetts Bay Colony grew very rapidly, and before 1634 there were nearly five thousand settlers. Those who settled Boston were of a very different temper than the Pilgrims who had preceded them. A number of them were well-to-do, gentlemen of learning, but the vast majority were humble people like those who came in the *Mayflower*. The biggest difference between the individuals comprising the two separate waves was that the Boston settlers were all Puritans still feeling attached to the Anglican Church. Their leaders had a profound dislike of democracy, a dislike only to be exceeded by their disdain for any religious view that was not their own. These Puritan leaders were intent on setting up in America the kind of church government they had wanted to see in England. Voting privileges were extended only to those who belonged to the Church of England (a practice that was enforced for the better part of fifty years), and everyone had to contribute taxes for the support of the Church; furthermore, they did not believe, any more than most people in their time, in the rule by all of the people. The Puritan priests ruled with an iron hand, a tragedy for that which was intended to be a noble cause. The end result was a denial of the privilege of religious freedom, the very dream that was sought by so many of the early settlers, and one that led to the persecution, ostracism and even death to those whose beliefs differed from those of the Puritans. There were remarkable inconsistencies in what the Puritans were attempting to do. First, the reasons the Puritans opted to go with the Massachusetts Bay Company rather than the Virginia Company and be required to settle in Jamestown, was that the Jamestown Colony was very much under the control of the Church of England and the King, the very bonds that the

Puritans were attempting to break. The second inconsistency pertained to the parish concept wherein individuals were taxed in order to provide the funding to support churches. Third, the stipulation that one had to be a member of the church in order to be a voting member of the community. Finally, many members of the church abhorred the zealous persecution of those persons whose religious preferences and views differed from their own.[5]

The New Englanders were always the most sturdily independent as well as the most sternly religious of the colonists; however, the inconsistencies between what the Puritan leaders and clergy wanted to impose upon their followers and those who chose not to be a part of the Church of England, inevitably led to conflict. This conflict was manifested in two ways. Initially, it created a barrier between the Separatists and the Puritans that took years to remove. Second, many members of the Anglican Church elected to move out of the reach of their leaders by up-rooting and settling in Connecticut, Rhode Island, New Hampshire, and what is now Maine. Over time, as more and more settlers came to Massachusetts from England, the influ-

---

5    The material for this section came from the following sources:

1. *Book of Knowledge,* Vol. 2. pp. 547–548 (Pilgrim's voyage, Plymouth Colony, and Puritan's Bay Colony).

2. *New Funk & Wagnall's Encyclopedia* (New York: Unicorn Publishers, Inc., 1954), Vol. 26, p. 9619 (Pilgrim fathers); Vol. 27, pp. 10015–10016 (background of the Puritans).

3. *Richard's Topical Encyclopedia* (New York: Richard's Company, Inc., 1953), Vol. 7, pp. 124–128 (advent of Pilgrims to Plymouth and Puritans to Massachusetts); Vol. 8, pp. 165–168 (Plymouth colony flourished while the Puritans expanded beyond Boston).

4. *World Book Encyclopedia* (Chicago: Field Enterprises Educational Corporation, 1968), Vol. 15, pp. 415–416 and pp. 803–804 (background material, basic beliefs, history).

ence of the Puritan clergy was diluted. These newcomers did not possess the religious zeal of those who came before them to this country; further, their reasons for migrating had more to do with their economic plight rather than the desire for religious freedom. Many congregational churches evolved in New England, each an independent entity unto itself. It took time but, ultimately, "voluntaryism" prevailed over the parish concept. The culmination of this struggle occurred with the adoption of the Great Bill of Religious Freedom (1784–1786). This model of separation, developed by James Madison and Thomas Jefferson was followed in the First Amendment to the Federal Constitution (1789–1791). As individual churches were formed, Puritan or parish church members who resigned and were formally accepted into another church of their choosing, were relieved from the taxes assessed by the parish church. Franklin Littell points out that, for the first time in history, "governments gave up the claim to use a preferred religion for political sanction, and guaranteed the churches their 'natural right' to pursue their own self-definition and self-identity."[6] This was a significant milestone in the development of America.

Having identified the major motivating forces that brought English families to the unknown shores of New England in the early 1600s, why did Roger Shaw elect to become one of the first immigrants to make this trip? From genealogical study, he was born on August 26, 1594, in London, Middlesex, England; further, he arrived in this country in or about the year 1632. From this information and again referring to the marvelous work by Harriett Farewell, *Shaw Records,* and the information she had gathered, several conclusions can be inferred that help to answer this searching question. First, Roger Shaw was a member of the

---

6    Franklin H. Littell, *Historical Atlas of Christianity,* pp. 260 and 263–264.

Church of England; second, he was a Puritan; third, he was a citizen in good standing; and, fourth, he possessed a keen business sense.

These inferred conclusions become more evident as one examines the data assembled.

Roger Shaw was identified as a man of prominence among the early settlers. In the early days of the colonies, laws were made by a quorum of the "Assistants" or "Magistrates" commissioned and sent out by the "Company" in London, England, that held the charter for the activities taking place in the Massachusetts Colony. As early as 1631 the Assistants passed a law that required church membership for the right to participate in local government. For example, in Boston, as late as 1676, five-sixths of the people were non-voters because they were not church members.[7] In 1636, Roger appeared before the General Court (a term applied to the legislative body of the Massachusetts Colony) and was made freeman, "having previously bought two hundred acres of land and built him a house on the south side of Arrow Street." In 1639, he was appointed as a drawn juryman (or juror) and the following year was elected Town Clerk of Cambridge, Massachusetts. He was also a selectman for this town for the year 1641, 1642, 1643 and 1645.[8]

In 1648, he moved to Hampton, New Hampshire, a settlement authorized by the General Court in 1638, and incorporated in 1639. Roger was one of the petitioners for this new settlement. After selling his property in Cambridge, he bought land in Hampton and, then, added to this property a grant of additional lands from Charles I (then King of Great Britain) thus acquiring a large estate. From 1651 to 1653 he served as a Representative to the General Court, was selectman in 1649 and 1654 and filled many

---

7     Harriette F. Farwell, *Shaw Records,* p. 17.

8     *Ibid.,* p. 18.

other important offices in Hampton. There was controversy arising from the occupancy of lands on the New Hampshire border that had been authorized by Massachusetts. In 1651 this matter was carried into General Court, and, as a result, added considerably to the responsibilities of the Representatives for that year. To resolve the issue required "unusual wisdom and ability," traits that Roger possessed. Also in 1651 Roger was appointed "Commissioner for trying small cases." In 1658 the town of Hampton appointed him as the first member to be on a committee of three, together with the Town Clerk to examine and record all grants and appointment of lands, highways and such-like; furthermore, that same committee was directed to "lay out and record convenient highways to men's land in the town and to allow satisfaction to the proprietors for the same according to their discretion." [9]

Finally, Roger was deemed competent by the General Court to be installed Vintnor and Keeper of the Ordinary at Hampton "to sell wine or any sort of strong liquors to Christians and the Indians, as in his judgment shall seem meet and necessary, on just and urgent occasions, and not otherwise." [10] What makes this last appointment so interesting is that Roger must have had some prior knowledge and experience in the wine and liquor business to be entrusted with this appointment. Further, his father, Ralph Shaw was Vintnor at the Sunne, on Cornhill, England. This fact links Roger that much closer to being the son of Ralph Shaw.

To summarize Roger's background, he was a man of the church, a landowner, a public servant, an entrepreneur, a risk taker, and one who was well educated. Certainly courage was manifested in his decision to leave England at an approximate age of thirty-eight to start a new life in America. Personal traits that he seemed to

---

9    *Ibid.*

10   *Ibid.*

possess were: integrity, intelligence, wisdom and vision. Roger Shaw married shortly after he arrived in New England. By his first wife Ann, he fathered eight children, two sons Joseph and Benjamin, and six daughters. He died in Hampton, New Hampshire on May 29, 1661. He set a high standard for those who were to follow behind him.

The only two indicators identifying Roger Shaw as a Puritan were the time of his migration to America, and his appointment to positions of responsibilities within a relatively short period of time. Although a more diverse group than those Separatists who came over on the *Mayflower,* the ones who arrived on these shores in the early 1630s allegedly had one trait in common— they were all Puritans; further, starting in 1636 when Roger was made a freeman after having purchased land and built his home, he seemed to progress rapidly from one position of responsibility and authority to another.

It is concluded that Roger Shaw came to America as part of that noble effort to purify, from within, the Church of England; further, that he was an entrepreneur who wanted very much to seek his fortunes in the New World. Another conclusion is that Roger was not a religious zealot, but he became increasingly disenchanted with the iron-hand rule exercised by the Puritan leaders over their followers. This could explain his moves away from, first, Boston to Cambridge, and, then, from Cambridge to Hampton, New Hampshire; in effect, moves away from the center of the Church's power. These moves also placed him in a better position to increase his land holdings by exposing him to an untapped frontier.

At the Musek home in Prague.

# 3
# The Joseph Thompson Shaw Family Genealogy

ROGER SHAW was the progenitor of this specific branch of the Shaw family. From Roger there were six generations of direct descendants between Roger and my father, Joseph Thompson Shaw. The biographical descriptions of these six descendants is shared with the intent of seeking to identify those traits that were passed from one generation to another, traits that, for the most part, form a common thread running throughout my ancestry.

*Joseph Shaw.* Joseph Shaw, the second child of Roger Shaw and his wife Ann, was born on January 2, 1635, and was a second generation member of the Roger Shaw family in America. Upon marriage on June 26, 1661, to Elizabeth Partridge, he and his wife settled on "the Falls side" of Hampton that was subsequently incorporated as Hampton Falls. He and Elizabeth had nine children, five sons and four daughters, Caleb being the third son and fifth child of the nine children born to this couple. In 1680 the area of New Hampshire constituted a Royal Province. The name Joseph Shaw appeared on a list selected from New Hampshire towns by the President and Council of the Province as being eligible for the office of councilman when three new members were to be selected. These selectees, who were granted the privilege of voting at meetings of the Council, were asked to appear at Portsmouth so that they could become acquainted with "his Majesty's commands in regard to the Province." Selection to this responsible position gives evidence of the integrity and intelligence of Joseph Shaw. He died on November 8, 1720.[11]

*Caleb Shaw.* Caleb Shaw, born in Hampton on January 31, 1671, the third generation of the Roger Shaw family in America, married in 1695, and settled near Hampton Falls. He and his wife Elizabeth Hilliard had ten children, four sons and six daughters, in which Ebenezer was the fourth son and ninth child. Caleb Shaw was a man of importance in the community having served as a member of the Board of Selectman. He was the Captain and part owner of a fishing sloop that plied the waters off the coast as far south as Boston. On March 19, 1715, while tacking in Hampton harbor, he was hit by the boom of the sloop, carried overboard and was drowned. Caleb was recognized as a leader, as well as a respected, responsible, and revered member of the community in which he served. His premature death was the cause of extensive sorrow.[12]

*Ebenezer Shaw.* A member of the fourth generation of the Roger Shaw family, Ebenezer was born on October 7, 1713, in Hampton, New Hampshire. Because of the early demise of his father Caleb, while he was still a child and until he became of age, Ebenezer lived with Moses Pearson, the first sheriff of Cumberland County. On November 19, 1738, he married Anna Philbrick of Hampton. They had ten children, five boys and five girls, Sargent being the second son and fourth child born to them. Because Ebenezer was a zealous churchman and believer, as children were born to his wife and to him, he desired to bring them up in a God-fearing manner. For this reason, Ebenezer moved his family from Hampton to Sargent's Island where the children could grow up in an environment uncontaminated by the impure associations of the town. Following this sojourn, Ebenezer moved his family in

---

11    Harriette F. Farwell, *Shaw Records,* pp. 19, 23–24.

12    *Ibid.,* pp. 24, 31–33.

1762 to Pearsontown, Maine, which is now called Standish. He took possession of a tract of land consisting of two hundred acres and a mill privilege, a privilege that was granted to him by the proprietors of the town. In addition to these holdings Ebenezer purchased additional land. He was a mechanic, carpenter, mill-wright and cooper. He also attended to a large farm and sawmill that he built by himself and was the first one ever operated in Standish. Ebenezer's success as a businessman was such that it enabled him to give each of his sons a farm when they started out in life on their own, farms that were located in close prox-imity to his own holdings. Ebenezer died on March 13, 1782, and his wife Anna died on December 12, 1804, both in Standish. They left nine children, eighty-two grandchildren, one hundred and nine great-grandchildren, and one great-great-grandchild. Ebenezer was the first settler with the surname of Shaw to arrive in Standish. From this point forward our kinsmen became a part of the Standish Branch of the Roger Shaw family in America.[13]

*Sargent Shaw.* Sargent Shaw, born to Ebenezer and Anna on October 23, 1745, was the second son, and fourth child of the ten children born into their family. Sargent, part of the fifth gener-ation of those descended from Roger Shaw, was born in Hamp-ton and came to Pearsontown with his father in 1762. His first wife Sarah bore him two sons and one daughter, his second wife Salome bore him one son and three daughters, and his third wife Anna bore him three sons and six daughters. Sargent's son Peter was born to his third wife Ann, Peter being the eleventh child of the sixteen born, and the fifth son of the six boys fathered by Sargent. Sargent and his brother were members of the first Baptist church ever organized in Standish; in addition, he was one of three early ministers of this church. He participated in the Revo-lutionary War, serving in Colonel Phinny's Regiment. Finally,

13    *Ibid.,* pp. 33, 106–107.

Sargent was the first constable of Standish. He and his family lived on a farm of one hundred acres deeded to him by his father Ebenezer. By occupation Sargent was a cooper; he was also an energetic and prosperous farmer. With respect to his community, he served on the Board of Selectmen for a period of several years. Sargent was a man much respected by his fellow townsmen; most importantly he was a man of unswerving Christian principles and fervent piety. Sargent died on December 3, 1823, in Standish.[14]

*Peter M. Shaw.* Peter M. Shaw, born on January 1, 1794, in Standish, Maine, was the sixth generation of the Roger Shaw family. He married Lydia Morton of Gorham, Maine, and they settled on the farm where he was born, and where he lived his entire life. Peter and Lydia had six children, four boys and two girls. Milton, my grandfather, was the fifth of six children and was the youngest of the four boys. Peter was a farmer, cooper and mill owner, a Selectman in Standish for a number of years, and a tax collector for three years. He, of whom it was said, "The memory of the just is blessed," must have had a very positive impact on those with whom he came in contact. He died on the farm where he was born and always lived, on July 2, 1866. Engraved on his tombstone were the following words: "Deal justly, love mercy and walk humbly." These seem to be very fitting words from one who was so highly respected for his integrity.[15]

*Milton Shaw.* Milton Shaw was born on March 29, 1837, in Standish, Maine, a seventh generation member of the Roger Shaw's family branch. He married Nellie Kimball Morse of Gorham, although she was actually born in Portland, Maine, on June 27, 1870. They settled in Gorham and had three children, my father being the youngest of the three. In the book *Shaw Records—1904,* from which the material for these biographical

---

14    *Ibid.,* pp. 107, 114–118.

15    *Ibid.,* pp. 118, 165.

sketches was extracted, the authoress indicated that Milton "has been in trade at Standish Corner and New York; now resides at Gorham where he is still engaged in trade. He was postmaster of Standish from 1861 to 1866." [16] The 1880 Census of the United States identifies Milton as a retail grocer, and the Census of 1900 identifies him as a lumber merchant who owned his own home that was free of mortgage; further, it was not a farm. From a photograph of their three sons taken in the early 1880s, the boys are well groomed and properly dressed. Also all three sons completed high school in Gorham, went to and graduated from Bowdoin College, and each went on to successful professional careers beyond college. These achievements by themselves would indicate strong parenting by Milton and Nellie with respect to the need for and importance of education and high expectations for responsible and productive behavior.

Before examining those traits that seem to have been passed through successive generations, three definitions are in order:

The first definition is of the word "privilege"—a right or immunity enjoyed by a person or persons beyond the common advantage of others.

The second definition is for the word "franchise"—the right to vote; a privilege arising from the grant of a sovereign or government; a privilege of a public nature conferred on an individual or body of individuals by a governmental grant.

The third definition is that of the word "freeman"—one who enjoys or is entitled to citizenship, franchise or other peculiar privilege; a man who enjoys personal, civil or political liberty.

By virtue of the Mayflower Compact, the first agreement for self-government ever put in force in America and usually considered to be the world's first written constitution, the foundation was laid for governance in this country by promising "just and

---

16    *Ibid.,* pp. 165, 181.

equal" laws. There were also constraints placed upon the early settlers by those companies whose charters were bestowed by the King of England. Looming above these controlling documents was the requirement of church membership as a condition for the privilege of voting. With the advent of the Great Bill of Religious Freedom (1784–1786) and the first amendment to the Constitution that became operational in 1791, this onerous constraint was lifted, truly allowing religious freedom. It is against this backdrop that, through successive generations from Roger to Milton, each of the seven men discussed was a "freeman" in the truest sense of the word and in light of those laws, rules and regulations governing their lives.

Of concern is whether or not these rights and privileges were used for personal gain or for the benefit of the community. It seems to have been for both. Each could claim ownership to real assets be it in the form of land, farms, home, sailing vessels, saw-mills and the like. And each was independent to the extent of making decisions as to where to settle, what responsibilities to shoulder, and which churches to attend. Further testimony to this independence was their tendency to push beyond the surrounding frontiers certainly because of the availability of land, but, even more so, because of the desire to move beyond the center of power that restricted their choices as to how their lives should be lived. Although none of the seven had been educated for a profession such as medicine, the clergy or law, they were intelligent and educated to the point where they could hold positions and master trades requiring the ability to read, write, and think critically. These men, who were self-sufficient, not only provided for their families but also held themselves responsible and accountable for their actions. On the other hand, each, with the exception of Ebenezer who was almost reclusive in his actions, showed no hesitancy in agreeing to serve the community of which each was a part. Whether it was by selection or election, and looking beyond Ebenezer, each served in some form of public activity and each was a respected, and in some cases, revered member of the community. One served in the Revolutionary War, while others had family members who served in the Revolutionary War as well as in the Civil War. As new churches formed, the Shaws were a part of the body of believers who helped initiate the churches. In one case, that of Sargent, he was one of three who served as a temporary minister when a new church was created in Standish. New Englanders took their religion seriously; in fact, many zealously. There is nothing in their backgrounds to suggest that the seven Shaws whose lives were examined were other than disciplined church members and believers in God. In review, these seven men, representing seven generations of Shaws descended from Ralph Shaw of England, were pillars in their respective communities and provided the leadership and vision as, at first, a series of colonies and then a new nation struggled through its first two-hundred and eighty years of life.

At the Waccabuc Country Club, Westchester
County, New York, April 8, 1923.

# 4
# Coming of Age

MY FATHER'S lineage has been defined. The next consideration is to determine the environment within which my father grew from boyhood to manhood. As one author has noted, "New England was the crucible in which the infant republic was formed; it in turn fanned the flames of its sons and daughters, shaping them into an amazing breed of self-reliant, independent and high quality individuals." As one studies the emergence of Maine as a frontier of expanding colonies, then as an independent province, then as a district within the State of Massachusetts, and, finally, as a state, what is apparent is that it too had to struggle for its independence. One marvels, not only at the beauty of Maine, but also at the individuality of its citizens a trait that has given these inhabitants the staying power to persist.

From a physiographical perspective there are many features of Maine that are reminiscent of Scotland. First, the land area of present-day Maine closely approximates the total land area of Scotland, and exceeds the combined land areas of the other five New England states. The terrain of Maine is predominantly mountainous with rugged uplands toward the west that gradually diminish in height until they reach the sea in the shape of bold headlands or pointed capes. As there are three distinct divisions of the topography of Scotland (the Highlands, the Central Lowlands and the Southern Uplands), so too does the terrain spread across Maine have three designations: the White Mountain Region, the Eastern New England Upland, and the Coastal Lowlands. The hydrography of Scotland is characterized by an abundance of streams and lakes, rivers and lochs. Maine has almost 2,400 lakes and over 600 rivers and streams. The geographic features of Scotland and Maine are characterized by deep ravines and valleys, precipitous cliffs and ragged coastlines. In fact, the general coastline from southwest to northeast Maine measures a mere 228 miles; however, including the coastlines of off-shore islands, and measured around bays, inlets and estuaries reached by tidal water, this extremely irregular coast has a length of 2,379 miles. There are also approximately 400 islands off the coast that serve as protective barriers for the many harbors. Where the two territories differ is with respect to the overwhelming forests in Maine that far exceed those found in Scotland; also, even though Scotland is ten degrees further north in latitude, the winters are more moderate than those in Maine by an approximate average of 15 degrees Fahrenheit. One explanation could be the tempering influences of the contiguous seas that surround most of Scotland including the Gulf Stream.

Although a colony was planted by the Plymouth Company when a group of English merchants sent 120 settlers to Popham Beach at the mouth of the Kennebec River in 1607, because of the bitter winter, sickness, disease and loss of leadership, by 1608 it was abandoned. Nevertheless, the people of Maine can remember with pride that theirs was the first of the New England states to give a home to settlers. In 1625 the first permanent English colony in Maine was established in Pemaquid, and others followed shortly thereafter. Also there was a steady trickle of emigrants from the Massachusetts Colony to her sister colony in Maine. These were independent folk who sought in the Church of England settlements in Maine the religious liberty that the stern Puritans denied them.

Unfortunately, through a convenient interpretation of her charter it was possible for Massachusetts to claim nearly all of the Province of Maine as its own, and bit-by-bit she annexed it until by 1658 she owned it all. A little later she added the land as far north as the Penobscot River. Actually there was conflict as to who the rightful owners were of the Maine Territory. The owners of the company that sponsored the colonists assumed ownership until it was discovered that a Sir Ferdinando Gorges had had the charter for the land conferred upon him by royal decree. It was not until 1677 that Massachusetts gained clear title to Maine by purchasing it from Gorges for about $6,000. By a new charter in 1691, the whole country as far as the St. Croix River ultimately became part of the Province of Massachusetts.[17]

Independence did not come easily to the Colony of Maine. At the same time as she was being swallowed by the Province of Massachusetts, Maine and all other New England colonists were under attack by the French aided and abetted by their Indian allies. The French were attempting to seize much of the territory between the Penobscot and the St. Croix rivers as well as other areas within New England. The resulting French and Indian wars persisted off and on throughout the New England colonies from 1689 to 1763 with the last of the wars consuming seven years and finally ending in 1763 with the signing of the Treaty of Paris. In this treaty, France gave up all its claims to Maine and most of the rest of North America. The treaty notwithstanding, the threat of conflict persisted. Land had been granted by the several London based companies to those settlers who would establish home-steads in those wilderness areas being occupied. To protect these settlers a series of forts were built across this frontier. Between wars and even after the wars ceased, Indian hostility was enough of a threat to make settlers hesitant about committing themselves to clearing the land and settling down in spite of the presence

17    *Richard's Topical Encyclopedia,* Vol. 8, pp. 149–151.
      *World Book,* pp. 62–77.

of the forts.[18]

Following the cessation of hostilities with the French, Great Britain passed a series of laws during the 1760s that imposed severe and unfair taxes on the colonists as well as restricted their trading activities. The consequences of this shortsighted action triggered opposition to British taxation and trade policies that in turn precipitated the Revolutionary War. What started as an effort to exact more equitable concessions from and to effect reconciliation with the British, turned into a war for independence, initiated by the signing of the Declaration of Independence on July 4, 1776. The brutal reprisals against the colonists invoked hardship and suffering throughout all thirteen colonies not only through trade blockades that immediately caused shortages of food and other vital goods, the burning of towns in punishment for opposing the king's policies, but also through overt military action that claimed the lives of many Americans. A full twenty-five percent of Americans remained loyal to the British crown; however, for those who resisted, through perseverance, and with the support of the French, Spanish and Dutch, the colonists prevailed. The Continental Army, under the leadership of General George Washington, forced the surrender of General Cornwallis' army at Yorktown, Virginia, on October 19, 1781. It is hard to imagine that America could have gained its freedom without the support of these three European countries. France recognized the thirteen colonies as a new nation as early as 1778 providing material and manpower support in the form of troops, ships and supplies. Spain declared war on Britain in 1779, and the Netherlands followed in 1780, both countries creating formidable distractions with which Great Britain had to contend. At the peace confer-

---

18   *Book of Knowledge,* Vol. 3, pp. 782–784.

     *Funk & Wagnall's,* Vol. 15, pp. 5302–5303.

     *World Book,* Vol. 13, p. 74.

ence held in Paris in 1783, Great Britain acknowledged that the colonies had become free and independent states. In effect, "out of trade laws and tea parties, rebellion and revolution, had been born the United States of America." For those who sided and fought with the British, their lands and holdings in the New World were forfeited. For those who fought against the British, there reward was free land notably in Massachusetts and Maine, but also in all of the other colonies.[19]

The trials and tribulations of this emerging nation were just beginning. The next war, the War of 1812, was a reaction by America to the growing intrusiveness by England in this country's affairs. In the western United States, the Indians had been stirred into actively opposing further intrusions into what they perceived to be their land; further, on the high seas, over a ten year period 900 American merchant ships had been seized, our sailors had been impressed into the service of the British navy, and England had blockaded our coasts. These offensives gave good cause for Congress to declare war on England on June 18, 1812. Victory at sea favored the American navy, but the majority of the land battles favored the British soldiers although there were notable exceptions such as the battle for New Orleans. Coincidentally, that battle inflicted enormous losses on the British troops but, unfortunately for the British, was fought two weeks after a truce with Britain had been signed in December 1814. The New England states did not necessarily favor this war because of the great profits that were being realized through ship building and trading. This sign of weakness and divisiveness was to be expected of a fledgling nation. On the other hand, this war

---

19    *Book of Knowledge,*
      *Funk & Wagnall's,*
      *Richard's Topical Encyclopedia,*
      *World Book,* Vol. 16, pp. 252–269.

demonstrated that America, with only eighteen states, was able to take its place alongside the greatest nations of the world. This country had strength, had confidence, and had the respect of other nations. A questionable war with an indecisive outcome became a watershed point in time when we were able to realize the tremendous potential that existed within America.[20]

In 1820 Maine became the twenty-third state. It was not a unanimous choice by its inhabitants. In spite of the heavy taxation by Massachusetts, poor roads, and the long distance to the capital city of Boston, many of its citizens preferred to remain as a part of Massachusetts. Although talk of separation had been a movement dating back to 1785, it was only after the War of 1812 that advocates for separation were voted into positions of influence and were able to sway a vote for separation in their favor. Even after voting for statehood, admission was contingent upon the Missouri Compromise, a compromise that called for Maine's entering the Union as a "free state" while Missouri was allowed admission as a slave state.

Ever since 1783 the boundary between Maine and New Brunswick, Canada had been disputed. The continuing argument led to the Aroostook War in which, fortunately, there was no blood shed; a boundary was finally set through a temporary agreement that was memorialized in the Webster-Ashburton Treaty of 1842.

In 1851, again showing its independence, Maine became the first state in the Union to pass a law prohibiting the manufacture and sale of alcoholic beverages, a law that remained in effect until 1934.

Another manifestation of its independent thinking pertained to anti-slavery feelings that were evident in Maine during the

---

20   *Book of Knowledge,* Vol. 5, pp. 1703–1707.

   *Richard's Topical Encyclopedia,* Vol. 7, pp. 209–211.

   *World Book,* Vol. 20, pp. 26–31.

early 1830s and persisted right up to and through the Civil War. Those who were especially vocal in their opposition to slavery were the state's Baptists and Congregationalists. During the four-year Civil War approximately 72,000 Maine men served in the Union Army.[21]

As one looks back on the birth and growth of Maine from its earliest years in the 1600s through the Civil War, physical and emotional conflict seem to have been the norm. The physical conflict was manifested through climatic conditions, impenetrable forests, and armed conflict with the Indians, British, French, and secessionists. The emotional conflict, although less evident, was certainly as pervasive. Tracing the history of Maine from the mid 1750s until my father's birth in 1874 there were many issues to be resolved by the inhabitants of Maine. The issues did not stand in isolation but, rather, formed a continuum that must have had an impact on each succeeding generation. Following the French and Indian Wars, the hostilities continued to the extent that the threat of violence precluded a safe environment for settlers to clear land and establish homesteads. The next critical issue was the Revolutionary War. This war forced the individual colonists to choose between their native country and their allegiance to their new life in a new world under unproven leadership. It was a difficult choice for most. Recognizing loyalty to the British monarchy in spite of oppressive taxes and trade laws was a viable option. On the other hand, should the independence sought from Great Britain through war fail, then, for those who rebelled, their dreams of freedom would perish. These two issues, as to when to settle virgin land and which side to support in the revolution, became life or death decisions. The War of 1812 found divergence of thinking between those who were realizing a profit from the British incursions on American maritime activ-

21    *World Book*, Vol. 13, pp. 62–77.

ities and those who felt that the English posed a legitimate threat to this country's independence. Following this war, at issue was statehood for Maine as an alternative to remaining as a province in the state of Massachusetts. Hand-in-hand with the issue was the fact that Maine, as a free state, became a bargaining chip that enabled Missouri to be accepted as a slave state. Unfortunately, this compromise did not allay the inevitable issue of a state's right to secede from the Union resulting in the tragic, frightful, and devastating Civil War. Prior to the Civil War its citizens were faced with the decision to force the issue of the state's northern boundary with Canada even if it meant war. Perhaps a small issue but one that had the potential to be very controversial was the prohibition on the manufacture and sale of alcoholic beverages.

Yes, these were all difficult issues requiring resolution, issues that had to have had an impact on the citizens of Maine as their families descended from one generation to another. Some of these issues were comparable to those faced by other citizens of other states; however, there were those issues unique only to the inhabitants of Maine, issues that helped to shape their individual traits and characteristics. An example of this reasoning pertains to my mother and father and the tremendous impact that the World War (WW I) had on each of them; however, this impact was not restricted to their generation. Both experienced the war first-hand but from very different perspectives. Subsequently, the emotional turmoil in which they were involved was passed on to their children influencing who they were and who they became. Yes, environment does have a profound influence in shaping who we are. It is certain that those emotional issues with which his previous generations had to contend had a significant impact on my father as he went from childhood, through the adolescent stages, and then on to manhood.

Also influencing the environment within which my father grew and developed was the extent of technology available at the time of his birth and those changes that transpired over the next twenty-five to thirty years. The steam engine had been invented much earlier but its potential applications were not truly realized until the latter half of the Nineteenth Century. Railroads were introduced into this country in 1830, at which time there were twenty-three miles of track. By 1850 there were about 9,000 miles of track: most of which were along the Atlantic seaboard. On May 10, 1869, the transcontinental railroad was completed, the greatest engineering feat of the nineteenth century. In 1876, two years after my father's birth, Alexander Graham Bell invented the telephone. In 1879, Thomas Edison invented the first operable light bulb. It wasn't until 1892 that the Diesel engine was invented. In the late 1890s and early 1900s Marconi demonstrated the efficacy of wireless communications. And it was during this same period of time that Orville and Wilbur Wright experimented at first with gliders and then with aircraft, developing the first engine-driven, propelled airplane in 1903. Henry Ford never introduced his first automobile until 1910, and the radio never burst upon the scene until 1920. In response to the question: What generation lived through the greatest change that transpired in this country? Author Stephen E. Ambrose said: "For me, it is the Americans who lived through the second half of the nineteenth century. They saw slavery abolished and electricity put to use, the development of the telephone and the completion of the telegraph, and, perhaps, most importantly, the railroad. The locomotive was the first great triumph over time and space. After it came, and after it crossed the continent of North America, nothing could ever again be the same. It brought about the greatest change in the shortest period of time." [22] These are the changes to which my father was exposed during the most critical years of his growth.

------

22    Stephen E. Ambrose, "The Big Road," *American Heritage,* Oct. 2000, pp. 60–61.

By 1836 railroad tracks had been laid; however, those tracks were used to carry freight not passengers. It was not until years later that passenger service was provided. There were no paved roads, and travel was by foot, horse, or horse-drawn wagon, coach or carriage. Home lighting was probably by electricity in the late 1800s; however, until then, it was by candles, lanterns and oil lamps, although gas-fueled streetlights were in cities. My father's family did not have all the amenities available to those living within a more developed area. However, it is also just as certain that, from a non-material point-of-view, within his community a church, a school, and the presence of traditional families were all a part of the normal expected environment. It was certainly not frontier living. In view of the fact that Milton Shaw was a grocery store proprietor at least until 1880 and a lumber merchant at least until 1900, he was able to provide for his family.

This then was the America that my father was born into on May 8, 1874, in Gorham, Maine, a settlement that had been founded in the early 1700s, incorporated in 1764, and where value systems had been inculcated into those descendants of the earliest colonists. These traits embodied thrift and industry as well as very strong feelings toward religion, morality and the need for education. My father's world was one of words, woods and water. He was a voracious reader of the best classical literature available. He was also one who thirsted to be out-of-doors, taking advantage of both water in the form of lakes, rivers, and the ocean, as well as the extensive forests of Maine that were all readily available to him. As a young teenager the words he read and the woods and water he experienced shaped his life. The knowledge gained became the cornerstone of his very being and was manifested in his course of study and activities he pursued at Bowdoin, the professions he elected to enter throughout the rest of his life, and the wisdom he imparted to me during my growing years.

My father's father and mother, Milton and Nellie Shaw, were

excellent parents. To receive a high school education followed by four years of college was an indulgence that not many families could afford or even wanted for their boys. Economically, life was a struggle thus necessitating that as many male members of the family as possible assist in providing support for the entire family, either by working on the farm, mill, or any other endeavor that would serve as a source of income. Milton and Nellie's three boys, their only children, completed their high school education in Gorham, and then went on to prestigious Bowdoin College where each received his bachelor's degree before moving into successful professional careers. Frederick became a teacher and then a salesman in several different lines of work, Philip in the banking profession, and my father as a writer and editor. Their success as students and then as professionals is evidence of not only the high expectations their parents had for them but also the fact that a family environment was provided wherein this individual success could be realized. In my father's case, his parents allowed him to have the opportunity to indulge in both his love for books as well as the great out-doors and all that was embodied in these activities.

MORE THAN forty years after my father first experienced the challenge of the outdoors, he put into words the exultation he felt when exploring new trails or running before the wind on the open sea. These thoughts were from an editorial my father had written in an issue of *Black Mask* magazine; the story resulting from these thoughts were then picked by the *Asheville Citizen-Times,* and run as an editorial on January 25, 1931. The introduction and the article itself read as follows:

> Joseph T. Shaw, who has been picking action stories for *Black Mask* magazine, one of the best known of the adventure publications, writes feelingly of the fellows who like to break loose from the grind and get out and chase rainbows once in a while.

"Most of us are not all the way grown up—and never will be, thank the Lord," says Mr. Shaw.

"Every now and then when we get a grumble against Old Man Economy, or whoever he is, who organized this scheme of things where we have to show up at such an hour, regular, stick on the job day after day, or else both ends will sort of get separated."

"Lots of folks have a yen to get out where there is plenty of elbow room and there's no concrete or slate underfoot and the skyline all the way 'round is where nature made it.

"Some fellows if they are young and spry and gingery, long for the hurricane deck of a horse that wants to go somewhere in an awful hurry, where there is only the wide, rolling prairie from horizon to horizon, cattle to be hazed, maybe the stranger on the way, a bad man or a right guy who'll make a good pal.

"Some men—and women, too—like to climb mountains, to dump the old duffel into the canoe, set her afloat and paddle off into the nowhere of deserted streams and woods.

"Others like to tote guns and go where covers aren't posted and animals are real and never heard of a zoo. And, perhaps, where men are still savage or bad and apt to mix it on sight.

"I know of a chap who had such a bad case of itchy foot that he has rigged himself a home on wheels and when he gets too restless simply steps on the starter and heads her off. But he's only half wild. Totes along a real comfortable bed, a radio and a gasoline stove. Yet he gets out and around.

"Me—I sort of like a boat—to let her keel over till the lower weather strakes come clear, to feel the buck and lift and pound of the head-on rollers, the sting and smart and salty taste of the spray whipping over the bow and the windward side

"Had me an old hooker once—schooner rig. Not much to look at. You could wear hobnail shoes and never get a kick from the skipper, and you'd leave part of your scalp on the hatch whenever you went below.

"But she was built like a ship and would carry her whole canvas when the nifty boys would reef down. And she'd take you out of sight of land and bring you back, too, straight on the course you'd set—only you had to reckon right which was part of the fun of the game.

"Yes, sir, lots of us like to get out and chase rainbows now and then and forget the guy who made life a grind of so many hours of a day."

Lady Alice and Bogie, August 20, 1922.

# 5
# The Bowdoin Experience

AT AGE seventeen years and four months, my father entered Bowdoin College in September 1891 as a member of the freshman class of 1895. To gain admittance to this college, a formidable set of requirements had to be satisfied including great emphasis on the Latin and Greek languages, as well as a comprehensive knowledge of the histories of both Greece and Rome. Specifically, candidates for admission were examined in the following subjects with textbooks being mentioned in some instances so as to indicate more exactly the amount of preparatory work required:

- Latin Grammar—Allen & Greenough, or Harkness.
- Latin Prose Composition—Daniell.
- Caesar—*Commentaries,* four books.
- Sallust—*Catiline's Conspiracy.*
- Cicero—*Seven Orations.*
- Virgil—First six books of the *Aeneid*, including *Prosody.*
- Greek Grammar—Hadley or Goodwin.
- Greek Prose Composition—Jones.
- Xenophone—*Anabasis,* four books.
- Homer—*Iliad,* two books.
- Ancient Geography—Tozer.
- The outlines of Greek and Roman History.
- Arithmetic—Especially Common and Decimal Fractions, Interest and Square Root, and the Metric System.
- Geometry—Plane.
- Algebra—Through Quadratic Equations.

- English Grammar and Composition. Each applicant was required to write a short composition based on standard works of English Literature.

In addition to the entrance examination, the Faculty would also examine candidates who had been "fitted" at any school having an approved preparatory course of study. This examination would take place at the applicant's school under the supervision of the Principal. The Principal would receive a series of questions to be answered in writing by the student. The resulting answers would then be returned to the Faculty for their review; they in turn would make the decision as to whether or not the applicant was an acceptable candidate for admission. It was a formidable series of obstacles to surmount in order to gain admission; however, once accepted, the curriculum to be mastered was even more daunting. For the first two years there were thirty terms of required work covering eleven separate subject areas. Each subject area required four hours of classroom and laboratory activity weekly for the duration of the term or terms prescribed. The majority of the subjects were spread over three terms with Modern Languages requiring six terms. The eleven subject areas were:

- Latin, three terms.
- Greek, three terms.
- Mathematics, three terms.
- Modern Languages, six terms.
- Rhetoric, one term.
- Logic, one term.
- Physics and Astronomy, three terms.
- Chemistry and Mineralogy, three terms.
- Natural History, four terms.
- Mental and Moral Philosophy, three terms.
- Political Science, two terms.

For the final two years there were twelve subject areas from which the student could choose. Again, thirty terms of study with each term requiring four hours of weekly classroom or laboratory work were required. The electives from which the student could select were:

- Mathematics, six terms.
- Latin, six terms.
- Greek, six terms.
- Biology, six terms.
- Physics and Astronomy, four terms.
- Chemistry and Mineralogy, three terms.
- History, four terms.
- Bible Study, two terms.
- Science of Language, one term.
- English Literature, four terms.
- German, two terms.
- French, three terms.

As one looks at the academic effort expected from the students, there was nothing easy about the challenge. It is interesting to note that of the fifty-three students who entered Bowdoin as the Class of 1895, all but three graduated within the four-year span, an attrition rate of less than six percent. The reason for those three students dropping out is not known; however, if reasons were speculated, academic failure would not be one of them. Rather, family or health problems could easily have been reasons for the student to leave college before completing the required curriculum.

In spite of the demanding curriculum, there was apparently time available for co-curricula activities. It is apparent that my father was a joiner and contributor demonstrating interests and talents most of which I was unaware, and none of which I inherited. He immediately received an invitation to become initiated into the Alpha Delta Phi fraternity. My father was one of three members of the Class of 1895's Committee on Odes, a committee responsible for creating and presenting an ode on special occasions such as Ivy or Class Day and Commencement. He became a member of the Banjo and Guitar Club and remained as one for four years; finally, starting as a freshman and for all four years, he was a Squad Leader and participant on the Class Athletic Team.

In his sophomore year my father continued to stay active. In addition to his original club and organization affiliations, he accepted membership in the Republican Club and the German Social Club. The *Bowdoin Orient,* the school newspaper, became an integral part of his college experience. As early as February 1892, my father was contributing to this journal, a practice that continued throughout his tenure at Bowdoin. In October of 1892, he quarterbacked a makeshift sophomore football team to a 36 to 10 victory over Brunswick High School indicating his zest for competitive athletics.

There was an intriguing entry pertaining to my father printed in one of the *Orient* issues during the 1892–1893 school year. It was in a section entitled "Odds and Ends" wherein the writer mocks fellow students. The entry was: "J. Shaw—Your face may be worth preserving, and you have an eloquent shape, but it was a big mistake to suppose that your gall would work you into the Ninety-five football picture when you did not belong on the eleven." Perhaps my father felt that this was an entitlement resulting from his success as a quarterback with the sophomore pick-up football team. Another possibility goes back to the interesting statement in the 1893 issue of the *Bowdoin Bugle,* the annual yearbook, made by the Historian of the Class of 1895: "Never did Bowdoin enter a class so per-eminent in brashness and verdancy." My father brash? Maybe he was one of those whose behavior prompted the statement. I had never perceived my father's behavior as that of one who was hasty, brash, presumptuous or impudent; however, at age nineteen there was certainly that possibility. Another interesting consideration is that his two older brothers were members of the Bowdoin class of 1893. Although born a year apart, Frederick Milton Shaw and Philip Morton Shaw were classmates, and as such had several interests in common including the same fraternity and the Bowdoin Republican Club. Philip was also one of the "first banjos" in the Banjo and Guitar Club, and Frederick was coxswain of the varsity crew team during the 1891 season. For all four years my father had the same dormitory room; for the first two years his roommate was Frederick, the older of his two brothers. I cannot help but feel that having two siblings paving the way made it much easier for my father's transition to college and could possibly have given him a level of confidence and aggressiveness that would not otherwise have been present. If nothing else, my father did not seem reluctant to stick his neck out even if he got whacked every now and again.

It was in his sophomore year that my father participated in varsity track an activity that he embraced for the next two years. The 220-yard dash and the 220 hurdles were his events; although I am not aware of any records set in these sprints, he must have enjoyed this sport by virtue of the fact that he persisted in it for the balance of his time at Bowdoin. The sophomore experience was, apparently, a very active period of time for my father. In the *Bowdoin Orient* issue of April 26, 1893, there was an entry that read: "Shaw, '95, has accepted a position for the spring, as teacher in Conway, N.H." It is difficult to understand how this could have been accomplished without his having dropped out of school for a semester; however, there is no indication that this had ever taken place.

With respect to his junior year, my father became one of ten members on the Bowdoin Editorial Board. Also he was the Odist for the Class Ivy Day, a "class day" for that academic year. Noteworthy during this academic year was an annual Exhibition Day that was, in effect, a demonstration of athletic prowess in a multitude of events. The activity was put on by members of all classes for the benefit of the entire college community and consisted of skills in gymnastics (which included parallel bars, the horizontal bar, tumbling, the flying rings, a dumb-bell drill, an Indian-club drill, Roman ladders, and the building of pyramids), pole-vaulting, sparring, wrestling and fencing (which included the art of fencing, broadswords drill, and the use of single sticks). In addition to individual activities, each class would, in turn, present a special group drill involving a specific area of expertise. In the spring of 1894, my father was involved with the broadsword drills, an individual broadsword exhibition, and the pyramid-building event. This is the first reference to my father's receiving instruction and submitting to the discipline of mastering the art of fencing. His proclivity for this sport was evident from thoughts expressed at an earlier age.

As a senior, my father added the Bowdoin College Snow Shoe Club to his multifarious activities wherein he was elected as one of the four officers, his office carrying the title of "Whipper-In" and the dubious task of whipping in members for united action. He concluded his four-year sojourn at Bowdoin graduating on June 27, 1895, with a bachelor's degree in Liberal Studies as a member of a graduating class of fifty-two (three members of the original class had dropped out, two new members were added along the way). Summarizing his four-year co-curricular career, he was the Odist for Ivy Day, a member of the *Orient* Editorial Board, on a varsity athletic team for three years, on his class athletic team, a squad leader for four years, and a member of the

Banjo and Guitar Club for four years.[23]

The salient features of my father's college career were his willingness to participate, his desire to write and critique the writing of others, and his fondness for athletics and the physical conditioning and competition evolving from this activity. As one reads the articles that were written by my father in the *Bowdoin Orient,* his love of words, woods and water become apparent as well as his innate creativity. My father was now ready to take on the challenges of the real world.

---

23    The material presented in this chapter were obtained from the eight Bowdoin College sources listed:

  1. *Bowdoin College Catalog,* circa 1895.

  2. *The Bowdoin Orient.* Published every alternate Wednesday during the Collegiate Year by the students of Bowdoin College.

  3. *The Bugle.* Published Annually by Editors chosen from the several Fraternities and from the Non-Society Men of the Junior Class.

  4. *Bowdoin College, Biographical Record of Joseph Thompson Shaw, Class of 1895.*

  5. *Bowdoin in the World War,* published in 1929.

  6. *Bowdoin Alpha Delta Phi in the World War.*

  7. *Bowdoin Alumnus, August 1952.*

  8. *General Catalogue of Bowdoin College—A Biographical Record of Alumni and Officers, 1794–1950,* Sesquicentennial Edition, Brunswick, Maine, 1950.

Camping, about 1934: Joe Jr., Sandy, Joe, Milton.

# 6
# The Art of Fencing[24]

FENCING WAS very much a part of my father's life, having captured his imagination when he was a boy. Years later, as a student at Bowdoin, that which was a boyhood fascination became a reality as my father immersed himself into those formal activities directly related to the art of fencing.

In essence, fencing is a by-product of the utilization of swords as a weapon of war. Man turned his skill to the making of weapons almost as soon as he discovered the art of working metals. The consequence was the sword, a device that became one of the oldest of all fighting weapons. Because dueling was introduced to the civilized world as a means of settling personal grievances, skillful swordplay became a necessary part of every gentleman's training. However, notwithstanding the fact that this form of judicial combat had been in vogue for at least three centuries, by the mid-1800s it had been outlawed in this country as well in most of the civilized world.

Evidence exists that fencing had been recognized as a competitive sport as early as 1100 B.C., and by the mid-1700s this concept of fencing had been universally accepted. Reasons abound for its ready acceptance, especially in urban areas: (1) the sport is

24    The material presented in this chapter came from the following two sources:

    1. *United States Fencing Association 2000, Fact Book.*

    2. Mr. Andy Shaw, Historian of the U.S. Fencing Association (history, general background of fencing in the United States, insight into activities of the USFA).

highly competitive requiring a high level of coordination, physical conditioning, and tactical awareness; (2) as more urban areas were created and there was a lessening of the agricultural pursuits in this country, especially throughout the 1800s, there was greater attention being paid to physical fitness; (3) the sport had its social implications providing opportunity for those in the white-collar world of work to interface with each other in a non-business environment; and, (4) for those who pursued fencing as a discipline, it represented the mastery of a skill.

IN SPITE of the foregoing observations governing the reasons why one would turn to fencing as an avocation, none of them apply to my father's decision to pursue this activity. His affinity for fencing was noted in his "rambling" autobiography, when he shared his enthusiasm for the sword as his weapon of choice. Elaborating, he explained that, as a boy, a stick felt natural in his grasp, striking and guarding a matter almost of intuition. His first formal training took place while at Bowdoin College where he participated in both broadswords drill and the use of the single sticks. Fortuitously, his tenure at Bowdoin from September 1891 through June 1895 came at a time when the sport of fencing was gaining recognition across the country.

For the first two years beyond college my father worked in New York City, first as a journalist for the *New York World* newspaper, and then as a clerk for the G.P. Putnam's Sons book publishing company. With regard to fencing, he became affiliated with the New York Fencers Club, thus marking the start of his amateur fencing career. In 1897, business opportunities necessitated my father's move to Boston where he became the Boston correspondent for the *Textile Manufacturer's Journal* as well an employee of the American Woolen Company. He remained with this firm until 1905. During this eight-year period my father continued to actively participate in fencing, commuting to New York City for specific events, activities and tournaments. This commuting to New York City from Boston was not unique, but, rather, an accepted practice by several distinguished fencers who worked in the Boston area; they realized the importance of competing against the best in New York City: the hub of fencing excellence.

WITH RESPECT to my father's amateur fencing career, the first of several first place awards he received was the YMCA "Duelling Swords," an award for competition held on March 20, 1902. Dueling swords implied that the contestants would duel until blood was drawn. The concept of dueling swords was discontinued in 1915, and the competition reverted to the use of the épée.

In 1908, my father received a second YMCA award for a first place finish. The YMCA was supported by J. Sanford Saltus, an independently wealthy individual who, in addition to being a fencer himself, made significant gifts to the YMCA, including the underwriting of the fencing tournaments staged by the YMCA.

In 1910, my father won the first of four national titles. A gold medal was awarded for his triumph in Sabers in the National Championship competition. He contested as a member of the New York Fencers Club one of the two strongest clubs then in existence, the other being the New York Athletic Club. The silver medal winner was J.W. Knox, and the bronze medal finalist was Frederick J. Byrne, an active, well-known fencer over an extended period of time.

The second individual national was awarded to my father in 1911 for demonstrated proficiency in the foil, épée and saber. The actual matches consisted of two touches with the foil, two with the épée and three with the saber. The silver medal finalist was Dr. John Ernest Gignoux, and the bronze medal finalist was E.B. Myers. The award was made in the name of the President of the Amateur Fencing League of America to my father for having bested the competition in these three weapons. In 1950, the three-weapon championship competition that involved either a five or seven touch bout, was eliminated.

On February 12, 1912, a gold medal was awarded to my father for his proficiency in foils. Competing as a member of the New York Fencing Club in a contest established in the name of J. Sanford Saltus, this activity was under the aegis of the YMCA.

In both 1914 and 1916, again competing as a member of the New York Fencing Club, my father was a member of the three-man team that won the National Saber Team Title Championship. For both years his teammates were Arthur St. Clair Lyon and Stediford Pitt. This tournament, sponsored by the Amateur Fencers League of America, was hotly contested and the title highly coveted. Opposed to the team on which my father participated was the team from the New York Athletic Club represented by August Anderson, Sherman Hall and Victor Curti, three highly proficient fencers. In fact, this three-man team had won the national title in the years surrounding 1914 and 1916. Many teams and their respective clubs were involved in this competition. Ultimately the top two teams competed in a series of nine bouts with the winner having to win a majority of the contests.

The best fencers in the country were affiliated with the two clubs that squared off against each other for the national team titles. Fencing-mates of my father in the New York Fencers Club were Arnold W. De La Peor, the French national champion: he was world renowned, and while in New York City represented Ireland. Also a member of this elite group was George Horace Breed, a fencer who excelled in both the foil and épée. Fencers with whom my father competed and practiced from the New York Athletic Club were August Anderson, five time national champion in sabers and purportedly the leading saber fencer in America during this general period of time. Also there was Sherman Hall, a top performer in the country during this same period of time in both the foil and sword.

MY FATHER was considered to be in the top echelon of fencers in the United States during this relatively short period of time from 1910 to 1916. He was the amateur fencing champion of the United States by virtue of the fact that he won four national titles of which two were individual titles and two were team titles. In the words of Andy Shaw, Historian for the United States Fencing Association, "Joseph T. Shaw was an awesome fencer, one of the best fencers in America, especially with the saber."

It has been said that my father had perfected an offensive move for which there was no defense. In view of the fact that for every offense there is a defense, this statement is probably attributable to his remarkable agility, and eye-hand speed and coordination. Physically he stood only five feet, eight inches tall, but my father had a powerful chest, as well as great strength in his arms and upper legs. He was an avid archer, golfer, sculler, rower, canoe-ist, runner and gymnast. These activities all point toward one who had developed the requisite skills, strength and stamina for success in the sport of fencing. With remarkable perseverance, his success with the weapons utilized in the art of fencing does not come as a surprise.

It is not known who instructed my father in the art of fencing. However, instruction did take place in that he indicated that he "was able to win the national championship in sabers after a little more than a year of instruction in the weapon." It is also sensed that there was a lot of self-instruction taking place; in effect, studying what others were doing and then adapting that information to his style.

Captain Joseph T. Shaw in Prague.

# 7
# Europe Beckons

DURING THE period 1905 through 1917 one can trace my father's active involvement with fencing in the Boston-New York areas; however, there is no available record as to which firms he worked for over this twelve-year span. My father did acknowledge that, during this period, a tempting business opportunity presented itself and that he was associated with other business enterprises up until World War I broke out. Whether he was alluding to his affiliation with the American Woolen Company from 1897 through 1905 as that tempting business opportunity is not known.

## THE PRE-EUROPE YEARS

SOME OF the missing information on my father's pre-European years was provided from his enlistment records when he volunteered for active duty with the U.S. Army in 1918. With respect to those questions dealing with his civilian occupation and specialty, my father indicated that he was the president of Visual Education, Inc., and that his specialty was "executive work."[25] When interviewed by Stephen Mertz, W.T. Ballard, one of my father's more prolific writers for *Black Mask,* indicated that my father had been president of a highly successful manufactur-

---

25   "American Relief Administration Personnel Files, Joseph T. Shaw," on file in Herbert Hoover Presidential Library, Stanford University, 1919.

ing company before the World War I.[26]

From bits and pieces of conversation, remembered from years ago, my father had been relatively wealthy but had lost a good bit of this wealth in the stock market panic of 1907. Whatever, my father did have the propensity to generate money as evidenced by the purchase of a schooner, his ability to invest time and money into his fencing activities, and the fact that he was able to take time away from his work in order to travel through Spain. Combining his Yankee background and his own built-in business sensitivities, my father's ability to earn a substantial income comes as no surprise.

As Europe exploded in fire, my father sensed that it was only a matter of time before the United States would be drawn into the conflict. To that end, he embarked on a program in 1916 and 1917 to train pre-draft men and members of the national Army on how to use the bayonet in close-in fighting.[27] Many of the moves utilized in fencing, especially the footwork, he incorporated into the bayonet techniques that were then being taught. As the Army manuals on bayonet fighting were revised, the modifications my father had introduced were factored into these training documents.

## EUROPE AT WAR AND ITS AFTERMATH

BECAUSE OF the wanton destruction of American shipping by German submarines everywhere on the high seas in 1916 and 1917, the United States declared war on Germany on April 6, 1917. The first American troops arrived in France on June 26, 1917. On July 20, 1918, my father, at age forty-four, volun-

---

26    Stephen Mertz, "W.T. Ballard; An Interview," *Armchair Detective, Winter 1979,* p. 3.

27    Autobiography (see Introduction).

teered for service with the United Sates Army. Commissioned as a captain and assigned to the Chemical Warfare Service, he boarded a ship and was on his way to Europe.[28] Although my father did not claim "a great part in sending Wilhelm to Doorn," he was able to maintain the tradition of having at least one member of the family take part in each war in which this country participated. He was one of nearly 1,400,000 American soldiers poured into France during that critical period of time.

My father was first assigned to the Gas School at Coigne, France, and from 15 November until the end of the year was attached to the Headquarters of the First Army, first stationed at Souilly, and later at Bar-sur-Aube. With the cessation of hostilities and the signing of the Armistice on November 11, 1918, my father started to explore other available challenges. In November he was offered the post of athletic director of the Ninth Corps, in the Army of Occupation; that option he refused in lieu of pursuing the opportunity to serve with the American Relief Administration.[29]

During and immediately after the war, the Allies sent food and supplies to war-shattered countries. In addition, new countries were being created from old empires that had disintegrated. Three independent countries—Austria, Czechoslovakia and Hungary— emerged from the old Austro-Hungarian Empire. Allied diplomats made a new Poland out of Austrian, German and Russian territory. They formed Yugoslavia by adding to Serbia, large portions of Austria-Hungary, Bulgaria and Montenegro. Romania was doubled in size. The peace conference awarded additional territory to Greece and Italy. The Ottoman Empire lost Armenia, Palestine, Mesopotamia (now Iraq), Syria and territorial claims in Africa. In 1917 to 1918, Estonia, Finland, Latvia and Lithu-

---

28    Edgar O. Achorn, editor, *Bowdoin in the World War* (published by Bowdoin College, 1929), p. 64.

29    *Ibid.*

ania declared their independence from Russia.[30] These many changes represented a remarkable shift in the geographic make up of Europe, with its attendant problems that included the many different racial, ethnic and language barriers that had to be surmounted.

During the war intense bombing and shelling had taken place in areas of military operations. The war destroyed the industrial and community lives of many cities, towns and villages in those areas. It closed or destroyed schools, factories, roads and railroads. In many countries, people had to depend on food supplied by their governments. In Eastern Europe and the Balkans, millions of persons fled from their homes in fear of invasion. Refugees moved helplessly from place to place in search of food, clothing and shelter. After the war, those who tried return to their homes often found that that their towns or villages no longer existed.[31] As a consequence, vast populations were at risk.

## THE CHILDREN'S RELIEF PROGRAM

IT WAS into this inferno of chaos that Herbert Hoover was moved, given the responsibility to direct Allied relief and reconstruction. He organized the American Relief Administration to specifically care for children in liberated and former enemy territory. Recognizing the challenge embodied in this effort, my father, who had been assigned to the Headquarters of the Chemical Warfare Service at Tours, France, since the beginning of January, initiated correspondence with Robert A. Taft and Herbert F. Hoover. On March 31, 1919, my father formally requested that he be transferred from the U.S. Army to this newly established organization, the United States Food Administration Program,

---

30    *The World Book*, Vol. 20, pp. 378–379.

31    *Ibid.*, p. 377.

headquartered in Paris. His commanding officer, a Colonel E.N. Johnston, Chief of Chemical Warfare Service stated that, although my father had given very excellent service, that he could be spared. Consequently, on April 8, 1919, the transfer took place; he was separated from the U.S. Army, and, while still retaining his commission as Captain, assigned to the American Relief Administration under Herbert Hoover. He was directed to proceed to Prague, Czechoslovakia, via Switzerland and Austria, where he was to be the Director of the Bureau for Children's Relief. This truly became a mission of mercy, and one that had to be initiated immediately.[32]

There were two duties assigned to my father by the American Relief Administration. The first duty was to extend relief to the physically needy children of the country, and the second was to effect, if possible, the establishment of the Czechoslovakian National Organization of Child Welfare. Not only were these objectives mutually supportive, but, since time was of the essence, both were undertaken jointly. Problems abounded. Existing relief organizations were incapable of providing support; the attitude of those who would be doing the work were conditioned to an autocratic bureaucracy where initiative was discouraged; there was deep divisiveness amongst the population because of race, nationality and religious diversity; and an infant democracy was taking its first small, uncertain steps.[33]

The Commission's first task was to mandate that the children would not be discriminated against: racial, national or religious considerations were immaterial—the only criterion was physical need. Next, the country was divided into fifteen zones or distribution centers. Doctors within each zone identified the

32    "American Relief Administration, Personnel Files, Joseph T. Shaw."

33    "American Relief Administration—European Operations, Czechoslovakia, Vol. VII."

physical status of each child from birth to fourteen and placed each of them in one of three categories of health: Class A, those children not in need of nourishment; Class B, those children who needed food to a considerable extent; and Class C, those children in critical condition. At the same time, experts were consulted as to which foods should be provided to the children; and the logistics for food ordering, delivery, storage and dissemination were established. Within the fifteen zones, sub-organizations were created with representatives from the community serving as members of each local board. Each board reflected the diversity of the population it served. Participation was encouraged from each member—cooperation was expected and received.[34]

The first trainload of food from the American Relief Administration reached Prague on May 13, 1919. Within six week's time, 400,000 children were being fed daily. A milk and cocoa ration was given to children up to six years of age as well as to nursing mothers and pregnant women. A soup ration was developed by those workers in the Commission who had had previous child relief experience for those children from six to fourteen years of age. The best experts on child feeding that could be found in the country worked in concert with the Commission team. Ultimately 428,318 children (of whom 150,681 were under six years of age) were being fed daily. These figures represented fifteen percent of the total estimated child population in Czechoslovakia, and sixty percent of the children estimated in need. During the implementation of the initial programs no relief was possible for Slovakia through lack of food and the situation brought about by reason of the Magyar invasion. These inhabitants of Hungary lost much of their land following the collapse of the Austro-Hungarian Empire and the resulting sub-division of its lands in 1919. In response, the Magyars invaded that part of Czechoslovakia that bordered

---

34    *Ibid.*

on Hungary thus precluding the ability of the Child Relief organization to provide for those children caught up in the conflict.[35]

The overall activities reflected the achievement of two of the three programs initially established. The third program was implemented between September 15 and December 15, 1919. This program provided for the feeding of 600,000 children, an estimated twenty percent of the total child population and about ninety percent of the estimated number in need of relief. It was initiated after the dissolution of the successful Children's Relief organization. Continued provisioning of supplies from the U.S. Government and private sources enabled the program to stay alive until the resources of Czechoslovakia were sufficiently developed to take over. One of the mainstays of the Children's Relief Program was the recognition given to it from the national level with both the country's President and Prime Minister serving as Honorary President and Honorary Vice President respectively of a National Committee. Every minister of the Government was a member of the Committee as were the chief representatives of the different religious and racial groups, heads of various relief organizations, and the heads of the banking and business associations. This Committee was truly inclusive of all the political government and all the people within the borders of the Republic, making it an organization of great national importance and effectiveness.

One of my father's great concerns was the discriminatory practices that were being exercised against Bohemian children living in the greater Vienna area, the capital of Austria located only about forty miles south of the southern border of Czechoslovakia. To that end, he wrote the following letter on May 19, 1919.

---

35   *Ibid.*

Dear Mr. Hoover:

Our attention has been called to the pitiable condition of 500,000 Bohemians living in and around Vienna, and learning of the principles which we have established in the country to minister fair treatment to all regardless of race, religion, or language, they have appealed to us to urge the application of the same principles in old Austria. We are informed that the poor Bohemian children in Vienna did not receive any of the clothes or shoes in the Christmas of 1917. In November 1918 all the organizations for the relief of the children, except those dealing with the Czech children, received biscuits, milk, coca and chocolate from the Swiss Republic; but the Czech children received none of these things.

General Legre, head of the Italian Mission in Vienna, made a gift of 400,000 kilograms of rice to the public kitchens, but the kitchens caring for 2,000 Czech children in nine different nurseries, did not receive its part. Dr. Perez, Argentine Ambassador, with the representatives of the Entente and neutral states, planned the segregation of 4,000 children in different camps for feeding provisions supplied by the Entente. The Jugdamt selected the children refusing those of Czech nationality, and Czechs were excluded from the number of 8,000 sent to Switzerland, and about 7,000 sent to Sweden. It is said that the only way in which food is safely sent to Vienna is by consigning it direct to the Czecho-Slovak Embassy in Vienna.

The foregoing items, together with a large number of statistics and records, have been given us by the secretary for care of Czech children in old Austria.

This gentleman was given the name of the head of the American Mission for Child Relief in Vienna. The principle of a fair apportionment of food among the neediest children within the borders of this country, regardless of their race or religion, has promptly become a slogan in Czecho-Slovakia, and is not only in the mouths of the delegations coming to us from the farthest border land, and in fact from all sides, but in the newspapers of the country and the letters that are pouring into the office. It seems also to have gone further, as Yugo Slavs have already made inquiries concerning our manner of work. Occasion of this letter was brought about by the expression of the desire that equal fairness be practiced in neighboring countries where children and people of this nationality have their homes.

If anything can be done in the present instance, it will go far towards encouraging a more amiable feeling on the part of the Czecho-Slovaks toward their neighbors, and I presume that you are so well advised of the feeling that exists between this country and the peoples who surround it on all sides, that you will appreciate the importance of helping along these lines.

A quick response to this letter was sent to Herbert Hoover from R. Hermann Geist, Commissioner for Vienna, dated June 4, 1919.

"I am in receipt of Captain J.T. Shaw's letter to you dated May 19, in regard to Czech children in and about Vienna. I have personally come in touch with the Ceske Srdce Videnske and have inspected its kitchens. I am supplying food to this organization for nine kitchens, approximating 2,000 Czecho-Slovakian children." [36]

MY FATHER'S letter of May 19 demonstrated his sense of righteousness and fair play, and extended well beyond the purview of his original assignment. Most importantly, it got results.

After my father had transferred to the American Relief Administration, the American Expeditionary Forces, headquartered in Paris, asked, by questionnaire, what his desire was once this duty assignment was completed. The choice was to be one of four options: To remain in the regular Army, to request an appointment in the Officers Reserve Corps, to request prompt separation from the Service, or to request immediate and final separation from the Service. My father elected the fourth option: namely,

---

36    *Ibid.*

immediate and final separation from the Service. His assignment in Prague ended on September 10, 1919, when the Children's Relief Program was demobilized. On September 30, 1919, my father returned to Paris and resigned his commission, receiving an honorable discharge. After fourteen months on active duty he was now returned to civilian status.[37]

In gratitude for the work he had done in Czechoslovakia, the Czech Government presented my father with a twenty-five inch sculptured marble statue of a Slovakian peasant mother and two children. One of the children is in his mother's arms, the other hiding in the folds of her mother's long flowing skirt—a beautiful testimony to work well done.[38]

## THE RESTLESS YEARS

MY FATHER remained in Czechoslovakia from 1919 until 1924. The only information available as to what transpired during that period of time is contained in his autobiography: "I remained in the country nearly five years and had the unique opportunity of observing and studying the birth and first infantile steps of a republic. Tempting business opportunities obtruded on every hand. A recurrence of an illness contracted in the war sent me to the mountains and gave opportunity for meditation. Business and the mere acquisition of wealth had lost their flavor. I turned seriously to writing."[39]

Apparently, my father had previously been married. The first acknowledgment of this marriage was in Harriett Farwell's book of the genealogy of the Roger Shaw family. A single entry reads: "Joseph T., b. May 8, 1874; graduated from Bowdoin in 1895;

---

37    "American Relief Administration Personnel Files, Joseph T. Shaw."

38    Autobiography.

39    *Ibid.*

is also engaged in mercantile affairs; m. Harriet Richardson; resides in Boston."[40] The book was published in 1904, with the data collected in 1903. This would place the marriage sometime after graduation from Bowdoin in 1895 and 1903. My mother, being exceptionally close to my wife, Nancy, told her that there had been a marriage to a lady who was a nurse, was either a widow or divorcée, and that there were two adopted children involved—adopted by whom is not known.

**Children's Relief Program statue.**

The third piece of information is that when my father filled out the necessary papers for entry into the Army in July 1918, the individual who was to be notified in case of an emergency was "Mrs. Joseph T. Shaw, 4 Rydal Place, Montclair, New Jersey."[41]

Unanswered questions are: (1) Was Harriett's last name Richardson a maiden name or the name of her former husband? (2) While in Montclair did my father and his wife rent or buy a home? (3) Why would my father give up the presidency of what was assumed to be a prosperous firm and volunteer for Army service? (4) If married, why didn't my father return to the United States

---

40   *Shaw Records, A Memorial of Roger Shaw, 1594–1661*, p. 181.

41   "American Relief Administration Personnel Files, Joseph T. Shaw."

either after his assignment with the American Relief Administration was completed, or upon resigning his commission as an officer in the U.S. Army? (5) If my father was not married when his work with the Czechoslovakian Children's Program was finished, why didn't he marry my mother sometime between September 1919 and 1924, before he came back to the United States?

Within my family there had never been any discussion about a previous marriage, and a search of marriage records in the State of Maine did not provide any answers as to the marriage having taken place. At this point in time, the above questions remain unanswered.

At the Musek home in Prague.

# 8
# The *Black Mask* Challenge

AT THIS point in the biography there are significant gaps in where my father was as well as what he was doing during critical periods of his life. The information that has been provided has, for the most part, come from biographical facts, encyclopedia explanations, and available records. Moving into this next phase of his life has its benefits. First, for a ten-year period, from the fall of 1926 until the fall of 1936, where he was and what he was doing can be clearly established. Further, there is extensive documentation available in the form of personal letters to and from those persons with whom my father worked, as well as magazine articles by those who knew him or were familiar with many of the principals involved in the growth and development of the thriving pulp industry.

## PULP LITERATURE

FOR AN outsider, examining an area to which there has only been limited exposure, basic questions come to mind. How did the pulp industry evolve? Who were these authors submitting stories for publication in pulp magazines? Was being a pulp magazine writer an end in itself or a means toward an end? Who were the editors who purchased stories for publication, and how did they fit into the picture? What was the extent of their responsibilities, and what were their expectations from the writers submitting material? Specifically, with respect to the *Black Mask* magazine, does the hard-boiled style of mystery story represent a unique niche in the field of American literature, and what was unique about the *Black Mask* magazine? Did my father attempt to Hammettize the *Black Mask* magazine? What kind of relationship existed between my father and Dashiell Hammett? What traits, capabilities, and strengths did my father bring to the editorship of *Black Mask* magazine? Was my father fired from his position as editor of *Black Mask* magazine, or did he resign on his own volition?

This is certainly a daunting listing of questions with no assurance that they can be answered with conviction and finality. For example, how did my father get involved in the "rough paper" magazine business, as he adamantly called it, or the "pulp" magazine, as labeled by most others? As indicated before, he had returned from Czechoslovakia in 1924 after having been there for the better part of five years. His return to the greater New York City area seemed natural enough in that his reported home address when he left for Europe in 1918 was in Montclair, New Jersey. Further his two older brothers were living and working in the area. Frederick was working as a salesman in various lines of business most notably as a commercial paper broker, and Philip as the senior partner of a firm that specialized in note and bond brokering. For an occupation, my father first turned to note brokering; in all probability because of the support he could realize from his brothers. However, his heart was not into this line of work—his desire was to write and to get involved in the literary field. Another factor at work was the condition of a society in turmoil. He was appalled by the disillusionment that followed the world war, the public cynicism, the increasing control over the cities by gangsters, and the lack of integrity of elected public officials. With a very strong sense of civic responsibility he felt obliged to get involved.

In 1926, in trying to sell a story to the editor of *Black Mask* magazine, my father ended up as its editor. It is not known why he approached this particular magazine. Perhaps it was one of several pulp magazines that he contacted in an effort to establish himself as a writer.

The origin of the pulp magazine tradition can be traced back to the 1830s when the availability of cheap wood pulp paper, the invention of the steam printing press, the expanding postal services and railways, and a growing literate working class made fiction affordable and accessible to the "common man." This cheap, popular and sensational periodic literature first appeared in the form of so-called weeklies, four pages long and printed on newspaper, containing reading matter plagiarized from the high-priced American and English magazines.[42] After 1860 dime novels were introduced as an alternative to the story weeklies. The two types of literature shared the same cheap fiction market, appealed to the same tastes, and made use of the same writers and popular characters. The weeklies and dime novels were awful for the most part, but they did create the first mass market for fiction in America.

It was in the early 1900s that the pulp magazines evolved, a seven inch by ten inch periodical repeating many of the publishing practices invented by their predecessors—the use of continuing series characters, hack writers, the exploitation of popular enthusiasms, and emphasis on action and sensation. They would also develop their own stale, repetitive formulas and bad writing. The pulp magazines flourished in the 1920s and 1930s, but in time, like the weeklies and dime novels, went from their birth, to widespread dissemination, to oblivion. For pulp magazines, their demise occurred by the 1950s.[43]

---

42    Lee Server, *Danger Is My Business* (San Francisco: Chronicle Books, 1993), pp. 17–18.

43    *Ibid.*, p. 137.

In 1920 the American mystery story was a literary form that lacked literary qualities; it was essentially lowbrow entertainment that constituted the adult reading material of the day,[44] and was looked down upon as publishing's poor, ill-bred stepchild.[45] At that point in time of their development, the resulting printed material was, irreverently, considered to be "throw-away" art.[46] Unlike the weeklies and dime novels though, pulp magazines generated "works of lasting merit and a level of creativity that would far outdistance the first, primitive pop-fiction magazines."[47]

Because of their extraordinary nature, the pulps magazines thrived on unconstrained creativity. Held accountable to few standards of logic, believability or "good taste," the pulps were literary dream machines, offering regular entry to intensive worlds of excitement, danger, glory and romance—almost all providing an escape from mundane reality.[48] "Without the sophisticated design, the pretty pictures, and the name-brand authors of the expensive slick (smooth paper) magazines, the pulps had to do with imagination and the power of the written word. This, as it happened, was their glory. Although it was not understood at the time, the pulps were creating an innovative and lasting form of literature—introducing new styles of writing and genres of popular fiction, discovering writers who would become some of the most widely read authors in the world."[49]

Of the many pulp magazines that were then on the market in

---

44    Richard Laymen, "The Changing Face of Crime Fiction: *The Black Mask,*" *American Bookseller,* May 5, 1986, p. 2074.

45    Lee Server, *Danger Is My Business,* p. 15.

46    LeRoy Lan Panek, *An Introduction to the Detective Story* (Bowling Green State University: Popular Press, 1987), p. 154.

47    Lee Server, *Danger Is My Business,* p. 20.

48    *Ibid.,* p. 9.

49    *Ibid.,* p. 15.

the early 1920s, *Black Mask* was relatively new. The magazine's original owners, H.L. Mencken and George Jean Nathan, formerly had been co-editors and then co-owners of *Smart Set,* a smooth paper magazine; as editors they encouraged authors to offer any work that they chose to write. The two ventured into the pulp fiction field with *Black Mask* in the hope that it would turn a quick profit enabling them to stabilize *Smart Set's* shaky financial condition. Frances M. Osborne was appointed as editor and the first issue was dated in April 1920. The magazine failed to realize a profit in its first year of operation; moreover, the burden of reading and making editorial decisions on manuscripts was too much for a magazine that the owners considered to be a paper "louse." Wanting nothing more to do with *Black Mask,* they took advantage of an opportunity to make another quick profit by selling the magazine to Eltinge Warner and Eugene Crowe who, by that time, had become the owners and publishers of *Smart Set.*[50]

For the first two years of its existence the quality of fiction published in *Black Mask* is considered by later standards as unreadable.[51] Fortunately for the magazine, a group of talented writers was starting to submit material, and, under the editorship of George W. Sutton, Jr., and his associate Harry North, the work of these developing writers began appearing in *Black Mask.* Carroll John Daly, who was the first to pioneer the hardboiled style of detective story writing, saw his first *Black Mask* story printed in the October 1922 issue. "Dolly" was followed in December by "The False Burton Combs." These two were the first of fifty-four Daly stories to be published in the *Black Mask* magazine through 1936. "Three Gun Terry" in the May 15, 1923, issue was significant in that the character of Terry Mack, the

---

50    Richard Layman, "The Changing Face of Crime Fiction: *The Black Mask,*" p. 2074.

51    *Ibid.*

world's first tough private detective, was introduced. The rough and tough, smart-alecky style Daly utilized in developing this character was such that some literary historians subsequently declared that a new type of writing was born.[52] Two weeks later the story "Knights of the Open Palm" appeared, featuring Daly's second hero Race Williams. This form of writing was the initial impulse toward what was later to be described as the Hard-Boiled School of Writing. A crucial element was that it emphasized action over the detection of clues. Daly's storytelling was "crude, repetitive, illogical, prone to exaggeration, artless, inconsistent, full of bad grammar, arbitrary paragraphing, and awkward binges of stream-of-consciousness; his cardboard heroes were brutal and ignorant, and frequently espoused the virtues of vigilantism."[53] He made no attempt at realism or objectivity;[54] however, this style of writing struck a responsive chord with the pulp-reading public

The next author of note was one whose writing talent had been recognized at an earlier point in time by H.L. Mencken. Dashiell Hammett made his debut in *Black Mask* in December 1922 with the "The Road Home." A year later Hammett's detective hero, Continental Op, made his first appearance in a story entitled "Arson Plus." Of the forty-nine Hammett stories published in *Black Mask* over the next eight years, the first four were submitted under the pen name of Peter Collinson, a disguise he used to conceal his real name until such time as he could assure himself that his work was being accepted by the reading public. "Arson Plus" instituted the distinctive style that changed the face of American mystery writing. Hammett's approach was characterized by the understated first person narrative; the terse,

---

52    *Ibid.,* p. 2076.

53    Lee Server, *Danger Is My Business,* p. 65.

54    Dave Lewis, "The Backbone of *Black Mask*," *Clues—A Journal of Detection,* Vol. 2, #2, Fall/Winter, 1981, p. 118.

hard sentences; and the methodical investigation employed. Lee Server states that Hammett was an innovative prose stylist with a profound vision of an America driven by violence and corruption; his writing was as spare and clear as any in the history of fiction.[55] A former operative with the Pinkerton Detective Agency, Hammett was able to give an authenticity to his stories that none of his peers could match. It was Hammett who laid the true foundation for what was to become recognized as the *Black Mask* school of objective hard-boiled literature. Whereas Daly penned mere pulp, Hammett aspired to something higher.

"By publishing 'Three Gun Terry' and 'Knights of the Open Palm' by Daly, and 'Arson Plus' by Hammett in 1923, *Black Mask* had made history; a revolution was underway, and the detective genre would never be the same."[56] The arrival of Erle Stanley Gardner in 1924, Nels Leroy Jorgensen and Tom Curry in 1925, and Raoul Whitfield and Frederick Nebel in 1926, followed closely behind the flow of stories from Carroll John Daly and Dashiell Hammett. These seven writers became the standard bearers for the *Black Mask* School of Detective Story Writing as it unfolded and evolved over the course of the next decade.

As editor from October 1922 until March 15, 1924, George Sutton seemed unaware of the effect that this new type of fiction was to have in the literary field. He continued to publish the work of both Daly and Hammett, recognizing the importance of the continuity of heroes from one monthly issue to the next. Phil Cody's contributions were even greater during the thirty-one month period from April 1, 1924, through October 1926 when he was editor. It was he who stated that: "the Hammett-Daly brand of tough, hard-edged storytelling represented a bold new step beyond the traditional school of crime fiction." He urged

---

55    Lee Server, *Danger Is My Business,* p. 67.

56    William Nolan, *The Black Mask Boys,* p.22.

Daly to write more about Race Williams, "recognizing that Daly's work was far inferior to Hammett's but he was wise enough to know that content counted more than quality in establishing the popularity of this new brand of fiction." Under Cody, circulation was increasing; in addition, he also followed Sutton's practice of encouraging hero continuity, and he felt confident enough to state that *"The Black Mask* magazine had found its stride and is forging to the front" in the pulp field.[57] In the latter part of 1926, Phil Cody moved into the position of vice president while continuing in his role as Circulation Director. He is the one who hired my father as his replacement.[58]

At this point two issues should be addressed. The first is the subject of who discovered whom with respect to new writers appearing on the scene. Both Daly's and Hammett's first stories received positive reaction from the readers of *Black Mask.* Does this mean that the editor discovered these two writers or was it, rather, the fact that the writers themselves sought out *Black Mask?* If the stories had not received any recognition, the authors would be passed off as just another pair of hack writers; however, because the stories were received with acclaim from the reading public, immediately everyone wanted to know who discovered them. It is interesting to note that Sutton totally disapproved of Daly's work to the point where he didn't even want to be identified with it. It was by a quirk of faith that Harry North, in his boss' absence, purchased Daly's first work; it was the readership that applauded the decision and clamored for more. Ray Chandler's first story was sold to *Black Mask,* and it was a smash hit. Did my father discover Chandler? No, he saw the genuineness of the work, purchased and published it, and then let the public judge

---

57    *Ibid.,* p. 23.

58    Richard Layman, "The Changing Face of Crime Fiction: *The Black Mask,*" p. 2076.

its worth. With respect to Hammett, his strength as a writer was ultimately going to come to the surface regardless of who was making the editorial decisions. There is much in the literature where individuals are arguing over the question of who made discoveries of certain authors. It is felt that this is a bogus issue.

The second issue pertains to pulp writers and the opportunities afforded them to continue to develop their craft. Rather than being a dead end street, pulp magazines provided a remarkable training ground for those who had elected to pursue writing as a career. Both Erle Stanley Gardner and Frederick Nebel rejected the opportunity to have their stories published in *The Hard-Boiled Omnibus* (1946) on the grounds that their work was dated and, therefore, would not accurately reflect the growth they had realized as writers in the ensuing years.[59] It is understandable that copy written in 1930 would not sell at a later point in time because it is dated and shows it glaringly;[60] however, it can also be said that the average writer for *Black Mask* was at the same level of expertise as the average writer for the "slicks."[61]

## EXPECTATIONS FROM AN EDITOR, AN AUTHOR'S POINT-OF-VIEW

ALTHOUGH MY father had no knowledge of the pulp industry, he was not a novice. As a youngster, reading had been a passion driving him to absorb everything between two covers on which he could lay his hands. By age fourteen he had read

---

59   Stephen Mertz, "Captain Shaw's Hard-Boiled Boys," *American Detective,* Summer 1979, p. 264.

60   Stephen Mertz, "W.T. Ballard: An Interview," *The Armchair Detective,* Winter 1979, p. 6.

61   Thomas Stuark, "Horace McCoy, Captain Shaw, and *The Black Mask,*" *Mystery and Detection Annual,* 1972, p. 147.

all of Scott's works, an extensive list of the works of both American and English authors, and a fair share of the Classics. While at Bowdoin he was on the college's newspaper editorial board, to which he contributed short stories. Upon graduation in 1895, with a bachelor's degree in Liberal Arts, his first job was as a reporter for the very reputable *New York World*. From that job my father went to a semi-trade weekly of which he became editor. In addition to writing short stories, about which publication information remains unknown, he also wrote a technical history of the country's woolen industry, *From Wool to Cloth,* as well as a book of impressions of Spain that followed his tour of the country, *Spain of Today.* Although only one hundred and fifty-three pages in length, this book provides entertaining reading. Its publication followed my father's travels through the country during the early fall of 1909.[62]

With this background and a world of confidence my father stepped into his role as editor. Regardless of the preparation, until one is immersed into the complexities of an editorship only then can one fully appreciate the intensity of its demands. An article entitled "A Penny a Word," authored anonymously, identified expectations from an editor of a pulp magazine. Anonymous declared that, if it is a monthly publication, having an assistant is essential. On the masthead of the *Black Mask* magazine there is no assistant noted, nor has a search of the literature identified anyone in that role within the *Black Mask* organization other than when Harry North was an assistant to George Sutton and, subsequently, to Phil Cody. My father was "it" although it has been suggested that Phil Cody as Vice President and Circulation Director may still have had his hand in helping to select stories for publication. Regardless, it was the editor's responsibility to

---

62    Joseph Thompson Shaw, *Spain of Today: A Guide to the Country of the Dons* (New York: The Grafton Press, 1909).

produce the magazine from reading manuscripts, to the checking of the final proofs, writing an editorial describing the current issue's stories, a public relations page announcing forthcoming articles, purchasing stories months ahead of when they would appear in the magazine, and maintaining the schedule for each issue.[63]

Discussions with Will Murray yielded additional insight. First, from an overall point-of-view the editor is responsible for the following broad areas: the flavor and the tone of the magazine and the consistency of this tone, the instinct to detect and move with changing tastes, the knowledge of specific areas, and the ability to operate within the boundaries of budgetary limitations.

From a narrower point-of-view the editor is responsible for the following activities:

—filling a varying number of pages in each issue, depending upon advertising

—determining the number of stories and the length of each

—taking raw typewritten manuscripts and turning this work into a professional magazine

—maintaining an inventory of stories to provide flexibility

—avoiding stories with similar themes in the same issue

—balancing character and story style types within an issue

—editing, then re-editing, and, finally, proof-reading the finished work in galleys and foundry proofs.[64]

Supporting staff, such as an illustrator or one to handle secretarial duties, is required, but pulp magazine staffs were lean at best; therefore, the responsibilities incumbent upon the editor

---

63    Anonymous, "A Penny a Word," *American Mercury*, March 1936, p. 16.

64    Telephone call with Will Murray, crime critic, and a remarkable source of information on pulp magazines in general and hard-boiled authors specifically.

were immense. The anonymous author also points out that the continued employment of an editor is extremely haphazard and subject to circumstances over which he has no control. Every change of policy, every poor guess by a publisher who thinks that a certain magazine should sell and it fails to do so, more often than not it means that the editor will be replaced. The survival rate of pulp editors was relatively low given the training and ability brought to the position, the responsibilities imposed upon the position, and the expectations of a publisher to realize a profit from his investment.[65]

In the "Penny a Word" article the anonymous author takes a very dim view of the lot of the pulp writer. In contrast to Anonymous' heartfelt sympathy for this poor soul are the words of Will Murray who senses that Anonymous represents "the flip side of what we usually hear from pulp writers who look back on their pulpateer days with the rosy nostalgia of remembered youth. Anonymous, whoever he was, was inconsolably bitter and disillusioned after a decade in the popular writing business. He cared little for his work and even less for his readers."[66] Contradictory to these feelings are those expressed by Todhunter Ballard when Erle Stanley Gardner was trying to push him into the writing of novels: "Books," Gardner said, "That's the way you have to go. You want to be a lousy pulp writer all your life? In ten years I will have thirty books under my belt. What will you have?" Ballard's response: "I couldn't see that far ahead, I didn't do the book. It was ten years before the death of the pulps forced me into the book field, and he was right. But I wouldn't have liked to miss the excitement of the pulps and their people."[67] Tom Curry shared

---

65    Anonymous, "A Penny a Word," p. 16.

66    Will Murray, "Postscript to 'A Penny a Word,'" p. 17.

67    Todhunter Ballard, "Writing for the Pulps," (unpublished sketch of a life writing the pulps), p. 18.

Ballard's attitude toward the art of writing. He rejoiced in the freedom of the writer's life. Drawing from the experience of twenty-five years he related as to how he made a living by writing pulp fiction and enjoying it. His essential point was that pulp fiction, or writing of any kind for that matter, enables one to be the whole show. You decide what you want to write, and you are as free as any man can be in this world of conventions and growing taboos.[68]

Unfortunately, Anonymous felt that the pulp writer was doomed to remain in the pulp field for his work-life, with very little opportunity to move beyond into the field of smooth paper magazines; even considering an attempt to move into the "slicks" he felt he no longer had the capability to eradicate his improper ingrown pulp habits, insisting that there had been a vast change in the craft since the early days. Anonymous felt that the pulps had lowered the age-level of their audiences with an appeal to the mental juvenile. This argument was supported by the observation that pulps were published at lower costs than their predecessors while enjoying the circulation of the old days, their profits accruing from mass production; the consequences of this action lowered financial risks and allowed new companies to enter the field with sweatshop methods and low standards.[69]

One feels a certain amount of empathy for Anonymous; however, it is sensed that he was not unique but, rather, was representative of a significant number of authors attempting to eke out a living by writing for the pulps. As is so often the case in all our endeavors, attitude seems to be the determining factor dictating success or failure. Of importance then is the identification of those who shape individual attitudes. Referring to the pulp field as an industry, separate and complete, Anonymous accepted the perception that there was an enormous gap between

68    Tom Curry, "It's Your Own Show," *Writer's 1945 Year Book*, p. 80.

69    Anonymous, "A Penny a Word," p. 14.

the pulps and other literary enterprises. In abject despair, Anonymous gave up any aspirations to move into the "slicks," and, in his own words, "he gratefully returned to the trough." [70]

It was into this milieu that my father stepped as the editor of *Black Mask* magazine. Granted that all publishers and editors were not erratic in the conduct of their respective responsibilities, nor were all pulp writers accepting their fate as the lowest members of the writing profession; however, there is no question that, as a profession, and especially during an economic down-turn, it was difficult for writers to make a living. As for my father, one who was not only an eternal optimist and visionary but who also was a believer in the potential of the individual to make significant contributions, he saw a remarkable opportunity for the magazine. "The story is people as Capt. Shaw so well knew." [71] This insightful observation is applicable to not only the writer of fiction but also to the game of life. My father was new to the profession but he was perceptive enough to recognize that through the spadework done by the two previous editors, George W. Sutton, Jr., and Philip C. Cody, and the recognition of the writing skills of seven authors in particular, the seeds had been planted. Before late 1922 detective pulp magazines were not that distinguishable one from another.[72] With Daly's and Hammett's submissions and their subsequent publication, *Black Mask* started to realize its own identity. One of the first actions my father took was that, in early 1927, he shortened the title from *The Black Mask* to *Black Mask*.[73]

---

70    *Ibid.*

71    S. Omar Barker, "Folks Make Fiction," *The Writer,* November 1955, p. 366.

72    *Hard Boiled Mysteries,* December 27, 1998, p. 1. (http://www.columbia.edu/~mfs10/pulp_hard.html)

73    William Nolan, *The Black Mask Boys,* p. 26.

# THE *BLACK MASK* HARD-BOILED
# SCHOOL OF DETECTIVE FICTION

MY FATHER'S intentions for *Black Mask* were contained in the June 1927 issue editorial page.

> *Black Mask* has a definite purpose and a definite aim.
>
> It is seeking to establish itself as the only magazine of its kind in the fictional world of today and the future.
>
> Its chosen field—detective fiction—is the most absorbing of all literature. This subject embodies mental and physical conflict in man's most violent moods. Its stories are essentially stories of suspense and action, with the thrill of chasing, the terror of pursuit, the triumph of successful analysis and the dread of discovery. They touch at the very heart of human emotions.
>
> However, to be convincing they must be real in motive, character and action. They must be plausible and not absurd. They must be clear and understandable and not confused. In a word, they must be written with the keenest thought and greatest skill.
>
> Therefore, word has gone out to all *Black Mask* writers of our requirements of plausibility, of truthfulness in details, of realism in the picturing of thought, the portrayal of action and emotion. All stories submitted to *Black Mask* are judged and selected with these cardinal requirements in mind, together with the necessity for swift movement in starting and in the development of plot.
>
> The reader of today gets his impression quickly. He judges the character of a man by what he does and not, as formerly, by the author's description of his physical appearance.
>
> And slowly but surely we are moulding the contents of the magazine along the lines of our purpose. We believe that now it more nearly expresses this purpose than it did even six months ago. From material now in hand and in preparation, we are certain that it will more closely approach our requirements in the months to come.

And yet we have an idea that detective fiction as we view it has only commenced to be developed. As a matter of fact, we expect the greatest and most noteworthy development in this particular field of literature than will be seen in any other. All other fields have been worked and overworked. This, as we visualize it, has barely been scratched.

This manifesto describes the salient elements of the *Black Mask* Hard-Boiled School of Detective Fiction. In essence, it is a style of writing that evolved over a period of several years. This style has three essential components: First, while the story is fiction it must create the illusion of reality. The stories must be told with compactness and drama. Second, "The formula or pattern emphasizes character and the problems inherent in human behavior over crime solution. In this new pattern, character conflict is the main theme; the ensuing crime, or its threat, is incidental." The third element of this style emphasizes action on the part of the characters and a fast tempo to the story as the plot unfolds. The interaction between these three components gives this school of writing its definition. Simplicity was stressed as was economy of expression. These constraints gave clarity, plausibility and belief to the story. It also forced the tempo to move quickly. The emphasis on character is predicated upon the ability to recognize human character in three-dimensional form, a condition that fosters character conflict. With this achieved the main crime and its victim are moved off-stage. The solution of the crime is still part of the story but no longer its essence; however, this does not become a distraction to a thrilling story. The beauty of this mode of story development was the fact that, with the writer moved out of the way, the characters are then allowed to define themselves as well as the environment within which they functioned. If the characters were defined as hard-boiled it was because they were given the opportunity to gain this distinction through their actions. In this form of story development, the plot was still important but it was subordinate to the interaction between the characters.

Dashiell Hammett said that: "If you kill a symbol, no crime is committed and no effect is produced. To constitute a murder, the victim must be a real human being of flesh and blood."[74] With respect to my father, not only did he embrace the several components of this hard-boiled style, but he also placed special emphasis on character development while relegating plot to a subordinate role.

The three elements of realism; character development; and the hard, brittle, fast-paced action are those features that separated this newly created *Black Mask* style of writing detective stories from the traditional form that is associated with a crossword puzzle paradigm, one that is deliberately lacking emotional values. My father recognized Dashiell Hammett's position in the genre of mystery detective stories by indicating that Hammett was the leader in what finally brought the magazine its distinctive form... "I wanted to make full use of his rare ability of observation and gift to analyze character beneath a surface appearance... Hammett told his story with a new kind of compulsion and authenticity. And he was one of the most careful and pain-staking workman I have ever known."[75] No other writer ever made such an impact on the magazine.[76] Clearly a new, uniquely American literary form of mystery story was emerging.[77]

In summary, the cardinal requirements to be met by his writers were plausibility, truthfulness in details, realism in pictur-

---

74    Joseph T. Shaw, editor, *The Hard-Boiled Omnibus* (New York: Simon and Schuster, 1946), Introduction, p. vi.

75    William Nolan, *Hammett: A Life at the Edge* (New York: Congdon & Weed Inc., 1983), p. 67.

76    *Ibid.*, p. 108.

77    Richard Layman, "The Changing Face of Crime Fiction: *The Black Mask*," p. 2076.

ing of thought and portrayal of action and emotion. Character and the problems inherent in human behavior over crime solution was emphasized; the ensuing crime or the threat of crime becomes incidental. Philip Durham made the following observations: Joseph T. Shaw had very definite ideas about the *Black Mask* style; for that reason he was determined to set a stylistic pattern to which all of his writers would adhere. The stories to be published would have a "new kind of compulsion and authenticity" embodied in action; however, he also held that "action is meaningless unless it involves recognizable human character in three-dimensional form." What is now referred to as a hard-boiled style is closely related to his demands on his writers to utilize a fast pace with short direct sentences, spare and uncluttered. My father disliked printing stereotyped stories of sordid banal crime; further, his detectives had to be familiar with, if not from, the sharp bright world outside the underworld in which they moved. My father was convinced that the work of his best writers would revolutionize American literature.[78]

My father also had a clear idea of the law-abiding reader for whom *Black Mask* was intended, a person who could relate to a fictional hero. *Black Mask* reflected the harsh realities of life in America at that time; consequently, the main characters were usually tough guys, loners, men who lived not only by strict ethical codes, but also "brought justice to the weak and death to those who preyed on them."[79] My father described this fictional hero as follows: Physically, he is "a pretty stalwart, rugged specimen of humanity—hard as nails, swift of hand and foot, clear-eyed, unprovocative but ready to tackle anything that gets in the way."

---

78    Philip Durham, "The Boys in the *Black Mask*," *UCLA Exhibit*, Jan. 6 to Feb. 10, 1961, Preface.

79    "Hard-Boiled Fiction: History of the Mystery," December 26, 1998, p. 1. (http://www.mysterynet.com/history/hardboiled/)

He is a man "who knows the song of a bullet, the soft slithering hiss of a swift-thrown knife, the feel of hard fists, the call of courage." This paragon who has experienced "grim life in the raw," also has a moral code. "He is vigorous-minded; hard, in a square man's hardness; hating unfairness, trickery, injustice, cowardly underhandedness; standing for a square deal and a fair show in little or big things, and willing to fight for them; not squeamish or prudish, but clean, admiring the good in man and woman; not sentimental in a gushing sort of way, but valuing true emotion; not hysterical, but responsive to the thrill of danger, the stirring exhilaration of clean, swift, hard action—and always pulling for the right guy to come out on top." To ascribe these traits to a *Black Mask* reader seems ludicrous, and my father had enough of a sense of humor to report in the subsequent issue of *Black Mask* that several of his readers suggested that he must have had Teddy Roosevelt in mind as a typical reader.[80] As one examines the underlying principles ascribed to many of these characteristics, one senses that my father described those virtues that were meaningful to him. At first blush they seem to be very naïve and inanely foolish, but they are from a man who experienced much of what he described. I don't know whether my father had ever experienced the song of a bullet or the soft slithering hiss of a swift-thrown knife; however, he was an experienced woodsman and a seasoned sailor. He had mastered the art of fencing and was an expert in the use of a bayonet; he had served in Europe as a part of the American Expeditionary Force in the Chemical Warfare Service; and he had gone to Czechoslovakia at the end of the World War, a newly-founded country that was struggling to establish itself as an independent entity, and, while there, was an integral part of that struggle. Yes, the above definition is a

---

80    Frank MacShane, *The Life of Raymond Chandler* (New York: Penguin Books, 1976), pp. 46–47.

portrait of an ideal; further, my father and his writers were showing courage by attacking not only gangster organizations but also the alliances between these gangs and the corrupt politicians and public officials. This also explains why my father was licensed to carry a pistol as well as the only man in New York authorized to carry a sword disguised as a cane.[81] When *The Glass Key* was presented in *Black Mask,* many of its readers felt that Hammett had "glorified crime and criminals." My father, in defending what Hammett had created, wrote a strong letter that was printed in *Writers Digest:* "*Black Mask* never has and never will make money by appealing to the appetite for stories which present crime in an alluring light. *The Glass Key,* a story of modern gangsters, is a seriously written and highly dramatic presentation of the present day alliance between corrupt politicians, public officials and organized crime. In this story, virtue comes out on top. The crook who has ruled a city is destroyed, his gang is broken up, and the politicians who made his career possible are swept out of office by the voters. Publication of it, and all stories like it, is a public service. Not until our citizens realize that modern crime cannot exist without the collusion of corrupt police and public officials, will it be possible to cure what is undoubtedly one of the most serious illnesses that our body politic has ever suffered."[82]

In October 1929, August Lenniger, a literary agent, interviewed my father seeking to crystallize the peculiar requirements of the *Black Mask* methodology and expectations from writers submitting manuscripts. The response to his first question: "Perhaps I can give you a better picture of what we want by telling you what we don't want. Writers seem to make the mistake of considering us a formula magazine. I get so many of the crime-solution variety of detective story that is nothing more than a crossword puzzle.

---

81   Lee Server, *Danger Is My Business,* p. 68.

82   *Writer's Digest,* September 1930, Letter to the Editor, pp. 9–10.

They usually begin with a murder, and the whole interest lies in finding the criminal. But there is no real character interest, no convincing real-life story! The dramatic events leading up to, and the actual commission of the crime lose their effect because they are brought out piece-meal."

A follow-on question: Then, you wish a story to proceed in chronological order as the events occur, followed by the criminal laying plans for a murder, how he carries them out and, finally, his apprehension? Response: "Well, the majority of stories we use are not primarily concerned with a murder. There is usually something else involved, and a killing accidental, or merely incidental to the plot. What I want first and last is a real story. The usual formula of the detective story found in most magazines is avoided, and the individuality of the writer is given full sway." [83]

In a subsequent interview in August 1932, Ed Bodin, New York correspondent for the *Birmingham News-Age-Herald,* as well as an editor and author's agent, narrowed the scope of the questions by asking: What chance does the unknown writer have to click with *Black Mask?* The response was immediate: "Best in the world, if he carries the *Black Mask* standard of craftsmanship as well as the story. You see—*Black Mask* demands fine workmanship. The names in the author list of our magazine are found in the *Saturday Evening Post, Collier's, Liberty* and the best magazines in the country; but names don't mean much unless the story is there too. That's why leading writers consider it a distinction to be on *Black Mask's* content page.

"Remember—when I read a story by a new author, I don't read it from the standpoint of that one story. I read it also as an example of that writer's workmanship. He might not click with that story—but if he writes *Black Mask* quality, he will know about it—for I am always looking for the fellow with the flair."

---

83    August Lenniger, *"Black Mask," Writer's Digest.* October 1929, p. 17.

When asked to mention names of his writers he most preferred, the tactful answer was: "This wouldn't be fair to the many *Black Mask* writers—for one never knows when one of the authors who write *Black Mask* quality will step ahead with a story that is exceptional. All my writers are fictional marksmen—that's why so many writers who get their first breaks in *Black Mask,* soon appear in the *Post* and others, along with their *Black Mask* appearances."

The best way then to know *Black Mask* is to read a copy? "Not exactly—but rather study the technique of the *Black Mask* writers—not one issue, but a dozen—and suddenly you will feel that fiction punch that tells why their stories were purchased. You'll find that expert swing and delivery in every story in *Black Mask.* Until you can sense and duplicate it—you are not quite ready to click."

It is presumed that the short length story is the best length to try? "Yes, *Black Mask* doesn't like novelettes over 15,000 words—and, of course, seldom does the new fellow hit the bull's eye with that length. His best bet would be the 6,000 word story, or a little less."

Bodin summarized the interview with the following observations: "Thus it is plain why *Black Mask* magazine holds such a high reputation in the all-fiction field. The editor is not just a purchasing agent of virile, adventure, western, detective or border stories that are usually found in such magazines—but a Judge of the Supreme Court of two-fisted fiction who knows quality as well as story substance and considers them with the eyes of his readers. As a popular author himself he has both the author's and the editor's vision.

"So don't send ordinary material to Joseph T. Shaw. While he wants to be friendly and helpful—his judgment cannot be fooled by inferior quality of workmanship or weak stories. When shooting at *Black Mask,* you are shooting at as fine a market as there is in the magazine field—and Mr. Shaw intends to maintain that reputation for *Black Mask.* Don't overburden him, or impose on his good nature. He will meet you more than half-way—but you've got to show him that you have the flair."[84] Eugene Cunningham identified my father as one of the country's two shrewdest judges of the Mystery Tale,[85] an observation with which George Harmon Coxe concurred when he said that Cap Shaw was "one of the shrewdest editors I ever met."[86]

My father had adopted an editorial policy that encouraged new writers and fostered their development through a close editor-author relationship including advice, help with revisions and simple kindness.[87] A short blurb in the May 19, 1934, issue of the *Los Angeles Tribune* refers to Ray Moffat, an aspiring author making his first sale to *Black Mask.* The story was "Death in the Dark," the unsolicited remark: "Incidentally, Ray tells me that Joe Shaw, editor of this periodical, is very much okay in his treatment of young authors."[88]

One point that is frequently overlooked in the development of a story is the importance of dialogue. My father always stressed the critical nature of action and tempo in effective writing, and its reliance on that which is physical action and that which is carried by dialogue. "Dialogue should never be used without purpose, without a definite contribution to be made. If it needs

---

84    Ed Bodin, "An Interview with Joseph T. Shaw," *The Author and Composer: A Digest for Songwriters, Dramatists, Scenario Writers, Fictionists,* August 1932.

85    Eugene Cunningham, "Editorial," *El Paso Times,* Sunday, March 9, 1930.

86    George Harmon Coxe, "Flash Casey," *The Great Detectives,* edited by Otto Penzler, Penguin Books, 1978, p. 72.

87    Frank Gruber, *The Pulp Jungle* (Los Angeles: Sherbourne Press, 1967), p. 77.

88    An article in the *Los Angeles Tribune,* Saturday, May 19, 1934.

introduction—and it can itself introduce a story, even a book—its most natural entrance is in the logical evolution of a situation, where characters have reached a point where they must talk it out, where the story demands it. Then let the characters you have portrayed tell the story you have set up, themselves; not in your language and with your own expression, but in their own.

"For essentially, dialogue must be real. It can be smart, if your characters are smart; it can be original, if your characters have that spark. But it must be in character, not only with respect to the personalities to whom you give speech, but also with regard to the actual situation and its natural requirements. If it's real, it strikes you pleasingly; if incongruous, it hits you like a slap in the face.

"Dialogue has practically all the properties which a story demands. It can be both a story builder and a character builder. Of course the attempt for realism can be carried too far. Several writers have gained a measure of renown for their reproduction of what purports to be actual speech; but what is good in one medium is not so good in another. Most people say too much anyway, and are often repetitious. If you have to read every word they say, even in a short dialogue, it grows monotonous and you easily lose the thread of the discourse. Written dialogue should be edited, like everything else borrowed from another medium. As a rule, it should be terse, with only significant expressions remaining.

"You must know your respective characters thoroughly, just what type of men and women they are, how they will act and react in a given situation. Of course you know your plot and just in what manner you want to develop it. Then cast yourself into the character that is to speak and express the thought, the feeling and meaning that particular character would naturally express under the circumstances and in his language and in his way of speaking."[89]

89    Joseph T. Shaw, "Dialogue," *Writer's Digest,* June 1939, pp. 24–28.

# MY FATHER AS A MAN AND AS AN EDITOR

WHEN MY father inherited the editorial reins of *Black Mask,* there were several fortuitous factors already in place. From a sociological point-of view, the 1920s were a traumatic period for America. As indicated above, it was a society in upheaval. The World War was not that far behind, thus leaving the country with the consequences of national mobilization and conflict. On January 16, 1920, Amendment 18 to the Constitution became effective prohibiting the manufacture, sale, or transportation of intoxicating liquors, as well as the importation or exportation of these beverages. The disastrous consequence of this action was the creation of an unlawful industry of liquor trafficking. Compounding the problem was the fact that the integrity of public office holders and law enforcement officials was in question by the general public, and inner city gangs and intra-city racketeering were running rampant. This unstable environment provided a natural setting for crime, murder and mayhem that ultimately coalesced into detective stories. A framework for a new style of mystery stories was evolving that was completely different from the classical, deductive style universally in vogue at that time. A group of imaginative, talented, creative writers gravitated to *Black Mask;* and the pulp reading public clamored for more.

When my father stepped in as editor he pledged to himself that he was going to make this fledgling magazine the best in the field. I am certain he did not initially know how this vision would be realized; however, he was astute enough to recognize the power of Dashiell Hammett's writing and its potential for this new style of Detective stories. My father never claimed to have discovered Hammett and the other *Black Mask* writers; however, he can correctly take credit for helping to develop their work into what became the mature era of *Black Mask*.[90]

Through definition and refinement my father guided the evolution of the hard-boiled style of mystery fiction writing. Time and again he said that he could not take credit for the type of fiction appearing in *Black Mask*. Years later, in his introduction to *The Hard-Boiled Omnibus*, my father stated: "We do not, and we cannot, claim credit either for the original work of these *Black Mask* writers or for their success. It is our conviction that no one person can bring forth successful writing from another. A discriminating editor may help toward skill and craftsmanship, but application of that skill and the thought behind it are the sole properties of the author himself." Regardless, one finds in the stories selected for the anthology powerful examples of the application of the formula, pattern, or elements of the *Black Mask* School of Mystery Writing. My father did not create the model of the hard-boiled detective story, but he was very much a force in both the evolution of the model and the authors who defined the unique and innovative style through their written work.

*Black Mask* flourished during the "golden decade" of my father's tenure as editor, November 1926 through August 1936.[91] He was the catalyst that made it all happen. No, he was not responsible for first accepting the writings of the original big seven: nor did he create the hard-boiled detective and the action-packed style of story that followed. But my father did bring to the table leadership traits that were directly responsible for the development of the *Black Mask* Hard-Boiled School of Mystery Fiction as a unique sub-genre in the field of American literature, and for *Black Mask* becoming the premiere pulp detective maga-

---

90    Lee Server, *Danger Is My Business,* p. 68.

91    Philip Durham, "Boys in the *Black Mask,*" Preface.

zine of its time.[92]

Who was this man, and what were these traits? First and foremost Joseph T. Shaw subscribed to the concept of servant leadership—he was there to serve others. The story of life for my father was people, and he never doubted the inherent greatness to which the individual could aspire and ultimately achieve. This explains why he so willingly expended his time, energy and resources to enable others to strive to grow to their fullest. He delighted in the success of "his" authors, urging them to grow beyond where they were even if it meant ultimate departure from the *Black Mask* family.

My father was a visionary, one who could see beyond the horizon. He knew early on the vast potential of the art that was being created by the *Black Mask* authors, perhaps not even aware that his own artistic beliefs were the result of his moral character.[93] He was well aware of the uniqueness of this new art form and the impact it was having on the entire field of mystery writing; furthermore, my father knew that elements of this hard-boiled school of writing would have applicability in other forms of literature.

My father was a gentle man in the truest sense of the word. He did not have a vindictive bone in his body, accepting all as equals. He recognized the inherent lows to which human beings could descend, but he was also well aware of the inherent potential goodness of the human soul. He never assumed that he was better than the next guy—as good as, perhaps, but not better. He railed against failures in ethics, integrity and morality, demanding the highest standards from himself before even attempting to judge others. He did set high standards for his authors, and

92    William Marling, "The *Black Mask* School of Hard-Boiled Fiction,"
p. 1. (http://www.ncsu.edu/encore/black.html)

93    Frank MacShane, *The Life of Raymond Chandler,* p. 46.

he did have high expectations from their performance, but he did not ask them to climb to the top by themselves—he was with each of them every step of the way encouraging, exhorting, suggesting, gently correcting, teaching all with patience, respect and sensitivity.

My father was truly inspirational. He believed in his writers and they believed in him; he was absolutely loyal to them, and they, in turn, reciprocated that loyalty; he would never pass up the opportunity to praise, promote, publicize, and extol the talents and accomplishments of his *Black Mask* authors. Richard Layman developed the argument that by the fall of 1926 Phil Cody had put together an effective literary team with the exception of one position. That exception was the need for a skilled publicist who could declare the importance of the team's work. Layman indicated that Shaw, a promoter with business savvy, understood that the fortunes of his magazines were directly related to the success of his writers. My father also realized that readers respect novelists more than short story writers, so he encouraged his stable to undertake longer works and to aspire to book publication. Meanwhile, he began promoting them as an elite group pioneering a new type of mystery fiction.[94]

Not only did my father publicly applaud Hammett for writing some of the best mystery fiction ever produced, for submitting his first novel unsolicited to Alfred A. Knopf, Inc., but also the astuteness of those who read the *Black Mask* offerings. My father had a romantic sense of his audience; consequently, he delighted in sharing with his readership those who regularly read the magazine for interest and/or relaxation. Cited were both President Herbert Hoover and President Franklin Delano Roosevelt; financier magnate J.P. Morgan; Dr. A.S.W. Rosenbach, the world's best

---

94   Richard Layman, "The Changing Face of Crime Fiction: *The Black Mask*," pp. 2076–2077.

known collector of rare books who claimed *Black Mask* to be his favorite detective magazine; and Bernard Smith, editor at A.A. Knopf, Inc., and Joe Lesser, Alfred Knopf's right hand man; in addition, others acknowledged were a well-known MGM director of pictures, a noted playwright, clergymen, bankers, and business leaders many of whom expressed their gratitude for the magazine through letters of support for my father.[95]

After examining this scrapbook maintained by my father which contained "a hodgepodge of dated and undated newspaper clips, little-known book reviews, movie interviews, stills, photos, magazine articles, ads for books published by his stars, blurbs or plants for *Black Mask* in various newspapers—anything and everything that pertained to his beloved rough-paper magazine," Hagemann had much to say. He lauded the techniques that my father used to keep his authors in full public view. "A promoter pure and simple," "a fierce competitor for sales," "a fierce defender of his product," "a combative editor" were descriptive of his evaluation of my father's approach to the outside environment. My father challenged the smooth paper editors; he exploited favorable comments about the magazine and its writers through his own editorials, interviews and newspaper articles; in short, he aggressively pursued any avenue he could to extol the magnificence of the literary product being sold. He reached out to newspapers countrywide with a complimentary copy of the most recent issue of *Black Mask*. Some of the recipients: *The Daily Argus-Leader,* Sioux Falls, SD; *The Rocky Mountain News,* Denver, CO; *The Boston Globe,* Boston, MA; *The El Paso Times,* El Paso TX; *The Weekly Bulletin,* Omaha, NE.[96] It is little wonder that his authors had

---

95    Joseph T. Shaw, *"Black Mask* Scrapbook," (unpublished), pp. 58, 60.

96    E.R. Hagemann, "Captain Joseph T. Shaw's *Black Mask* Scrapbook," *The Mystery Fancier,* Vol. 7, No. 1, January/February 1983, pp. 2–6.

an overwhelming desire to have their work published in *Black Mask.*

My father shared with Eugene Cunningham his ideas for keeping ahead of the procession in this popular fiction field of mystery writing. "Naturally," says the Captain, "our ambition is to make each issue of the magazine more interesting than the last. To accomplish this purpose requires a combination of several elements. First and foremost is demanding an increasing capability of the writers to please the readers.

"We know from a cold blooded analysis of our field that a detective story reader audience can be one of the most particular to which a magazine is ever directed. We believe that our audience is particular and we move as if commissioned to choose fiction of the highest quality.

"Our policy then, calls for the best stories obtainable. What is meant by 'best'? Why, stories that grip, interest, thrill; with characters that one can feel exist; characters with motives and engaging in action logically born of those motives. Both motive and action to be so realistic as to insult the intelligence of none; to seem, not only possible, but inevitable.

"Doubtless this is a high standard. I hear that *Black Mask* is getting to be one of the hardest magazines in the country to make. I must confess that I regard this authorial cry as a compliment—since a large number of writers do make our pages, to the great satisfaction of a growing audience." [97]

A highly principled man, my father took his editorship very seriously. He had a profound sense of responsibility to his writers, his publisher and to the public. He also held himself accountable for that which took place under his watch. As editor, he was both insightful and imaginative, dignified yet humble, compassionate and generous, and, fortunately, blessed with a great sense of

---

97    Joseph T. Shaw, *"Black Mask* Scrapbook," p. 29.

humor. Finally, he welcomed work, never backing down from that which had to be done, but, rather, relishing the challenges and opportunities confronting him. Most importantly, my father believed in the power of prayer. The manifestation of these many admirable traits were such that they created within him a remarkable ability to shape and influence the attitudes of those with whom he interacted.

Although these observations may seem to be hyper-inflated, the 1920s and 1930s were extraordinary times, and the high literary achievements by many remarkable individuals required strong, bold, aggressive yet compassionate leadership. As talented as the *Black Mask* writers were, and they were talented, they also were a diverse group of individuals. They came from different socio-economic backgrounds, levels of formal education, age, writing experience, temperament, self-discipline and in many cases struggled with poverty, depression and alcoholism. To work with these individuals so that their separate efforts could be part of a cohesive whole was indeed a formidable challenge unto itself.

My father never hesitated to use the monthly editorial page of *Black Mask* as a bully pulpit to expound such social issues as gun control, the problems left behind after the repeal of the Eighteenth Amendment concerning prohibition, those public officials who lacked integrity and allowed themselves to be compromised, and the need to re-establish law and order.

In the above paragraphs I have described an extraordinary man, using superlative terms to properly identify him. One would say that these things would be expected of a son talking about a beloved father; however, the descriptive words are from those who worked and interacted with "Cap Shaw."

# THREE OF THE EARLY MASKETEERS

THE WRITINGS of Dashiell Hammett, Carrol John Daly and Erle Stanley Gardner demonstrate the multi-faceted aspects of the hard-boiled detective stories. These men were three of the earlier members of the group that influenced this new form of writing.

## DASHIELL HAMMETT

SOME OF these distinguishing qualities of character can be seen by examining the relationship between my father and Dashiell Hammett. The most insightful and comprehensive information available is that provided by William Nolan in his biographical studies of the life and times of Hammett. Initially, it would seem that the personalities and life styles of the two men were about as alike as day and night. Hammett's love of the night life, his failure to constrain himself to the responsibilities of marriage and parenthood, his affinity for alcohol and womanizing, his fits of depression, and his sardonic tendencies were the antithesis of my father's traits. For my father, the marriage vows were inviolable, family was central to his life, and he did not indulge in self-destructive activities or fits of depression; on the contrary, he was very much the optimist and always bursting with enthusiasm and new ideas. He was not a teetotaler but I never knew him not to have alcohol consumption under control. Whereas Hammett seemed to do a lot of introspection, my father did not. Whereas Hammett had many career concerns, recognizing that his recurring illnesses often dictated which jobs he could or could not hold, my father was not burdened by indecision. He put his hand into several different ventures, but he never hesitated to move on when he found something more challenging. More often than not, my father's activities kept leading him closer to the literary field, a field that, in spite of his love for the woods and water, inexorably became his primary calling. The disparity of these two men with regard to their formal education was amazing. Hammett gave up his schooling at age fourteen, my father graduated from prestigious Bowdoin College. Also there was a difference of twenty years to the month in their age. Dad being the elder could have been Hammett's father.

In spite of their differences, there were many similarities between these two men. Both had ancestral roots in Scotland, both were stubbornly independent non-conformists, both thrived on adventure and had a passion for books. Neither shied away from hard work; both had a deep sense of civic responsibility; both were unflagging patriots, my father volunteering for service in World War I at age forty-four, Hammett volunteering for service in World War II at age forty-eight; both had an untouchable level of integrity; and both were gentle men. They were quite a pair.

Fortuitously, my father and Hammett were brought together through unique circumstances. An observation by William Pronzini is revealing: "Two events made *Black Mask* the great, pioneering magazine it was in the detective field. One was the decision of Dashiell Hammett to submit the bulk of his early work for publication in its pages; the other was the hiring, in 1926, of Joseph T. 'Cap' Shaw as its new editor." [98] Yes, this was the coming together of two great literary men, one an editor, one an author.

Upon his arrival at *Black Mask,* the first thing my father did was to peruse previous issues of this magazine in an effort to understand what the magazine was all about so that he, in turn, could build on what Phil Cody had already established. Two areas he focused on were first the originality and authenticity of Dashiell Hammett's writing. Hammett alone seemed to realize the full

---

98    William Pronzini, Compiler, "Horace McCoy: Mopper-Up," *Arbor House Treasury of Detective and Mystery Stories from the Great Pulps,* 1983, p. 51.

potential of hard-boiled detective fiction beyond its gun-slinging appeal. As an ex-Pinkerton detective turned self-taught writer, Hammett was uniquely qualified to give his characters the three dimensions of which other writers of the tough detective story were incapable.[99] My father's other observation was that Hammett was no longer submitting stories to the *Black Mask* magazine. The reason for Hammett's departure from *Black Mask* was related to three hundred dollars that he felt was owed to him by Phil Cody.[100] Through correspondence with Hammett, my father was able to develop the story format of what he would like to see in the magazine. "We wanted simplicity for the sake of clarity, plausibility and belief. We wanted action, but we held that action was meaningless unless it involves recognizable human character in three-dimensional form." My father hit a responsive chord with Dashiell Hammett that enabled them to establish a pattern of story telling that emphasized character and the problems inherent in human behavior over crime solution.[101] My father gave Hammett a free hand in creating this fiction, paid him premium rates for his work, and urged him to attempt longer more fully developed stories. Feeling that Continental Op in novel form could reach a large audience of book readers, my father suggested extending the Op's fictional range to allow greater depth and character expansion.[102] In effect, my father was laying the foundation for the novels that followed. In 1926, Hammett considered himself a retired fiction writer. Inability to provide the money for a second impending child prompted him to turn away from pulp writing

99    History of *Black Mask,* June 13, 2002, http://www.ncsu.edu/encore/ black.html, p. 2.

100   Richard Layman, editor, *Selected Letters of Dashiell Hammett, 1921– 1960* (Washington, D.C.: Counterpoint, 2001), p. 28.

101   Frank MacShane, *The Life of Raymond Chandler,* p. 46.

102   William Nolan, *Hammett: A Life at the Edge,* pp. 67–68.

and to enter the field of advertising. Hammett might never have produced *The Maltese Falcon* or any of his other novels had it not been for my father.[103]

A relationship was being forged, one that centered around their common effort to produce stories calculated to expand *Black Mask* circulation, but there was also a warm personal relationship developing. Dashiell Hammett had been a guest at our home in Scarsdale, New York, on at least one occasion. At age two I retained nothing, but a picture dated 1929 does reveal his presence in Scarsdale. At another time, on a trip to the West Coast, my father personally gave a present to Dashiell Hammett's daughter Mary Jane.[104] My father wanted to know his authors at more than a professional level. Over a four-year period, he became something of a father figure to Hammett. He provided a ready market for Hammett's best fiction, extolled the strength of his stories in editorials, and raced to his defense when critics wrote demeaning appraisals of his work.[105] He was a source of encouragement to Hammett and paved the way for him to write his first full-length novel, *Red Harvest.* It was indicative of their relationship that this first novel was dedicated to Joseph T. Shaw.[106] On the other hand, my father didn't hesitate to exercise his editorial prerogatives of censorship, to make suggestions for changes in his stories, and to urge Hammett to set character before situation.[107] With respect to censorship, sex and homosexual references were taboo, as was the use of vulgarities and blasphemies in any story printed in *Black Mask.* My father was a stickler on the implementation of this policy; however, this same policy subjected him to the antics

---

103   *Ibid.,* p. 65.

104   *Ibid.,* p. 73.

105   *Ibid.,* p. 101.

106   *Ibid.,* p. 79.

107   *Ibid.,* pp. 93–94.

of Dashiell Hammett, who once baited him with the terminology of "gooseberry lay" and "gunsel." A manuscript from Hammett contained both expressions. Dad thought the worst of "gooseberry lay" and had it expunged from the story. It also prompted a letter from my father to Hammett stating that *Black Mask* would never publish vulgarities of that sort. In truth "gooseberry lay" refers to a tramp who makes his living by stealing freshly laundered clothing from a clothes line and then selling this clothing for a few pennies for food. On the other hand, "gunsel" is a mischievous word with homosexual connotations. My father assumed that, because Hammett used the word so casually that it pertained to a hired gun, and allowed it to pass untouched.[108] I don't know what Dad's reaction was to this duplicity of words but I cannot help but believe it was with a suppressed scowl.

It was a fruitful relationship, Though it only lasted four years, Hammett did codify the model by which my father not only reshaped *Black Mask* but also established a whole new style of detective writing, namely, the *"Black Mask* School."[109] *Red Harvest,* a "literary landmark" bound in hardcovers, moved the hard-boiled school of detective fiction from the back room of the pulps into the bright lights of bookstores; the Conan Doyle image was completely shattered.[110] This novel gave expression to Hammett's anger against injustice. This anger was genuine, bitter and unrelenting. He projected a strong personalized viewpoint into a fictional framework thus enabling *Red Harvest* to be an expression of moral outrage exposing "the cancer of crime." What was encouraging about the utilization of a novel to share a personal predilection is that my father understood what Hammett

---

108   Erle Stanley Gardner, "Getting Away with Murder," *The Atlantic Monthly,* Vol. 215, No. 1, Jan. 1965, pp. 73–74.

109   William Pronzini, "Horace McCoy: Mopper-Up," p. 51.

110   William Nolan, *Hammett: A Life at the Edge,* p. 80.

was doing, respected it, and supported it. As my father stated: "We knew he was great... but it took the *Black Mask* stories published in book form to wake up the country as to how great he really is."[111] Unfortunately for *Black Mask* and its readers, Hammett stopped writing fiction for pulp magazines because he believed he could do better by concentrating on smooth paper magazines and developing novels. His last Continental Op story for my father was published in the November 1930 issue, almost eight years to the month when his first *Black Mask* story appeared, and four years after my father and Hammett started working together. My father realized the immense loss this was to the magazine and tried to entice him back but to no avail. Hammett saw greener fields beyond. It is interesting to note that, shortly after his departure, Hammett had three short stories about his protagonist Sam Spade published, two in *American Magazine,* and one for *Collier's.* These stories lacked intensity and the wry passion of the work he had done for *Black Mask.* This Spade was far inferior to the complex, richly textured Spade that Hammett had created in *The Maltese Falcon;* the new Spade was bland, all but invisible. Hammett had moved beyond the emotional environment of the series.[112] In addition to the many individual articles published, four of his five novels were serialized in *Black Mask.* No other writer had made such an impact on *Black Mask* as did Hammett. With respect to my father, he, more than any of the other previous editors, defined the form of realistic detective fiction originated by Hammett; my father is the man most closely associated with "the *Black Mask* School" of objective hard-boiled literature.[113]

As Hammett moved off the scene, his place was taken by

---

111   *Ibid.,* p. 108.

112   *Ibid.,* p. 124.

113   *Ibid.,* p. 67.

Raymond Chandler. Hammett and Chandler were the two *Black Mask* writers in particular who symbolized hard-boiled fiction. Their stories, with their harsh realism, violence, and terse dialogue, remain the best examples of a style of writing acknowledged to be the most important contribution the United States has made to the mystery genre.[114] *Black Mask* had a secure place in American literary history because it stimulated a generation of genre writers who perceived a style of writing that would accurately reflect the modern world. With the exception of Hammett and Chandler, these writers are as important for their influence as for their writing—their influence was profound.[115] My father was the one who created the editorial environment within which individual growth could take place, and then pointed the way.

## CARROLL JOHN DALY

CARROLL JOHN DALY not only preceded Hammett to the pages of *Black Mask* by two months, but his main character, Race Williams, was the progenitor of all hard-boiled detective protagonists.[116] The toughness of the hard-boiled approach, laced with lots of realistic action, was empathized in Daly's work. But the freewheeling, trigger-happy, one-dimensional, vigilante hero—as well as the non-sensible convoluted plots—did not fit the restraints of the writing pattern being developed. Consequently, Daly was never acknowledged as one of the geniuses in the evolution of this new school of writing. By Daly's own admission, *Black Mask* editors had little affection for his work; but, fortu-

---

114   "Hard-Boiled Fiction: History of the Mystery," p. 2.

115   Richard Layman, "The Changing Face of Crime Fiction: *The Black Mask*," p. 2078.

116   Thomas Stuark, "Horace McCoy, Captain Shaw, and *The Black Mask*," p. 139.

itously, his stories sold magazines, and the editors, including my father, had the good sense to continue to publish his writing.[117] In total, Carroll John Daly had sixty of his stories published in *Black Mask:* twenty-four from September 1922 through October 1926, thirty between November 1926 and November 1934, and six after November 1934 with his last story being published in July 1944. Allegedly there was a falling out between my father and Daly in 1934; there may be some truth to this because Daly vanished from *Black Mask* in 1934 for the balance of my father's tenure as editor. It had been suggested that there was conflict over self-plagiarism; however, it is also noted that Daly had not altered his style much, and by the 1940s his gun-slinging Roaring Twenties detective had finally gone out of favor.[118] This could also explain why only six of his stories were published over the ten-year span from 1934 to 1944. As late as 1981 Michael Barson also questioned the motives for Daly's departure offering the following thoughts: "While still near the peak of his popularity, Daly up and left *Mask* in 1934 and took up with *Dime Detective,* dragging Race with him. Was the move prompted by a higher per-word rate? Had Cap Shaw at last grown weary of stale plots and clunky prose? Perhaps the parting was mutually agreeable."[119]

Be that as it may, my father did not harbor grudges. Of all his *Black Mask* authors, the only one I remember meeting was Carroll John Daly. It was in 1934 or 1935. I was seven or eight years old and my family was visiting him and his family. I cannot remember his physical traits but I will never forget his generosity. In his attic he had an extensive layout of Lionel electric trains. Even

---

117   Lee Server, *Danger Is My Business*, p. 65.

118   William Marling, "The *Black Mask* School of Hard-Boiled Fiction," p. 3.

119   Michael S. Barson, "There's No Sex in Crime: The Two-Fisted Homilies of Race Williams," *Clues,* Fall/Winter, 1981, Vol. 2, No. 2, p. 108.

at that early age I was into electric trains, and he, realizing this, gave to my older brother and me train accessories that I still have.

Two other incidents surrounding Daly give better definition of who he was and how he became unwittingly a victim of circumstances. The first, as reported by Erle Stanley Gardner, went as follows: "Now, Carroll John Daly had never had the slightest experience with actual crime or criminals, much less with bullet wounds, except the one night he spent in the Tombs, in New York City, when an ingenious confidence man, wanting to give an address which would bear checking, simply took the telephone book of White Plains, New York, and selected a name at random. The name happened to be that of Daly.

"When the police officers rapped at the door, Daly answered. They asked him if his name was Carroll John Daly. He said it was. That was enough. The next thing Daly knew he was on his way to jail." [120] My memory of the incident was the flurry it caused in our household when word came to my father that one of his authors was locked in the Tombs. I believe it was my father who sprung him loose after verifying for police officials that Daly was an innocent author.

The second incident was described by William Nolan: "Daly's world of crime and violence was purely imaginary; he had never had the slightest experience with crime or criminals, but he once made up his mind to buy a .45 automatic. Since Race Williams was always killing hoods with his two big .45s, Daly felt he should know what one was like. He purchased the gun and, on the way home, was arrested for carrying a concealed weapon. As one friend observed: 'That was the end of Carroll's research.'" [121] These are examples of just how diverse my father's writers were. It is also amazing how far a vivid imagination can take an indi-

---

120   Erle Stanley Gardner, "Getting Away with Murder," pp. 72–73.

121   William Nolan, *The Black Mask Boys*, p. 38.

vidual even without the real world experience. If Daly had incorporated sex into the later stories of his writing career, he might have pre-empted Mickey Spillane and his detective hero Mike Hammer.

"Hammett liked Daly and felt that he had contributed to the eclipse of Daly's career because Daly had been unfavorably compared to Hammett as a practitioner of the hard-boiled style."[122]

## ERLE STANLEY GARDNER

ALTHOUGH FEW writers would achieve anything like the success of Dashiell Hammett and Raymond Chandler, the writers in Shaw's stable were by and large a remarkably talented group, creating a rich array of effects and characters within the bounds of the hard-boiled style.[123] One of those writers who did receive significant acclaim was Erle Stanley Gardner. He was a lawyer and became a successful writer, ultimately becoming the most widely read and translated of all American writers through his Perry Mason mysteries. His writing was considered to be on the fringes of the hard-boiled mainstream to the point that even his less dreadful pulp stories were closer to Daly's standards than to Hammett's.[124] Gardner confessed that in the early stages of his writing career his "stories were terrible... I didn't know how to plot [and] I had no natural aptitude as a writer." Early on when Phil Cody was editor of *Black Mask,* he rejected all of Gardner's stories; however, Harry North, the associate editor, took a personal interest in Gardner and gave him the "expert guidance"

---

122   Richard Layman, *Selected Letters of Dashiell Hammett, 1921–1960,* p. 29.

123   Lee Server, *Danger Is My Business,* p. 69.

124   *Ibid.,* p. 67.

he needed to acquire the skills that enabled his material to sell.[125] Gardner's pulp fiction was written in a fast-moving but slapdash manner without style or resonance; it was a no-frills, compulsively readable style of storytelling that was born and bred in the pulps.[126] However, these flaws notwithstanding, Gardner did finally master the art of mystery writing, and, in time, became *Black Mask's* most prolific writer, having one hundred stories accepted, seventy of them during the Shaw era. In addition to the earlier support provided by Harry North, my father provided further guidance for many of his stories while outright rejecting others. Gardner was a prodigious writer and a tireless worker, ultimately culminating his writing career having sold well over 315 million copies of his books and having had them translated into thirty-two languages. It was quite an achievement for one who thought of himself as a "lawyer who wrote" rather than as a writer who practiced law.[127]

There is nothing to indicate that my father and Gardner did not have anything but a very good working relationship during the years they were together. Acknowledging Gardner as a man of immense energy and enthusiasm, Todhunter Ballard related one incident involving Gardner that unfolded as follows: "Tom Curry tells of the early *Black Mask* days when the eastern writers would gather in Grand Central Station and catch the train to Scarsdale to Joe Shaw's parties. Tom claims you could hear Erle from one end of the train to the other.[128] The implications were two-fold. One, that he was no shrinking violet, and, two, that he was very much a part of the family of *Black Mask* writers. However, there was another side to Gardner that seemed to manifest itself in

---

125   William Nolan, *The Black Mask Boys,* p. 96.

126   Lee Server, *Danger Is My Business,* p. 67.

127   William Nolan, *The Black Mask Boys,* p. 94.

128   Todhunter Ballard, "Writing for the Pulps," pp. 16–17.

resentment of my father and jealousy toward the leading role that Hammett played in the success of *Black Mask.*[129] These emotions became evident when my father asked Gardner to participate in *The Hard-Boiled Omnibus* to be published in 1946, and he refused to allow his work to be reprinted. The reason given was that neither his best nor even his typical work had not been done for *Black Mask,* and it would not be fair to have it stand side by side with authors who had been doing their best work while writing for the magazine.[130] This is a specious argument. All the writers were on a learning curve using the pulps to strengthen their storytelling crafts. My father had assumed responsibility for the growth of each of his writers and very few were beyond the pale wherein they had no more growth to realize. Hammett and Chandler were exceptions but each had studied long and hard before mastering his trade. Perhaps there is a trace of ego involvement at the thought of being compared unfavorably with Dashiell Hammett.

The second concern expressed by Gardner was that because of my father's alleged infatuation with Hammett's work, he was Hammettizing *Black Mask;* in effect, my father was requiring every one of his authors to write as Hammett did. Several responses seem to be in order. Several of my father's authors openly acknowledged that they did try to imitate Hammett's style. Ray Chandler was one of those who studied Hammett's work with care and his own grew out of it.[131] In the 1930s some of Gardner's earliest Perry Mason novels were said by reviewers to be imitation Hammett, a statement that resulted in an angry rebuke from

---

129  Ron Goulart, *The Dime Detectives,* Mysterious Press, 1988, p. 39.

130  E.R. Hagemann, "Cap Shaw and His Great and Regular Fellows: The Making of the Hard-Boiled Omnibus, 1945–1946," *Clues—A Journal of Detection,* Fall/Winter 1981, Vol. 2, p. 148.

131  Frank MacShane, *The Life of Raymond Chandler,* p. 48.

Gardner.[132] Lee Server sensed that some of my father's writers did mimic the Hammett style, "either by natural inclination or in calculated deference to Cap Shaw's buying patterns."[133] Tom Curry claimed that my father's expectations from his authors underwent a transition following the success of *The Maltese Falcon* in the early 1930s. "Joe Shaw built *Black Mask* into about the best crime magazine that ever came down the pike. For years it was known as such, here and in England, too.

"Shaw gave his writers the rein, let them do the writing while he did the editing... Hammett wrote one brand of stuff, Gardner another, Daly a third, Nebel his own; and Curry had his line. There was real variety in the magazine... but when Hammett's work became such a tremendous success, Shaw began to require that each story have the Hammett elements. The magazine became a monotone in Hammett's style, and to sell to it you imitated."[134]

W.T. Ballard, whose first story was not published by my father until September 1933, well after the success of Hammett's *Maltese Falcon* had been trumpeted, stated that "without the freedom for growth Shaw gave his 'boys' we might never have had Sam Spade, *The Thin Man,* Marlowe, Perry Mason and their fraternity."[135] Ballard also acknowledged that Hammett's writing served as a source of inspiration rather than as a formula that should be copied.[136] An article written by Thomas Sturak about Horace McCoy has a revealing footnote. "You will hear it said," Lester Dent has written, "Joseph Shaw told his writers what to write and how, demanded they do *'Black Mask'* style. This was not true. He

---

132   Ron Goulart, *The Dime Detectives,* p. 39.

133   Lee Server, *Danger Is My Business,* p. 69.

134   Tom Curry, "It's Your Own Show," p. 88.

135   Todhunter Ballard, "Writing for the Pulps," p. 8.

136   *Ibid.,* p. 9.

demanded nothing of the sort."[137] On the other hand, Erle Stanley Gardner has charged Shaw with trying "to get writers to follow the Hammett style. One of my big differences with Shaw came when I accused him of trying to 'Hammettize' the magazine."[138] Gardner vigorously defended this opinion in correspondence with Thomas Sturak; however, Sturak responded by stating that nowhere in some fifty letters concerning eighteen story manuscripts for *Black Mask* between 1927 and 1934 did Shaw ever suggest to McCoy that he follow "the Hammett style." Much the opposite, as the letter quoted in my text indicates, he was always sensitive to the least "suggestion of Hammett" as he put it another time in McCoy's writing. About another manuscript, Shaw noted a resemblance to Hammett in minute gestures, and admonished, "good as Hammett is, Horace McCoy doesn't need it."[139]

Specific observations can be confirmed from this discussion. First, under my father's leadership a *Black Mask* hard-boiled school of mystery writing evolved. Second, many elements of the basic tenets that comprise this formula for mystery writing were embodied in the work of Dashiell Hammett. Third, my father clearly expounded these principles, exhorting his writers to follow this formula (Note his manifesto in the June 1927 issue of *Black Mask*). Fourth, it is also true that many of the *Black Mask* writers, on their own volition, sought to imitate certain aspects of Hammett's style. Finally, it must be recognized that, as the *Black Mask* School of mystery writing evolved, it moved beyond

---

137   Thomas Sturak, "Horace McCoy, Captain Shaw, and *The Black Mask*," p. 157, footnote #13 (reference to the October 27, 1958, letter from Lester Dent to Philip Durham and, then, confirmation through his own experience with Horace McCoy and correspondence with Joseph Shaw).

138   Erle Stanley Gardner, "Getting Away with Murder," p. 73.

139   Thomas Sturak, "Horace McCoy, Captain Shaw, and *The Black Mask*," p. 157, footnote #13.

Dashiell Hammett. This is not a put down of Hammett. He was peerless. His influence on writers who followed behind him was enormous. At his death in 1961, a *New York Times* editorial stated: "His prose was clean and entirely unique. His characters were as sharply and economically defined as any in American fiction. His stories were as consistent as mathematics and as intricate as psychology. His gift of invention never tempted him beyond the limits of credibility." My father, as has been cited earlier, gave his writers free rein as to what to write and how to write. He was astute enough to realize that each writer had his own style and that he could not teach them to write. What he could do though was to guide, suggest and bring them back to those principles that made this mode of writing so unique. Sturak noted that this language—the "hard brittle style" that Chandler said belonged to everybody and to no one—was the most widely imitated characteristic of the *Black Mask* "formula." It was not its essential constituent; for example, the differences among the writing styles of, say, Ray Chandler, Erle Stanley Gardner and Horace McCoy are apparent. "The critical qualities were of intention and emphasis; and herein the *Black Mask* writers anticipated the existential trend of serious twentieth century fiction." [140] As interest in the pulps waned in the latter part of the 1930s, the fundamental elements of the hard-boiled school of writing did not become out-dated. In fact, Hammett, as a teacher years later, stressed less liberal use of slang, a need for continuity, further development of character, and that tempo must be recognized as a vital ingredient. He also emphasized the need to keep things moving.[141] It is concluded that Cap Shaw, in no way, attempted to Hammettize the *Black Mask* magazine.

---

140  *Ibid.*, p. 140.

141  Julian Symons, *Dashiell Hammett* (Orlando: Harcourt Brace Joranovich, Publishers, 1985), p. 66.

The third concern expressed by Erle Stanley Gardner in his letter to my father of January 25, 1946, was that he in some way or other had belittled Phil Cody by not giving him enough credit for creating the *Black Mask* hard-boiled school of mystery writing. Cody was the editor before my father; in addition, he was my father's immediate boss for the ten years my father was with *Black Mask*. Certainly Cody was in at the beginning as the foundation pieces were starting to come together for this radical change in detective stories; as vice president of Pro-Distributors Publishing Company, Inc., and director of circulation, he was interested in reader reaction to the stories being printed. But it has not been established that he was involved in the creation of the hard-boiled formula and its component parts.

The direction from which Erle Stanley Gardner often came is not clear. For example, he took full credit for bringing Dashiell Hammett back to *Black Mask* after Hammett's one-year hiatus from fiction writing. In truth, it has been clearly established that it came about from communications that my father had initiated with Hammett. Hagemann identified Gardner as "one of the greatest bores ever spawned," and then he goes on to cite Gardner's complaints against my father stating that he had falsely claimed to have discovered Hammett, that *The Hard-Boiled Omnibus* was a self-aggrandizement to Joseph T. Shaw, and that my father erred when he called Frederick Nebel the best writer of the group. Hagemann also observed that Gardner was "cynically unjust." [142] Ron Goulart states that "Gardner felt he was slighted in *Black Mask* because only those authors who would imitate Hammett received first class treatment." [143]

The following correspondence between my father, Willis Wing

---

142   E.R. Hagemann, "Cap Shaw and His Great and Regular Fellows," p. 148.

143   Ron Goulart, *The Dime Detectives*, p. 40.

(Gardner's literary agent), and Erle Stanley Gardner is revealing. Gardner had directed that correspondence to him should be transmitted through his agent. Further, an apparent letter from Gardner to my father through Willis Wing is not available. The first of what is a series of letters, dated January 17, 1946, was from my father to Willis Wing:

Dear Mr. Wing:

I presume it is healthful, shocking though it may be, to get an occasional glimpse of the opinion in which the other fellow regards you.

For my side, if I were ever interested in fame I certainly would not seek it as Johnson's Boswell; which is another way of saying that I have never on my own claimed credit for the discovery and development of any writer, be he Gardner or be he Hammett. What other people may have said or may say is beyond my control and responsibility. I have disclaimed any such credit time and time again, and the only thing I can do about it is expressed in the closing paragraph of an introduction, prepared by request of publishers a couple of months ago, copy of which I enclose.

Along this same line of thought, I have always valued a man's friendship above any word of appreciation he might extend to me, and I have never criticized a writer's work without the sincere hope that, in my feeble way, it might be of benefit to him, and this applies to Erle as distinctly as to many others. I had thought that Erle was keenly aware of this.

This projected anthology is no attempt to aggrandize myself, either as editor or individual. The thought is silly and absurd. Rather, I look upon it as dedicated to a group of writers, remarkable because almost without exception they have achieved outstanding success in their profession.

My own contribution to it, outside of assisting in selections, is an impersonal recital of the magazine as I found it and what these writers made of it when once in stride.

In my opinion, Erle has missed the one important point in its progress, and this, I think, explains to me why so many of my comments to him went so far afield. Hammett was the leader in the thought that finally brought the magazine its distinctive form. Without that, it was and would still have been just another magazine.

What Hammett wrote before, what Erle wrote then, Whitfield, Nebel, Daly and others, did not set the pattern it was later to assume. It was only when Hammett began to set character before situation, and led some others along that path, did he in any way attain recognition. This change, as can readily be seen by an examination of all his republished stories, shall I say, chanced to happen shortly after I came to the magazine, in 1926. Whether the reams of correspondence we exchanged during that period had anything to do with it is not for me to say. My own opinion is that its only help was to permit him opportunity to work out and express his new ideas to sympathetic ears. The claim that I could teach Hammett, Erle or anyone else to write is too absurd for at least my intelligence to entertain.

Replying categorically to points in Erle's letter:

I have quite forgotten the Nebel incident; but I'm hanged if I can see how I could consciously have called Nebel the "best" writer when, let us say, Hammett and Ray Chandler were there at the same time.

I have the warmest admiration and liking for Phil Cody, but Phil was an advertising man and not an editor and the impression I was given immediately was that he was thankful to be rid of all responsibility for it. In fact, I found the magazine without definite aim or purpose and was, indeed, told within the office that it was wobbly on its last legs.

I expect that Erle was not aware of that. Nor, possibly, does he know that it was Warner, the publisher, who told me to keep Hammett out of the pages, because he could not read him, who threw out Whitfield's short stories, which *Cosmopolitan* immediately took over, who rejected the last story Nebel would submit, who rejected over my protest, the series following the Ken Corning stories.

As to the contributions of the several names that Erle mentions, it seems to me it would be more fitting to go back to Nathan and Mencken who started the magazine, if it were not that I am limiting my observations to the moment I came to the magazine and personal knowledge of it.

I am sorry to give you such a long letter. It has stirred me considerably. Let me say that if I had a suspicion that such resentment was entertained toward me by any of the old group, as is expressed in Erle's letter, I would not have agreed to go on with the proposition. However, the selections are in and I presume it will have to proceed.

**The letter from Gardner to my father, dated January 25, 1946, followed:**

Dear Joe:

I note from your letter to Willis Wing that if you "had had a suspicion that such resentment was entertained toward me by any of the old group, as is expressed in Erle's letter, I would not have agreed to go on with the proposition."

How any man of ordinary intelligence could have ever participated in the editorial battles that we had without feeling that I bitterly disagreed with your editorial concept of my work is far beyond me. And how anyone saw me come forward with financial donations at times when you were on your uppers can feel that I didn't have a feeling of friendship for you is equally beyond me.

I suppose it is because of the fact that I have practiced law for so long that I can bitterly resent a man's business attitude and still have a personal liking for him amounting to affection. Apparently you have not been able to grasp that quirk, trait, or vice—whatever it may be—in my character.

I am astounded that a man who should know as much as you do about it could feel Cody was only an advertising man and not an editor. Phil Cody never wanted to be an editor but the fact remains he was one of the best editors I have ever known.

Phil Cody is a friend of mine. Frankly I am getting damn sick and tired on the part of your friends to belittle Cody's part in *Black Mask* Magazine. If you have not inspired this attitude, you have at least done nothing to correct it, and your letter seems to indicate that this is the way you yourself feel.

So far as I know, Phil Cody was the first man to appreciate the real genius of Dashiell Hammett. I remember when he came out to the coast he went up to see Hammett and told me he thought Hammett was destined to be one of the great mystery writers of this country. He did everything possible to encourage Hammett.

In your letter to Wing you state that you were "told within the office the magazine was wobbly and on its last legs when you took over and that you found the magazine without definite aim or purpose." This is a broad statement and I think it's inaccurate. I'd be willing to bet that *sales* under the Cody regime, including the issues for which he had purchased the material when you took over, were fully as high as they averaged later.

However, that's beside the point. Phil Cody was editor of the magazine during the period when Hammett developed his "Continental Op." He bought stories of Race Williams by Carroll John Daly, and he bought stories by Gardner for nearly three years before you became editor.

If by the words "without definite aim or purpose" you mean the magazine under Cody didn't cater merely to one style of fiction, then and then only, you are right. I wrote you dozens of times that your attempt to make the style of the magazine uniform would put it over into the red ink. It did. During the time *Black Mask* was steadily falling behind in sales, your competitive magazine at Popular Publications was earning enough money to make possible the big publishing business that exists there at present.

That detracts only from your business judgment, however, not your ability to discover and to inspire enthusiasm in the writers who followed the style you could correctly evaluate and appreciate. Surely my ideas on this can come as no surprise to you.

If any story of mine appears in an anthology in which it is assumed that the literary standard of *Black Mask* was developed exclusively through your editorial guidance, it constitutes an implied endorsement of a false premise and a slur on Phil Cody. This explains my attitude and the reason I felt it necessary to write the letter I did to Willis Wing.

I am deeply sorry that that letter seems to have shocked you. I am damned if I know why it should. You have had enough tangible evidence of my friendship to realize that my business differences with you have not affected the way I feel toward you. But those business differences are just as profound as they ever were. I personally resent the tendency on your part to belittle Phil Cody's editorial ability and his influence on the course of the magazine. While you were editor you discovered enough famous writers to have all of the credit any ordinary mortal should want.

I have been waiting for years hoping that I would notice some effort on your part to give Cody his share of credit. So far, I have failed to observe any. Your letter to Wing shows you don't feel he is entitled to any. I am sorry you have this attitude.

I hope you understand that despite the sharp differences of opinion I am still your friend if you want it that way. If, however, you feel my differences of professional opinion have changed your desire to have me for a friend, you have only to say so. I have my deep-seated convictions in this matter and I am not going to change them merely to hold a friend.

## My father's response to Gardner in a letter dated January 28, 1946:

Dear Erle:

I thought you knew me better. I have never deviated in my friendship for you. Willis Wing can tell you that, before he handed me your letter, I said: "Erle and I have had our differences of opinion but he is one of my best friends." I have had plenty of reason to believe it and never thought to question any other feeling on your part until certain expressions in your letter to Willis hit me rather hard.

I've seen lots of fellows argue and get mad but I've always held that a difference of opinion was not a cause of enmity. Why, I have warm friends who are Democrats, New Dealers and what have you. I even edited President Roosevelt's Foreign Policy.

I'm glad that you got all this off your chest. You've made a grand success and I don't think you can name anyone who is more pleased over it than I.

Now, as I understand it, the particular gripe is that I have and am still am trying to claim credit for the success of all you fellows. I am trying to disprove that in the statement which I presumed Willis had sent on to you. Whenever anyone has mentioned anything like that to me I have always denied it and said that I was simply lucky to be along at that time.

I have always considered Phil Cody one of my best friends, and he never had to question my feelings toward him. However, I know what that situation was better than anyone else possibly could; the situation of the magazine; what he thought of it; what he and North were doing with it. Phil never resented my coming in. The only feeling he ever expressed was relief. And that ought to tell you plenty. Now, Erle, credit me with one of the streaks in your own character; I cannot say what I conscientiously know to be different. My own great debt to Phil was helping me to fight Warner until it became hopeless. And how can I express that? What the magazine was under Henry Mencken and George Nathan, under George Sutton, Phil Cody, Harry North—there may have been others—is not for me to say. The point is, the magazine changed its form, pattern, style, or whatever you want to call it, and in so doing it tripled its circulation, to which I am not calling attention. I would not consider it fair to anyone who preceded me. I'd like to give Phil credit for my debt to him, and I'm trying to scheme how to do it without comparisons in the magazine's life.

But let's have an end to disagreements. You have stated your points of view, I have told you of the things I know. Although I have no credit in it, I am proud of your success as I am proud of your friendship, and believe you me, Erle, I have not forgotten the tangible evidences of it. By all counts you should be in this anthology, of that group at that time. Willis says you probably have a copy of "Heavenly Rat." If not, I can send it to you. Please have Willis let me know.

The last letter in this series was Gardner's response to my father on February 1, 1946:

Dear Captain Joe:

Atta boy!

It bothered me to think you and I couldn't take up the cudgels in the old spirit of give and take, cussing out each other's opinions, going round and round, but still being friends.

As you suggested, let's forget the whole thing.

I have certain ideas and you have certain ideas. Of late I have had a very strong feeling that my best work or even my typical work was not in *Black Mask* and I don't think it would be good to have some of that work published side by side with the work of writers who were doing their best work in the magazine, nor am I too certain that it is fair to my present book publishers to have earlier and inferior work contained in an anthology.

My best to you for your continued success and the next time I'm in New York, I'm going to grip your hand, look into your familiar countenance across a desk, grin at you and probably start the same old arguments all over.

Lots of the best.[144]

Gardner was a very difficult man with whom to work, and he was one who did extensive grumbling. He was highly opinionated and on occasion did go off on tangents without caring to know the facts. It is questionable as to whether or not he ever grasped the vision of that which was being developed before his very eyes in *Black Mask* mystery writing. Nevertheless, he was a monumental figure in the field; he found a niche and admirably filled it. In spite of my father's efforts, in the years beyond *Black Mask,* his relationship with Gardner can best be categorized as strained.

---

144    UCLA Library, Special Collections.

# YES, THE STORY IS PEOPLE

ALTHOUGH MY father's life was laced with achievements, these were only the by-products of his ability to work through and with people. Each of the authors cited on subsequent pages, in chronological order in which they first appeared in *Black Mask,* was unique; each had his story to tell as well as the manner in which it was told. Their common denominator was Cap Shaw and the influence he had on their development as exponents of the *Black Mask* mode of story telling.

Erle Stanley Gardner complained that my father gave first class treatment only to those authors who would imitate Hammett. In spite of an unpredictable Hammett, an inflexible Daly, a contentious Gardner, and erratic behavior on the part of many of his authors, my father had that magnificent trait of treating all his authors as equals. Each of his authors was his favorite. After my father's death my mother related to me a letter that she had received from one of his authors with whom he had worked. What struck me from this conversation was the statement that "when I was with Cap Shaw he made me feel that I was the most important person in the world." While assembling *The Hard-Boiled Omnibus,* my father wrote: "A grand fellow, Lester Dent. Well, they were all great and regular fellows, unafflicted by 'successful author' phobia on their rapid climb upward." [145]

My father had a vision to make *Black Mask* magazine the best in the field; he was instrumental in redefining the elements of the hard-boiled detective story; and, he did establish standards for the magazine and expectations from his writers; and, yes, he did point the way for this pulp magazine. However, it was the writers who made the *Black Mask* magazine so successful; my

---

145    E.R. Hagemann, "Cap Shaw and His Great and Regular Fellows," p. 143.

father provided the inspiration for these writers to excel. He cared about each of his authors and they knew it, and they, in turn, realized his sincerity in helping them grow to their fullest. My father was a gentle taskmaster. Stories were returned to writers more than once for revisions, but most of the regular contributors were inspired by his detailed, serious response to their work.[146] This is the essence of who my father was and why the *Black Mask* magazine flourished under his leadership.

## TOM CURRY

TOM CURRY'S first publication in *Black Mask* magazine was in the October 1925 issue, his last in the December 1933 issue. Curry observed that my father was one of those editors who believed in using a stable of writers rather than buying whatever came through the mails. He picked eight or ten men and steadily bought from them. Hammett was a member of this group, Gardner, Nebel and Daly were other members. Later on George Harmon Coxe and Prentice Winchell (using the pen name of Stewart Sterling), came in.[147] This approach made perfect sense. It gave my father more time to spend with individual authors, he knew what to expect from these writers, and it gave him far greater inventory control as he planned subsequent issues of *Black Mask.*

Two other insightful comments were made by Curry. The first comment pertained to my father's tremendous enthusiasm, an enthusiasm he sought to impart to his writers.[148] My father refused to allow his writers to get down on themselves or to get discouraged with their work. It was this enthusiasm that kept many of his writers moving forward, enabling them to see the

---

146   Lee Server, p. 68.

147   Tom Curry, "It's Your Own Show," p. 87.

148   *Ibid.*

vision he had, not only for themselves but also for the magazine and the hard-boiled style under development. The second insight was directly related to his concern for the individual writer's growth even at the expense of that writer leaving *Black Mask* for greener fields. In Curry's words, "Shaw begged me, pleaded with me, to make *Murder Chains* into a book and to do so quickly. Magazines have supported me for the most part; and I still have to get at the book." [149]

## FREDERICK NEBEL

WRITER DAVID LEWIS identified Frederick Nebel as "the backbone of *Black Mask*," one of five heavyweights who produced good, reliable stories for the magazine. Given my father's predilection for realistic dialogue, objective narration, powerful emotion and plenty of action, he cultivated strong series characters as a vehicle to explore these objectives. Lewis felt that no other writer more epitomized these ideals and stressed their development over a ten-year period of time than Nebel. He noted that Daly made no attempt at realism or objectivity; Hammett, in spite of his importance, wrote only four years under my father's guidance; and, although Erle Stanley Gardner and Raoul Whitfield supplied scores of stories, their leading characters were only on the fringe of the hard-boiled mainstream. From March 1926 until August 1936 Nebel had sixty-eight pieces published in sixty-six issues. All but eleven stories concerned police or private detectives and all but thirteen featured series characters. Several stories had sequels of sorts but all were "complete" in accordance with my father's guidelines.

Although Nebel was on the scene when my father was appointed as editor, and even though the dialogue Nebel had

---

149   *Ibid.,* p. 88.

developed was already tough and believable, his approach was more subjective than the stories developed over the next two years with my father as his editor. "In a magazine known for its style, Nebel took a backseat to no one. His dialogue was crisp and true, his narrative lean and crackling with energy. Nebel developed his characters through action and interaction." Lewis maintained that Hammett's protagonists hid behind multiple masks and were prisoners of their own reserve, while Nebel's were straightforward. They heeded their emotions but stopped far short of the histrionic single mindedness displayed by Daly's Race Williams.[150] Lewis also maintained that, even though *Black Mask* was Nebel's lowest paying market, he did find his niche under my father's guidance with a series originally called "The Crimes of Richmond City." Further, he kept that series going through more years out of loyalty to my father as well as through the recognition of how much his enthusiasm and encouragement had meant to him during his developmental years.[151]

After my father left *Black Mask* in 1936, Nebel apparently chose not to offer any more material to the magazine. A disappointment for my father was the fact that, in 1946, Nebel declined to have his work published in *The Hard-Boiled Omnibus,* stating that his old work was dated. Obviously my father felt that his work was excellent and wanted to see Nebel's work recognized in this seminal anthology. The loyalty between these two men was beautiful to see.

## HORACE McCOY

HORACE McCOY was one of my father's more interesting writers. Between December 1927 and October 1934 he furnished my

---

150   Dave Lewis, "The Backbone of *Black Mask,*" p. 118.

151   *Ibid.,* p. 122.

father with seventeen stories. Thomas Sturak made some keen observations of this talented writer whose pulp fiction reflected not only the conflicting interests of his everyday life, but the emotional self-division that was at once the source, subject and undoing of his creative imagination. McCoy's professional writing, professional work, moods, health and whatever else were a series of ups and downs. Of the stories he submitted to my father, he never did much rewriting or polishing, but upon receiving manuscripts back from my father, never hesitated to make the corrections taking the approach that "your wish is my command."

My father recognized the latent talent possessed by McCoy, had received favorable comments on his work, and was unquestionably his most loyal champion. For these reasons, my father was quite willing to work with him even though his professional patience must have been taxed to an extreme. In response to the often carelessly written and uneven stories, with characteristic tact my father wrote to McCoy in 1930, with the following observation: "You know, I have an idea you write so easily and fluently that you are apt to give less thought to the logic of the plot and action than the man who does not write so well." While certainly not agreeing with his actions, my father understood McCoy. The fatherly advice he proffered to him concerned advice about "sacrifices" contributing "directly to the strength of a writers work, and of the value in maintaining an unshakable sense of humor—a rare and mighty gift." Not only did my father devote time and energy to McCoy, but he was very responsive in forwarding checks for stories still under scrutiny, and, even beyond that, he would also throw in additional funding when extensive rewriting was required.[152] After examining extensive correspondence between Joseph T. Shaw and Horace McCoy,

---

152   Thomas Sturak, "Horace McCoy, Captain Shaw, and *The Black Mask*," pp. 145, 147 and 149.

Sturak observed that "Captain Shaw is always sincere and gentle, courteous and patient. These Christian virtues tempered his blue-pencil idealism; therein lay his greatness as an editor." [153]

The high point of McCoy's writing career was the novel, published in 1935, entitled: *They Shoot Horses, Don't They?* It was not a hard-boiled detective novel, nor was it remotely like any other story McCoy ever wrote. Unlike Hammett, Whitfield, Chandler and almost every other writer of the *Black Mask* School who graduated to hardcovers, McCoy did so extra-curricularly. He applied the crucial lessons learned under my father to original themes and novel techniques beyond the range of any popular magazine formula.[154]

## WILLIS TODHUNTER BALLARD

W.T. BALLARD, one of the later arrivals to the formative *Black Mask* stable of authors, was as good for my father as my father was for him. Ballard possessed an open-mindedness and genuineness that enabled them to bond very easily. His first story was published in *Black Mask* in September 1933 and forty-three stories followed, the last being printed in May 1945. While with my father, twenty-two of his stories were accepted for publication.

Ballard, inspired by the first of Hammett's movie *Maltese Falcon,* starring Ricardo Cortez, submitted his first story to *Black Mask*. "I mailed the story and ten days later had a letter from Joe Shaw. He liked the manuscript; true it had a couple of minor holes that he wanted plugged, but in the meantime he would not hold up the check. To a writer in the bottom of a depression that alone was enough to endear me to him. The check was for two hundred and fifty dollars—two and a

---

153   *Ibid.*, p. 147.

154   *Ibid.*, p. 156.

half cents a word. I had been working for one cent or less and usually on publication. I was rich, so rich that I lost a hundred and a quarter at the Caliente Race Track. But the headiest part of the sale was that I was working for Joe Shaw, writing copy in which I could believe." [155]

Thirty-five years later Ballard put into words his reminiscence of those three years working for my father: "Captain Shaw was quite a person. He had great talent as an editor and under Cap's shepherding *Black Mask* magazine flourished. He reoriented the direction of the American detective story." These observations clearly define the personal chemistry that developed between these two men. As Ballard realized: "It has been said that for every successful writer there must be an editor who believed in him, an assessment I heartily endorse. It was certainly true in my case, for until I began to work for Joe Shaw at *Black Mask* I was drifting without any real direction."

"One of Shaw's greatest strengths as an editor was his ability to impart a spirit of high morale to his writers. He made us all feel that we were the elite, the chosen few, and as a result drew from us our best work and a devotion that I have never seen equaled in the business. He made us sort of a family, invited the boys who lived in the New York area to parties at his Scarsdale home and encouraged those of us on the west coast to have periodic dinners together." And then Ballard off-handedly stated that: "not that the crowd ever treated Joe with reverence. They were always putting him on in one way or the other." At one of the west coast dinners, with my father present and knowing his distaste for four letter words particularly in polite society, two writers, Paul Cain and Horace McCoy, were outdoing each other with outrageous brags of their adventures in various whorehouses. Amusingly, the gag to shock my father backfired when another writer acknowledged

---

155   Todhunter Ballard, "Writing for the Pulps," p. 9.

the true story that he had been raised in a whorehouse operated by his mother and aunt.[156]

Another story, that is indicative of my father's desire to encourage his writers to bond, involved his sending a telegram to Ballard intended for Dwight Babcock. Once he realized his mistake, instead of firing off another telegram to Babcock, my father asked, by telegram, Ballard to deliver the first telegram personally to Babcock. "That was pure Shaw. Instead of wiring Dwight direct I was to be the messenger boy." Dutifully, Ballard and his wife traveled from Pasadena to Tujunga, California, an extensive trip to deliver an incorrectly-sent message to an individual he had never met. The message got delivered and in the process there was a reciprocal visit from the Babcocks who were joined by another aspiring author, Norbert Davis. The end result was that these three writers became very close friends.[157] It is apparent that my father's gambit was successful.

As a prolific author, Ballard wrote eight Bill Lennox stories over a period of six weeks, all of which he sold to *Black Mask.* Phil Cody, who had been moved to the presidency of the Pro-Distributors Publishing Company, Inc. (at that same time my father was moved up to the position of vice president), suggested that Ballard's inventory was big enough and that my father should refrain from buying any more stories from him for several months; however, over the years that my father remained with *Black Mask,* Ballard sold him more copy than any other writer.[158]

In testimony to the relationship existing between my father and Ballard, Ballard noted that Joe Shaw was never arbitrary, and that he did not always trust his own judgment. "Once he sent me a manuscript and asked me to read it and tell him whether he

---

156   *Ibid.,* p. 10.

157   *Ibid.,* pp. 12–13.

158   *Ibid.,* p. 9.

was nuts to believe he had discovered a near genius. I found the dialogue somewhat contrived, but the characters jumped out of the pages and in most cases were bigger than life. This was the first submission to Shaw by Raymond Chandler." [159]

In an interview with Ballard by Stephen Mertz, Ballard was effusive in his praise of my father. They were not empty words. On two occasions he expressed his genuine love for my father. When my father finally left *Black Mask* and Fanny Ellsworth took over as editor, Ballard continued to submit manuscripts. "It was a living. But although Fanny was a good editor it was never the same as with Joe Shaw. At the risk of sounding euphoric, there never was a relationship between editor and writer to equal my connection with Cap Shaw." [160] "Through the years I have worked with the leading editors of the business: Ray Long, Fanny Ellsworth, Dorothy Hubbard, Erd Brandt, Ken McCormick, Ken Littaur, Ken White, you name them. But none of them offered the help, the assurance, the patience that Joe Shaw gave to his writers. It is too bad that he has been so overlooked in the history of the craft." [161]

## RAYMOND CHANDLER

MY FATHER'S influence on Raymond Chandler is what gave him the courage to pursue writing. Chandler was an apt student and through persistence and my father's inspiration mastered the art of writing mystery stories. He analyzed the work of many authors and imitated where he felt appropriate. Chandler most admired Hammett's attention to detail and his ability to transform a physical observation into something that reveals character. This

---

159   *Ibid.*, p. 11.

160   Stephen Mertz, "W.T. Ballard: An Interview," p. 3.

161   *Ibid.*

Hammett influence and imitation on his own work placed Chandler implicitly in the central tradition of contemporary American letters.[162] My father had great respect for Chandler and almost without exception placed his stories in the lead position in the magazine. My father indicated that Raymond Chandler came to *Black Mask* full fledged, that his very first stories were all that could be desired, and that there never was any question or doubt about his ultimate success.[163] In spite of the bouquets thrown to Chandler about being a finished product upon arrival, learning to write mystery stories was a tedious task. The key to his success was that he persisted. In making the transition from a very able writer in the Romantic tradition to a hard-boiled author, he had to master the fundamentals: he did this by analyzing the work of authors like Hammett and Gardner. He had always written in British English. Now he had to master his own American language, a task that was comparable to learning a foreign language.[164] In comparing Chandler with Hammett, Hammett lacked Chandler's verbal facility and the vision that illuminated a scene. Here Chandler exceeded Hammett in a fundamental way.[165]

Chandler's ambition was to write for *Black Mask;* in total, he had eleven stories published between December 1933 and January 1937. In 1947, looking back on his early literary career Chandler identified those reasons why he had selected the pulps as the medium within which he wanted to begin his apprenticeship in detective fiction. He believed that "some of the pulps at that time had very honest and forthright stuff in them; the literary standard was flexible and there was a chance to get 'paid while learning;' and, although the average story in *Black Mask* was not too good,

---

162   Frank MacShane, The Life of Raymond Chandler, p. 47.

163   *Ibid.,* p. 50.

164   *Ibid.,* p. 49.

165   *Ibid.,* p. 48.

there was a possibility of writing them very much better without hurting their chances of being read." [166]

Despite their critical differences, both Shaw and Chandler worked well together. Through correspondence, Shaw would gently teach and provide Chandler with helpful suggestions on each story—trim here, bulk up this. Shaw was an instrumental man with respect to Chandler's early success; he would teach Chandler not how to write, but rather how to write a good mystery. [167]

Chandler was older than most of the *Black Mask* writers and, therefore, was not as dependent upon my father to the extent that most of the other writers were. However, he looked upon my father as a "very kind and warm editor" who had "the ability to get better writing out of his own men than they could really do." While still an active contributor to *Black Mask*, he wrote that Cap Shaw had "a great insight into writing and he can give a man a buck up when he needs it as nobody else I know can, or does." [168] In a letter to Erle Stanley Gardner, dated January 29, 1946, Chandler emphasized this point with the following observation: "The proof of that is that some writers we both know have never reached the standard again that they attained in the *Black Mask* under Shaw." [169]

When my father left *Black Mask* so too did Raymond Chandler. Part of the reason for his departure was because of loyalty to my father; however, he also wanted to follow Hammett out of

---

166    Robert F. Moss, "Ray Chandler and the pulps," from Frank MacShane, *Criticism and Scholarship, Selected Letters of Raymond Chandler* (New York: Columbia University Press, 1981), p. 86.

167    Jason Barr, "Faded Ink Spots, February 1998," *Sabine Magazine* (http://www.sabine-mag.com/archive/ar05008.htm), p. 2.

168    Frank MacShane, *The Life of Raymond Chandler*, p. 50.

169    Frank MacShane, *Selected Letters of Raymond Chandler*, p. 68.

the pulps. My father, as always, wanted to see his authors grow, and, in all probability, suggested to Chandler to turn some of his novelettes into a novel. *The Big Sleep* was the result and was sold to Alfred A. Knopf, Inc., in 1939. This success enabled him to move away from pulps completely.[170]

## DWIGHT V. BABCOCK

IT WAS with trepidation that Dwight V. Babcock submitted his first story to *Black Mask* heeding the blurb inserted by my father in *Writer's Digest:* "Only the very best will appear here." Expecting a prestigious rejection letter (and they were hallmark letters) he was pleasantly surprised when my father accepted this story for publication in the January 1934 issue of *Black Mask,* sending him a check for one hundred dollars. My father followed this by accepting his next story on November 10, 1933, for inclusion in the February 1934 issue. Fortunately for Babcock, my father paid upon acceptance not publication.[171]

Two diversionary points of interest: The first relates to a letter of rejection received by an aspiring author by the name of Carroll Rheinstrom who responded with the following observation: "If all authors received rejection slips as nice as yours, they would feel almost fully compensated for their literary efforts, as I do." [172] This touch of grace comes as no surprise. He would, in a gentle manner, always try to point out the reasons why he was rejecting a story. The second point pertains to my father's notation that he felt that the February 1934 issue of

170   Ron Goulart, *Cheap Thrills—An Informal History of the Pulp Magazines* (New Rochelle: Arlington House), p. 127.

171   James L. Traylor, "Murder Up His Sleeve," *The Armchair Detective,* Winter 1990, pp. 57–58.

172   Philip Durham, "The Boys in *The Black Mask*," p. 11.

*Black Mask* magazine was the high point of his many editorial achievements.[173]

All in all, Babcock had twenty-one stories published from January 1934 until December 1939. Babcock was one of the last of my father's elite group known as the *Black Mask* boys.[174] However, it was not all smooth sailing for Babcock's growth as a pulp writer. With his first story, Babcock had done his research well. The story closely replicated the classic *Black Mask* style with the narrative straightforward and the writing crisp. There were the usual hard-boiled characters, but somehow more alive than usual.[175] Having accepted his first two stories, when my father rejected Babcock's third story he immediately contacted him asking for specific criticism and advice for future stories. My father's response, dated November 24, 1933, was: "We favor stories that will immediately create sympathetic character appeal to offset the sordid brutality which is a part of the criminal atmosphere. Without this there is no real interest in a story merely of crime." [176] My father then rejected the next Maguire story from Babcock because of the absence of respectable characters. Babcock's success with *Black Mask* is a reflection that he clearly trusted my father's judgment and tried to incorporate all of his suggestions into his *Black Mask* submissions.[177]

My father felt very comfortable with Babcock and wrote to him frequently requesting his assistance on occasion and confiding in him at other times. My father's interest in bringing his writers together to enable them to feel as if they were part of a family led his asking for Babcock's assistance in rounding up the west coast

---

173   James L. Traylor, "Murder Up His Sleeve," p. 57.

174   *Ibid.*

175   *Ibid.* p. 58.

176   *Ibid.*

177   *Ibid.* p. 59.

*Black Mask* writers. The result was the "famous" January 11, 1936, dinner at the Nickabob Café in Los Angeles.[178]

Babcock not only bonded easily with my father but also with other *Black Mask* authors, especially W.T. Ballard and Norbert Davis. The *Writers Review* of September 1935 confirmed that Babcock, Ballard and Davis were fast friends and also reported that the three of them were in a " 'high ball huddle' telling each other what a swell guy Joe Shaw was."[179]

## LESTER DENT

IT WAS in 1936 that Lester Dent, who wrote the popular Doc Savage novels under the name Kenneth Robeson, made the decision to break into *Black Mask* magazine, a magazine that he considered to be the holy grail of the pulps and one of the hardest to crack.[180] His first submission, entitled "Sail," was rejected by my father. In a letter, dated July 19, 1936, the following guidance was provided:

> Dear Lester Dent:
>
> We're simple folk; really—we've kidded ourselves so long in trying to gauge average intelligence receptivity that for all practical purposes we're it.
>
> Style—we were unwary enough to state that we weren't concerned with style, method or technique so long as entertainment should be provided. Perhaps we are still right about that, since understanding must introduce entertainment and stand by throughout.
>
> You've done things with this darned good story "Sail"—particularly with the first half. You've given a series of pictures that are designed to provide

---

178   *Ibid.* p. 64.

179   *Ibid.* p. 62.

180   Will Murray, *Lester Dent* (biography in progress), p. 1.

movement, plot and its development. Some of these pictures are gorgeous in their plentitude of descriptive material of a rare authenticity and almost as rare recognizability. Mr. Average Reader would have to go through a dictionary a score of times to a page. In the first place he hasn't a dictionary, and, in the second, if he had, it is extremely doubtful if he would bestir himself to do so even once. He doesn't appreciate the value of such pearls, and he'd say "Nuts" or "Rats"—or some equally absurd and irrefutable New Deal argument.

So what?

Your method of presenting the story by the disjointed picture system, plus the remarkably full amplification of each, ties up Mr. Average Reader in a confused maelstrom of noodle aches more severe than Sail's cramps.... You are altogether too nimble for him in their swift sequences and in the still remaining too abrupt and angle changes.

There are approximately seventeen pages of this—and it's a darned good story. And would it lose any of its effectiveness if these seventeen pages were told in the straight-running, non-switching, simple language of Mr. Average Reader?

Confidentially—many of these pictures fascinate me; but that was when I relapsed from my role. And in it once more, I am convinced that this method does not beget clarity and constant understandability, and without these we are gutted and sunk.

Man, can you write.

Incidentally, this is not the *Black Mask* method. It is not Hammett's. Curiously, it chances to be exactly Jim Moynaham's conception of Hammett's style or method. Jim is so far wrong that his machinery creaks and groans. Yours does not; you have oiled it so darn well. But it is there—in places in the first seventeen odd pages, and it confuses and obfuscates, when the narrative should ring as clear as the winding of the silver horn on a winter morning.

How's your patience?

I'd tackle the do-over on this part myself—for sake of the work you've given it—but I couldn't do it justice. I'm not that much of a sailorman, and there are some pearls that must be saved.

In a post-script, my father added:

> How about thinking of the angle of having the characters informing
> the reader in these pages—whereas now the author does it for the most
> part? [181]

My father's response to Lester Dent was symptomatic of the
manner in which he worked with all of his writers—gently yet
pointedly. As Phil Durham was assembling "The Boys in the
*Black Mask*" Exhibit in the UCLA Library, January 6 through
February 10, 1961, he requested a statement from Lester Dent as to
his experiences with "Cap" Shaw. The response, in a letter dated
October 27, 1958, was an insightful analysis of my father and his
inter-relationships with his authors as well as an emotional testimony of his affection for my father.

> Dear Durham:
> I don't foam easily, I'm pretty sure. But this chip of recognition you
> toss toward Cap Shaw and his *Black Mask* stirs my juices quite a bit.
> Shaw was the finest coachwhip I ever met in an editor's chair. In
> my thirty-five years of freelance fiction, no one stands out so. Hence I
> presume when you speak of *Black Mask* you speak of Joe Shaw.
> *Black Mask* in Cap Shaw's hands was akin to a writer's shrine. I don't
> mean today but in the Twenties and Thirties when Shaw presided. That
> was the brief wonderful time when American literature was endowed
> with the most effective training ground in all history—the pulp magazine.
> The writers whom Shaw published in *Black Mask* were sort of automat-
> ically endowed with a hair shirt that they wore with pride and some
> dubiousness, because where writers got together you were pointed out
> as a *Black Mask* man, not a *Post* writer, a *Collier's* writer, a *Doc Savage*
> writer or an *Argosy* writer, but as a *Black Mask* writer.

---

181   UCLA Library, Special Collections.

So Cap Shaw had recognition in his day.

His writers regarded Captain Shaw with—if any writers ever truly gave an editor such—reverence. At least I never heard a *Black Mask* writer be casual about Shaw.

My tenure with Cap Shaw was short. I sold him, I think, only three pieces. Then he gave up the helmsmanship of *Black Mask* over a policy dispute, which, I am convinced, is what kept me from becoming a fine writer. Had I been exposed to this man's cunning hand for another year or two, I could not have missed. Cap did try to work with me and guide me after he left *Black Mask,* and became an agent. But in those days I was feisty and greedy, and also Joe no longer had the money-apple to dangle in front of me—a sale to *Black Mask.* Instead I wrote reams of saleable crap which became my pattern, and gradually there slipped away that bit of power with words that Shaw had started awakening in me.

Cap was gentle with his writers. You went in to *Black Mask* and talked with him, you had feelings of stature, you felt you were doing fiction that was powerful. Cap gave this strength to his writers. He could, because he was so convinced it was the truth.

Cap himself was the personification of English culture. This was so sincere in him that it was almost a spiritual garment he wore. This facet struck me hard. I was a Missouri hillbilly, and I think I was at all times a bit skeptical of Cap Shaw's reality. For one thing he was an expert at fencing, and this was enough to make him incomprehensible to me.

How did Shaw find and develop so many great writers? I wish I fully understood.

In my own case, I'd written a lot of published pulp, many millions of words of it, before I assembled enough guts to decide I might, just might, be able to do something near Cap's standard. So I telephoned him. Could I have a talk with him. I could. I went to the *Black Mask* office, expecting to get the customary puzzling generalities about what he wanted.

My first shock: Here was a cultured man editing a pulp. Second, here was an editor who thought his writers were truly great. I never did feel fully at ease that afternoon—three or four hours as I recall—because culture makes me itch, and an editor who didn't pretend his writers were crude factories was unbelievable.

But here was a man who could breathe this pride of his into a writer. Cap didn't think I was a pulp hack. Joe felt that I was a writer in step with the future. He thought that of all his writers. He had a way, with this device or some other device, of breathing power into his writers. I am sure all of Cap's writers—Hammett, Chandler, Gardner, the rest, probably felt this.

That day Shaw showed me a bit from a letter from Chandler, a piece so delicate and sensitive and perceptive that it forever moulded my view of Chandler, whom I have never met. The bit concerned some value Chandler was seeking, a thing that Shaw might congeal. Showing me the note from Chandler did exactly what Shaw probably wanted it to do—it sold me on the idea that I was not to sit down and do a hack hardboiled piece of pulp for *Black Mask*. I was to believe and feel I was doing a great piece.

Joe used his coach whip in strange gentle ways. He would start discussing his writers, their skill, and before you knew it you would find some Hammett or Chandler in your hands along with a blue pencil and Cap would be asking, "Would you cut that somewhere. Just cut a few words." The idea, of course, was that there was no wordage fat. You could not cut. Every word had to be there.

You will hear it said Joseph Shaw told his writers what to write and how, demanded they do *"Black Mask"* style. This was not true. He demanded nothing of the sort. He did demand that every word mean something—he must be able to hardly touch your piece with a blue pencil. And he didn't rewrite himself—if there was one paragraph off, you got it back to re-do. That may be the secret of realism Shaw writers acquired. Anyway, when you did something lean and powerful, no excess wordage anywhere, then you had *"Black Mask* style."

Cap had above all the power to impress you incredibly with the importance of the things he considered made a good story. This may have been partly the force of his dignity, his culture. As I wrote in the beginning, I have never met another like him. Possibly as a measure of my respect for him, I never troubled to submit another piece to the *Black Mask* market after he left, a thing I certainly did not discuss with him or with anyone but myself.

You ask about my own published material. It amounts to several hundred book lengths and shorts. My most recent, a short earlier in the year in the *Saturday Evening Post;* a *Wagon Train* TV story; then in *Collier's* and other slicks, pocket books by Gold Medal and others, books by Doubleday, and for seventeen years and a bit more a book length published yarn every month about a character called Doc Savage under Kenneth Robeson, a house name for Street and Smith. I think I did two hundred and eighty-seven Doc books.

I do hope you fellows grasp the idea that *Black Mask* was Joseph T. Shaw. He created its power.[182]

Lester Dent had only two stories published in *Black Mask,* "Sail" in October 1936, and "Angelfish" in December 1936. He is almost invariably cited as one of the major exponents of the *Black Mask* School by scholars and researchers who seem unaware that his total contribution in numbers of pages was so slim.[183] After my father left *Black Mask,* Lester Dent was one of several writers who elected not to submit any more stories. Fanny Ellsworth repeatedly tried to coax stories from him. Dent declined. It was out of loyalty to my father, and with the feeling that without him at the helm things could never be the same. Among those who chose not to seek further publication in *Black Mask* were Raymond Chandler, who went on to greater accomplishments in hardcover, Frederick Nebel who went on to slicks and undeserved obscurity, and Lester Dent.[184] Unfortunately, with my father's departure

---

182   *Ibid.*

183   Will Murray, "Lester Dent: The last of Joe Shaw's *Black Mask* Boys," *Clues—A Journal of Detection,* Vol. 2, Fall/Winter, 1981, p. 128.

184   *Ibid.,* p. 133.

the greatest casualty of all was Lester Dent himself. "Had Shaw remained, Dent would have unquestionably produced more 'Sail' stories and who knows what else. But this was not to be."[185] In retrospect, even before Dent became a *Black Mask* writer he had already developed in his writing the fast movement, the brittle violence of emotion and action; in effect, the unmistakable *Black Mask* style.[186]

## *BLACK MASK* IN PERSPECTIVE

IN THE 1920s other detective pulps gave little space to the kind of story my father was championing. When speaking of his authors who wrote during that period my father often said "that their product, in its best examples, was several years ahead of its time. These writers were blazing new paths. After the Great Depression the paths were clear enough to follow; the imitations came."[187] When my father stepped in as editor, he was determined to raise the level of the magazine to make it readily distinguishable from other pulps. He wanted to encourage his best writers by using them consistently and more often. He also was prepared to pay higher rates.[188] These inducements were certainly a part of my father's strategy but his impact went well beyond them. He took his job seriously as if he had been at the helm of *American Mercury* or the *Atlantic;* he was never apologetic about what he preferred to call rough paper writing.[189]

At its best, *Black Mask* published the sparsest prose of any

---

185   *Ibid.*

186   *Ibid.,* p. 129.

187   Ron Goulart, *Cheap Thrills,* p. 130.

188   Julian Symons, *Dashiell Hammett,* p. 33.

189   Thomas Stuark, "Horace McCoy, Captain Shaw, and *The Black Mask,*" p. 147.

magazine in the country. Joe Shaw used to admonish his new writers: "Prune and cut, don't use a single word that you can do without. Read Hammett, Gardner, Nebel, Daly. Try to write like they do." [190] Gruber then continued by offering an intriguing insight: The *Black Mask* writers did attempt to write like those who went on before them. "So did many, many other writers. Hemingway's style when he finally found it in *The Sun Also Rises* and a *Farewell to Arms* is right out of *Black Mask*. Even though he never published anything in the magazine, he most certainly read it." [191]

My father maintained the highest standards in pulpdom.[192] According to one of his authors, he could become evangelistic: "He insisted that each line of good writing contain all the harsh splendor of revelation, brought forth in an agony of discipline and a sort of ecstasy of mystic communion with ultimate reality." [193] My father also said that many of the writers with whom he worked "observed the cardinal principal in creating the illusion of reality; they did not make their characters act and talk tough; they allowed them to. They gave their stories over to their characters and kept themselves off the stage, as every writer of fiction should. They did not themselves state that a situation was dangerous or exciting; they did not describe their characters as dead shots or infallible men. They permitted the actors in the story to demonstrate all that to the extent of their particular and human capabilities. As a consequence, they wrote convincingly." [194]

For ten years my father had had an unparalleled run as editor of the *Black Mask* magazine. His resolution to make it foremost

---

190   Frank Gruber, *The Pulp Jungle,* p. 145.

191   *Ibid.*

192   Lee Server, *Danger Is My Business,* p. 68.

193   Philip Durham, "The Boys in *The Black Mask,*" Preface.

194   William Pronzini, "Horace McCoy: Mopper-Up," pp. 51–52.

of the detective pulps was achieved. But that was only the beginning. He realized many achievements beyond developing *Black Mask* into a respectable and prestigious pulp magazine.

First, he moved mystery writing away from the crossword style of trying to deduce, through logic, who committed the crime, to a hard-boiled, fast-moving, sharply-worded story in which character development and reaction to a created environment became the focal point of the story. This approach was a momentous contribution to the art of mystery story telling earning for itself a remarkable niche in American literature.

Second, he made writing for the *Black Mask* magazine a training ground for the development of ambitious authors. Yes, even Hammett, Gardner, Chandler and a small coterie of highly talented writers. He did not teach them how to write, this they had already achieved; but through instruction, guidance and infinite patience he showed them how to write a better hard-boiled mystery story in a style that encapsulated the very essence of the established doctrine.

Third, and perhaps most important, was that those who embraced his influence grew into better, stronger craftsmen as a result. They allowed themselves to be touched by the magic of his presence, and my father reveled in the successes that they realized by moving from "rough" paper writing to the "smooth" paper magazines, hardcover novels in book form, and, in some cases movies. He never failed to express this pardonable pride in their achievements, a trait that was one of his hallmarks.[195] What Cap Shaw created became a legend. Popular culture scholar Russell B. Nye wrote: "The greatest change in the detective story came in 1926 with the emergence of the *Black Mask* school of fiction." [196]

---

195   E.R. Hagemann, "Captain Joseph T. Shaw's *Black Mask* Scrapbook," p. 4.
196   William Marling, "The *Black Mask* School of Hard-Boiled Fiction," p. 31.

There was always a part of Hammett that despised what he called the *"Black Mask* junk." He sometimes adopted, as did Chandler a few years later, the attitude of a literary man stooping to work in a low-grade medium.[197] How quickly one can forget his roots, for it was in the pulps, specifically *Black Mask,* where both Hammett and Chandler honed their skills in the art of crime story writing. Both authors had acknowledged this, realizing that the road to their subsequent successes led through the *Black Mask* experience.

In a letter to Babcock in June 1936, my father expressed his concern about his writers: "I'm very glad to see you swing in with this fast story of Chuck Thompson. All the boys seem to be going pretty well now. Chandler is, of course, Chandler, but Ballard and Butler, Eric Taylor are all hitting it off nicely, and, of course, I include you in this group. I do wish there was some way in which Norbert Davis could come to see how very easy our slant is." [198] As my father's tenure with *Black Mask* was winding down, on August 28, 1936, he sent a poignant letter to Babcock: "I don't want to break relations with you and other members of the group... as I've just written to Ballard, I'm darned if I want to quit the fellows when they're are almost there." [199] Apparently, in September, my father kept writing his impressive missives to Babcock. His sense of mission about the *Black Mask* School had not diminished. All of the West Coast boys had written of their feelings and support for him. On September 10, 1936, my father responded to their concerns: " I knew damn well how I felt about all you boys out there but I didn't know it was quite that way the other way around. Further, he congratulated Babcock on his career decision: "You are wise in aiming consciously for

---

197    Julian Symons, *Dashiell Hammett*, p. 47.

198    James L. Traylor, "Murder up His Sleeve," p. 65.

199    *Ibid.,* pp. 65–66.

a more difficult market. The danger lies in being satisfied with the easy going."[200]

Babcock was moving toward novels. As always my father was concerned about "his boys." He recommended Jane Hardy as an agent, a recommendation that Babcock accepted. My father expressed great concern and possible "embarrassment" as to whether or not he had given Babcock advantageous advice as to representation. "Shaw was truly rare among editors," praised Babcock.[201]

An anecdote concerning Jane Hardy is appropriate. In the July 1934 issue of *Writer's Digest* the following letter to the editor was printed:

> Dear Editor:
>
> Anent your editorial box in the article by Joe Shaw... I this morning wrote to the Dean of Men, U. of W. Va., in answer to his request asking me if I could recommend any course of books for writers. This was after his reading short story of mine in current *Atlantic Monthly*, which seemed to make him think I was an authority.
>
> I was, anyhow, able to endorse Hoffman's three books and to tell him that seventy-five of the top flight of authors would back my opinion. This is of course a fact. Next to A.S.H., Bob Davis should be placed.
>
> Joe Shaw has very limited views as to what he likes. Beyond those limits one could hardly call his education catholic.
>
> J. Allan Dunn,
>
> Explorer's Club, New York City

In the August issue of *Writer's Digest,* a response to Dunn's letter was printed:

---

200   *Ibid.,* p. 66.

201   *Ibid.,* p. 62.

Dear Editor:

Some of us are a little bit upset about that remark of Mr. Dunn's about Joe Shaw, which appeared in a recent issue of *Writer's Digest*. I have a sort of personal weakness for Mr. Shaw, for I think he is one of the really outstanding editors in New York, and I think he is one of the squarest shooting men I've ever known.

I just can't see why anyone has to take what I consider an unfair crack at him.

As a rule, I don't bother about other people's affairs, but I, personally, feel that someone should say something. You see, Mr. Shaw is my friend, and I'm from Texas, where if you hate a man, he knows it, and if you're his friend, you stand by him.

Jane Hardy

New York City

## And then the Editor's response:

Jane Hardy's letter was one of fifty received to date by *Writer's Digest* in reference to Mr. Dunn's note in our "Forum Department." May we again reiterate that the Forum Department of *Writer's Digest* is used to express the opinions of our readers, and that most certainly we will not edit those letters sent to us because we disagree with them. Mr. Dunn is an able writer and entitled to his opinion. Mr. Shaw has been commented on too often in our columns for us to express again our thanks to him for the aid he has given writers.

An observation about my father is that as one writes about his relationship with one writer after another, he never truly acknowledges, or gives himself credit for the influence or impact he has had on these authors. It was profound.

NOW IT was time to move on into the final phases of his life's work. Whatever forces governed the change, a decision was made and my father's back was turned on his ten year run with *Black Mask* magazine.

## WHY THE DEPARTURE?

IN RETROSPECT, a pertinent question is: Why did my father leave *Black Mask?* In seeking a viable answer, a search of the literature offers some possible reasons, but they are all speculative. It is probable that pulp magazines in general and *Black Mask* more specifically were losing subscribers throughout the 1930s. General factors can be identified one or more of which could have been the determining factor or factors for loss of sales. The Great Depression, or as my father grandly euphemized it as the "Universal Retrenchment," [202] was a bear market that prevailed for thirty-five straight months from 1929 to 1932. One impact of the depression was that personal disposable income had diminished to the point where fifteen cents a copy was perhaps a nickel too much. In addition to the havoc wreaked on the economy, pulp magazine competition was intense. As my father correctly predicted, *Black Mask* success would attract many imitators. This did occur as the number of pulp detective and mystery story magazines increased considerably.[203] It is obvious that one could crank out pulp fiction that could be sold, but one could not artificially create stories in the *Black Mask* style. As a result, few of the imitations had much long-term impact. In the end, the hardboiled school survived them all, and became one of the most

---

202   Thomas Stuark, "Horace McCoy, Captain Shaw, and *The Black Mask*," p. 149.

203   John L. Apostolu, "Norbert Davis: Profile of a Pulp Writer," *Black Mask Magazine,* p. 7. (https://blackmaskmagazine.com/blog/norbert-davis-profile-of-a-pulp-writer/)

popular genres in the pulp era and beyond.[204]

Another source of competition was the introduction of a flood of pulp romance magazines into the market that not only diluted the existing number of readers for individual magazines, and, redirected female readers away from the hard-boiled style toward those publications that favored romance, but it also attracted a whole new female audience. It can be argued that the hard-boiled style of mystery stories was no longer popular; however, this supposition is doubted by virtue of the fact that mystery story writing is still very much in vogue even today, albeit with the inclusion of sexual promiscuity as Mickey Spillane discovered with his protagonist Mike Hammer.

The above information notwithstanding, my father's separation could have been provoked by sales alone. The high point of *Black Mask* sales was in 1930. By 1936 sales had plummeted dramatically to a level less than when Dad first arrived at *Black Mask* in 1926. Eltinge Warner, owner and publisher, may have felt that change was necessary, and that was all there was to the decision.

Whatever the reason, Phil Cody, as President of Pro-Distributors, had to trim overhead costs. The move from 578 Madison Avenue to 515 Madison Avenue was a first step. The next step would have been to not only cut my father's salary but also the price per word that he was then paying his authors. This also could have been the determining factor in my father's departure from *Black Mask;* however, knowing that my father had sustained financial setbacks much earlier in his professional life, and that money was not that big an issue with him, it is doubted that loss of salary would have been the motivating factor. If my father still believed in what he was doing and still had the opportunity to continue performing the remarkable services he was providing to

---

204  *Hard Boiled Mysteries,* December 27, 1998, p. 1 (http://www.columbia.edu/~mfs10/pulp_hard.html)

his authors, he would never have turned his back on the editor-ship of *Black Mask.* The reason for separation had to be some-thing more complex than the money factor.

In a letter from my father to Dwight Babcock dated March 20, 1936, he indicated that there were problems brewing: "We have been more or less tied in a knot over some new matters that have come up for decision."[205] James Traylor, the author of this article on Dwight Babcock and the source of this extract from that letter, hypothesized that, because *Black Mask* was the most prestigious pulp, it did pay the highest rates and did sell for a higher cover price than many of other pulps; further, problematically, Shaw's insistence on absolute quality in *Black Mask* may have worked against it. Finally, the magazine was becoming too predictable, almost too pat in its approach to the detective story; consequently, Shaw's tenure was coming to an end.[206]

Austerity certainly was a problem, but it was not a dire condi-tion in that after my father's departure issues of *Black Mask* continued to sell at fifteen cents a copy and stayed at that level until June 1940 when the cost was increased to twenty cents. Further, the new editor continued to pay Babcock at the one and one-half cents per word that my father had been paying him. As far as the magazine being too predicable, a new corps of talented writers was being introduced to the readers of *Black Mask,* each with his own individual style of writing. There was diversity even though there was adherence to the hard-boiled tenets of mystery writing. No, the problematic reasons introduced by Tray-lor should be discounted.

In another letter to Babcock from my father dated August 28, 1936, three days before his effective date of resignation, another element was introduced. It was a personal letter sent from Scars-

---

205  James L. Traylor, "Murder up His Sleeve," p. 64.

206  *Ibid.,* p. 65.

dale, New York, and tells in very general terms the reason for his resignation: "On a matter of policy." [207] Dad was not one to discuss private matters in public nor would he besmirch others when there was a difference of opinion being expressed. A September 10, 1936, letter to Babcock revealed more about his resignation saying that "the decision was definitely pulp, and that would be good to none of us." [208]

An educated guess as to why my father left *Black Mask* is predicated on a seed planted by Will Murray, whose observation was that a whole new audience was turning to the reading of pulp magazines, namely women, because of the introduction of female characters and romance. Referring to a detailed letter to Babcock written on January 17, 1935, my father said: there is a need for "more appealing characters, more appealing plots and situations. We don't mind the brutal characters in a story... we don't mind the hard action; we want it; but we do want... a man that is a hero; a girl... that is very likable and appealing—a man and a girl that the reader feels just must come through." My father was sending this same message to all the other writers whom he looked upon as the newer group in *Black Mask*.[209] Traylor then observes: "Shaw had evidently heard the same complaints about *Black Mask* stories—just consider the toughness of Paul Cain, Raoul Whitfield, and Frederick Nebel during this time period—and wanted to start the stories going in a slightly different direction.[210] In effect, pressure was building to introduce women into the stories that would appeal to a new and rapidly growing female audience.

However, the rigid editorial stance had already been tempered. For example, in March 1926, months before my father came to

---

207   *Ibid.*

208   *Ibid.*, p. 66.

209   *Ibid.*, p. 61.

210   *Ibid.*

*Black Mask,* editor Phil Cody in advertising for new writers was quite explicit: "We are seeking new stories; nothing weird, no horror stories or occult or experimental or romances. The feminine element is not desired."[211] Then, in February 1931, my father, in seeking new authors and stories, suggested; "a touch of romance is not objectionable in its fiction."[212] The door was cracked open, although not far enough to change the philosophical bent of the magazine.

If the assumption that the role of women and romance in future crime stories would be radically shifted is correct, then this change in editorial philosophy would be contrary to everything that my father was effectively doing for the previous nine years; unfortunately, there would now be incompatibility of perceived mission between those responsible for determining the future direction of the *Black Mask* magazine and my father. The bottom line was that my father was a man's man, and *Black Mask* was primarily a magazine for men. The focus could not be on soft-boiled romance without destroying the very essence of the publication. The directional change requested was of such magnitude that it could have been debated whether or not, given the foundation undergirding the success of *Black Mask* and the proclivity of its writers, these changes could have taken place under my father's leadership.

In editing a Dwight Babcock submission, to the suggestion that the author's protagonist was contemplating marriage, my father's response was, in effect, to not let him get married too soon: "it would be fatal."[213] Was this an attempt to dampen any romance in the story? Also Frederick Nebel was one of my father's authors who did write romance stories, but these stories were written

---

211   *Author and Journalist,* March 1926.

212   *Author and Journalist,* February 1931.

213   James L. Traylor, "Murder up His Sleeve," p. 61.

separately from the hard-boiled material. In no way are these examples shown to identify my father as an anti-feminist—quite the contrary. He was highly respectful of women and very sensitive to those of the opposite sex.[214] In fact, three of the five novels my father wrote could have been characterized as romantic, and only one of these five would be considered as hard-boiled. It is felt that my father left *Black Mask* because he felt that the introduction of romance into the magazine compromised the essential mission for which the Hard-Boiled School of Mystery Writing was developed. This could not be considered just a gentle change, but, rather, a major change.

To further substantiate the argument, it is noted that within three days after my father's letter of resignation, the new editor, Fanny Ellsworth, had already been in contact with the *Black Mask* writers. Recognizing that my father would not compromise the hard-boiled style in deference to a soft-boiled style, Cody must have been under pressure to find a replacement editor who would factor these changes into the magazine without leaving any gaps in *Black Mask's* editorial leadership. For that reason, Ellsworth must have been already appointed and was just waiting in the wings for my father's resignation to become effective; further, she was already the editor of *Ranch Romances,* a magazine that, in the words of Will Murray was "wildly successful." [215] Knowing well ahead of time that he was leaving *Black Mask,* my father laid the foundation for those articles that should be used in the four-month spread from September through December, with at least one for January 1937. This action is very much in accord with his highly established ethical standards, and it demonstrated his great love for this publication as well as his respect for his authors. My father left *Black Mask* magazine with grace and with dignity.

214   Dave Lewis, "The Backbone of *Black Mask* (Frederick Nebel)," p. 118.

215   Will Murray, *Lester Dent* (unpublished biography), p. 8.

# THE AFTERMATH

IN A letter, dated September 1, 1936, from Eve Woodburn of the Jane Hardy Literary Agency to Dwight Babcock, she disclosed changes in *Black Mask's* story acceptance policy; "There has been a change in the policy... Hereafter, they don't want stories about tough cops. They do want a bit more emotion... they will continue to want stories in which cops or G-men star, but they want these leads played up in a more sympathetic manner."[216] It was the start of a long year for Babcock. In 1937 he only placed two stories with *Black Mask,* whereas, as late as October 1935, my father was asking Babcock to give him one Chuck Thompson G-man story each month.[217]

In October 1936, Fanny Ellsworth assigned J.B. Magill to be the managing editor, overseeing the *Black Mask* magazine. She also announced that: *"Black Mask* will continue to be a market for the better types of detective fiction."[218] In January 1937, there was some back-treading with the announcement that *Black Mask,* under a new editor, has a slightly broader policy than when it was under Joseph Shaw. "The magazine will still publish the most realistic fiction found in the detective field; nothing soft, sentimental and emotional is welcomed; women interest is acceptable, although sex itself is not used."[219]

By April 1937, the solicitation policy became more declarative: *"Black Mask* is a more open market than *Ranch Romances;* the magazine can use a good detective story of almost any kind except horror and fantasy; armchair type is not favored; plots should be well rounded and logically developed; the editor is

---

216  James L. Traylor, "Murder up His Sleeve," p. 66.

217  *Ibid.*

218  *Writer's Digest,* October, 1936, pp. 4–5.

219  *Writer's Digest,* January, 1937, p. 16.

looking for the detective who is different; a touch of mystery is desired."[220] By necessity, an explicit statement about injecting romance into the stories could not be made by virtue of the fact it would place *Black Mask* in direct competition with its sister magazine *Ranch Romances.*

Unfortunately, times were perilous for *Black Mask* in 1938 thus necessitating combining the July and August issues into a single August issue.[221] By July 1939, the word went out. "All kinds of detective stories are used: Direct action detection, occasionally the psychological case, off-trail stories, a few even from the crook's viewpoint."[222]

Unlike the criteria emphasized by my father (character development, effective dialogue, fast moving action, and a hard, brittle style), the hard-boiled formula was diluted. Writers whose work was rejected when my father was making the editorial decisions were introduced while the familiar hard-boiled writers were dropping away. Sales were still declining, and the magazine never did regain its lost momentum. In the early 1940s the magazine was sold to Popular Publications.[223] The editor of *Dime Detective,* Ken White, became *Black Mask's* newest and last credited editor. In its declining years the magazine became a bi-monthly publication with a change to a smaller format, one with fewer pages.

Years later Richard Layman offered a sad commentary on the fading and ultimate demise of the *Black Mask* magazine: "The glory days of the old *Black Mask* were over when Shaw left. Fanny Ellsworth took over as editor and she and her successors kept the magazine alive for another fifteen years, but it was just

---

220   *Writer's Digest,* April, 1937, p. 16.

221   James L. Traylor, "Murder up His Sleeve," pp. 67–68.

222   *Writer's Digest,* July, 1939, p. 18.

223   Frank Gruber, *The Pulp Jungle,* p. 127.

another pulp magazine by then, trading on its past glory. Cornell Woolrich, Cleve Adams and John D. MacDonald were among the notable contributors after Shaw left, but if new talent came, old talent left. By the early 1940s all of Shaw's star writers were gone." [224] *Black Mask* died a lingering death in 1951.[225] The last issue of this magazine was published in July 1951.[226] Thus ended the thirty-one year saga of *Black Mask.*

---

224   Richard Layman, "The Changing Face of Crime Fiction: *The Black Mask,*" p. 2078.

225   *The New Black Mask Quarterly,* No. 1, A Harvest/HBJ Original, Introduction, p. vii.

226   *A History of Pulp Magazines: Black Mask.* (http://www.ejmd.mcmail. com/hardboil.htm)

Hana and Joe: Eisenstein, Czech Republic, February 1922.

# 9

# The Final Phase of the Professional Journey

MY FATHER was moving into a future, on a trail that he had not previously marked. He was truly a pioneer, blazing a new path, taking an approach that had served him well for all of his life. Like the good woodsman he was, at age sixty-two, he adjusted the pack on his back and moved on to the new challenge: his next career. This newly blazed trail has not been an easy one to retrace. In general terms, it consisted of three separate endeavors: author, editor and literary agent.

## AS AN AUTHOR

IN AN interview in 1979, one of my father's former writers, W.T. Ballard, was asked the following question: "Joe Shaw was a strong guiding force where many of his writers were concerned. Did you have any memorable experiences in your relationship with him as an editor?" In his response, Ballard expressed his love, admiration and respect for my father, and cited the special relationship the two of them had. He also said that he made a fine editor; he could point the way for his writers, contributing much to helping them work out their problems with sympathy and understanding, but he could not do the same for himself though writing was most what he wanted to do.[227] This observation was echoed by at least two other *Black Mask* writers some years after my father's departure from *Black Mask,* and obviously pertained to him as a hard-boiled mystery writer. Lee Server added that Cap Shaw wrote some mystery fiction that showed no sign of approaching his editorial standards.[228] Some observations: First, my father was an educated man, a man who conveyed his thoughts beautifully as seen in the extensive dialogue he established with his writers through written correspondence. It was a florid, flowing style that was quite expressive and always upbeat and encouraging.[229] Next, my father authored seven books that were published. Of the seven, four were mystery stories. One of the non-mystery stories was *Out of the Rough,* a book focusing on golf and romance, that definitely was a winner. It was published in 1934 in the United States, England, Australia and New Zealand. The reviews by newspapers in all four countries were very positive. The following literary notice was indicative of the accolades received upon the book's publication: "This novel should be read by all who delight in a breezy humorous story, and studies by all those who play golf or think they can play golf. First and foremost, *Out of the Rough* is an entertaining account of how a young American, keen on reducing his score, comes to Elie, in the Kingdom of Fife, to take lessons from a grand old pro, Sandy Macgregor. Sandy is not an orthodox teacher, and his methods are highly original but wonderfully successful. For example, he takes his pupil on a fishing expedition, and teaches him the correct way to hit the ball by making him cast a fly, and he follows this up by driving home a second lesson by getting his pupil to thrash his corn with a hand flail. A mere man might be excused for doubting the usefulness

---

227   Mertz, "W.T. Ballard: An Interview," p. 3.

228   Server, *Danger Is My Business,* p. 69.

229   Traylor, "Babcock, Murder Up His Sleeve," p. 62.

of such training, but Mr. Shaw's methods of improving a duffer's play have been enthusiastically backed up by such champions as Harry Vardon, Mark Seymour, and Abe Mitchell. The seal of their august approval is a guarantee of the soundness of the instruction, and readers need not hesitate to follow the advice given. As for the other aspect of the book, no one who reads it will need to be told that it is outstanding for the sureness of its characterization, its gay situations, and its witty dialogue. It can be unconditionally recommended as an enjoyable novel and as a book of instruction in the art of golfing." [230]

In addition, F. Popplewell, twice champion of Australia and professional of the Royal Sydney Golf Club, said, "The golf instruction is particularly sound. It is exactly my idea of how this great game should be played." [231] Hugh M. Kahler, in *Collier's Weekly* magazine, remarked: "As a recovered golfer I protest against the publication *Out of the Rough.* I defy anybody to read it without making experimental swings with the nearest umbrella handle." [232] Joseph Murdoch said that *Out of the Rough* was the greatest golf book ever written.[233] (The Murdoch Golf Library. Worcestershire: Great Books, 1991). *Out of the Rough* is still being published today.[234]

As to why my father was not an adept mystery storywriter, Will Murray offers the following explanation. Essentially, my father never experienced an apprenticeship wherein when manu-

---

230   Joseph T. Shaw, *Out of the Rough* (London, England: Williams and Norgate Lt'd, 1934), Literary Notices, Galkirk Herald. May 25, 1935.

231   Shaw, *Out of the Rough* (Sydney, Australia: Angus & Robertson, 1934), "Pleasant Golf Lessons," Sept. 29, 1934.

232   Joseph T. Shaw, *Out of Rough*, Bendigo Advertiser, New Books, Sept. 15, 1934.

233   "The Murdoch Golf Library" (Worcestershire: Great Books, 1991).

234   Ailsa Inc., 444 Madison Avenue, Suite 704, New York, N.Y., 10022.

scripts were submitted they went through a series of rejections and refinements as the stories were reshaped to conform to the desires of the editor. With his background, it is a certainty that if he had had the opportunity, either by necessity or by choice, to go through this grueling process, he too would have mastered the art of being an effective word mechanic. Not one of the *Black Mask* contributors escaped this process of maturation, including Dashiell Hammett, Erle Stanley Gardner, and Ray Chandler. The traits required to become a good editor are not the same as those required to be an effective storyteller. Also recognize the difficulty, or perhaps inability, of being able to critically evaluate one's own work. All of this seems to make sense.

With respect to *Black Mask,* my father did have a Western story published in the December 1926 issue. In all probability this was the same one that he was trying to sell to Phil Cody at the time they first met, when Cody extended the editorship to him. In 1931, a four-part serial entitled *Derelict* was published under my father's name even though the story had already been published as a novel in 1930. Also, in 1932, another four-part serial he had authored, entitled *Fugitive,* was published in the *Black Mask* magazine. Additional novels authored by my father were *Danger Ahead* (1932), *Blood on the Curb* (1936), and *It Happened at the Lake* (1937).

Under the pen name of Washburn Thompson, two stories appeared in the magazine *Boy's Life. Wings of an Eagle* was published as a five-part serial in the September 1935 through the January 1936 issues, and *Lee Rails Awash* appeared in the April through July 1935 issues.

Another outlet for my father's writing was thirty-six individual mystery stories authored between September 1938 and May 1943 and published in different mystery magazines using the pen name Mark Harper: *All-Star Detective Stories, Black Mask, Clues-Detective Stories, Crime Busters, Detective Short Stories,*

*Detective Story Magazine, Dime Detective Magazine, Doc Savage, Mystery Magazine,* and *The Shadow.* Eleven of the thirty-six stories featured Cass Manning, the chief of police of a large metropolitan area. This hero expended his time and energy maintaining law and order among the many criminal elements flourishing in that environment.

John Nanovic, executive editor of the Street and Smith magazine group, deserves a great deal of credit for having accepted most if not all of the Mark Harper stories. In commenting on Mark Harper's work he specifically mentioned the fine restraint my father used to advantage. As an example, Nanovic refers to the novelette "The Rolling Heads" that first appeared in *Mystery Magazine* in the March 1940 issue was well as the 1941 *Detective Story Annual.* To quote: "Harper's strongest point, in my opinion, is the quiet restraint which he puts into his best work. You see that great things are happening; you feel that they are bound to happen; yet every word, every line in the story, seems to belie this. No word in the story tells you how tragic the circumstance is; no paragraph explains the difficult situation which hero or villain faces. But, by indirect reference, by gradual tone, by careful comparison, you get the sensation of things about to topple all around you."[235]

Much of my father's writing was produced during the period when he was editing the *Black Mask* magazine. In response to the question: "When do you get the time to do this writing?" he indicated that the planning and writing of such novels as *Danger Ahead, Derelict,* and *Out of the Rough* constituted his recreation.[236] W.T. Ballard was quite correct when he observed the

---

235  John Nanovic, "The Personality of a Detective Story," *The Writer's Year Book,* 1941.

236  Joseph T. Shaw, *Out of the Rough* commentary. "Clearing the Desk," *El Paso Times,* Aug. 11, 1935.

extent of my father's zeal to write. My father was consistent on this point. In his "rambling" autobiography he states: "Analogous to my tendency for roaming, my preference for an occupation has always been that of writing. This too was subjected to the same conflict with business. If I prepared for anything in college, where I was editor of the college periodical, it was for the writing game."

## AS AN EDITOR

AS MUCH as my father aspired to be a writer, being an editor was in his blood. When he first left *Black Mask* it was not to step into a pre-ordained position he had set up for himself. Fortunately, he had established strong enough bonds with many who were delighted with the opportunity to give back to him some of that which he had so graciously given to them. Jane Hardy as the head of a literary agency was one,[237] and Lester Dent was another. In the few short months Lester Dent had worked with my father, he had developed an incredible loyalty toward him; as a result, he began opening doors all over New York City for my father.[238]

One of my father's first projects was to create a magazine that would replicate *Black Mask.* It would be designed as a new high-quality detective pulp. This thrust made good sense in that the Pro-Distributors Publishing Company, Inc., owner of *Black Mask,* had pretty much abdicated its role of trumpeting the *Black Mask* magazine as the leading exponent of the Hard-Boiled School of Mystery Writing.

My father, always the visionary, perceived the void that would be created by the change in direction planned for the *Black Mask* magazine and felt that there was still a market for the Hard-Boiled mystery stories. Further, there was available a cadre of

237  Traylor, "Murder Up His Sleeve," p. 66.

238  Murray, *Lester Dent Biography,* p. 6.

*Black Mask* writers who chose not to submit any more stories to the magazine out of loyalty to my father, or, if they did, would have willingly followed him into this new enterprise. To this end, Lester Dent set up a meeting between my father and two representatives of the Street and Smith Publishing Company, Henry William Ralston and John Nanovic. This endeavor came to naught.[239] Another meeting, again made possible by Lester Dent, was set up between my father and a magazine publisher by the name of Reardon. The second meeting also was not fruitful.[240] It is postulated that the falling subscription rate for the *Black Mask* magazine was indicative of a falling demand that did not bode well for another mystery pulp magazine. As cited before, competition from imitation pulps, comic books and paperbacks mitigated against something new; furthermore, there was no clear knowledge of which variables were most critical in causing the market decline and the time at which these variables would shift. Apparently, the organizations contacted were averse to risk taking with respect to this new proposal. These meetings occurred during the fall of 1936 and the early months of 1937.

It was not until 1945 that my father was able to get back into the editor's chair. It was as the editor of an insightful anthology that depicted what he considered to be the best of the *Black Mask* stories authored by those writers he considered were the chief contributors to the *Black Mask* School of Mystery Writing. In the 1945 to 1946 time period, there was not that much interest in looking back to that period when my father had been the editor of the *Black Mask* magazine; however, he "persisted, believing something important had happened in the decade he was with the magazine. He did not claim credit for what had happened in the decade he was with the magazine but he was pleased to

239   *Ibid.*, p. 6.

240   *Ibid.*

be around when it did. During the years 1926 to 1936 the hard-boiled detective story had grown up and been perfected in the pages of *Black Mask*. And it was in those years and this magazine that the private eye first became an important American hero." [241] Originally the anthology was given the working title "A Treasury of Early *Black Mask* Stories," but was then formally changed to *The Hard-Boiled Omnibus; Early Stories from Black Mask*. The introduction is quite revealing in that it clearly depicts the evolution of this new style of mystery story telling:

> ... Obviously, the creation of a new pattern was a writer's rather than an editor's job. Consequently, search was made in the pages of the magazine for a writer with the requisite spark and originality, and we were amazingly encouraged by the promise evident in the work of one. Not that his pattern was different from that of others, but he told his stories with a new kind of compulsion and authenticity.
>
> So we wrote to Dashiell Hammett. His response was immediate and most enthusiastic: "That is exactly what I have been thinking about and working toward. As I see it, the approach I have in mind has never been attempted. The field is unscratched and wide open."
>
> It was apparent that Mr. Hammett shared our hope for a medium in which he could achieve his aim while developing his talent into a highly skillful instrument. We pointed out that this particular medium—the magazine mystery story—was both constrained and restrained. We felt obliged to stipulate our boundaries. We wanted simplicity for the sake of clarity, plausibility, and belief. We wanted action, but we held that action is meaningless unless it involves recognizable human character in three-dimensional form.
>
> Dashiell Hammett had his own way of phrasing this: "If you kill a symbol, no crime is committed and no effect is produced. To constitute a murder, the victim must be a real human being of flesh and blood."

---

241  Goulart, *Cheap Thrills*, p. 114.

Simple, logical, almost inevitable. Yet, amazingly, this principle had been completely ignored by crime writers—and still is, in the deductive type of mystery story.

In physics, an explosion sends out sound waves. But if there are no ears within their range, there is no sound. If you read of a thousand aborigines wiped out by earthquake or flood, you are abstractly interested. But let a member of your own family be even remotely threatened and you are at once intensely concerned, emotionally aroused. This is true in real life. Why shouldn't it hold true in fiction, which must create the illusion of reality?

It was on this philosophic concept that we began to shape the magazine we wanted, the kind of story it would print.

The formula or pattern emphasizes character and the problems inherent in human behavior over crime solution. In other words, in this new pattern, character conflict is the main theme; the ensuing crime, or its threat, is incidental.

For a clear demonstration of this pattern, consider *The Thin Man* by Dashiell Hammett, and *The Big Sleep* by Raymond Chandler. In approach and structure, both are singularly alike, since both adhere closely to the pattern. Otherwise they are as dissimilar as any two novels, which demonstrates the infinite variety attainable under this pattern. Neither can be tagged "just another detective story."

In both, characters, in full three dimensions, and character conflict are set up. The main crime and its victim are off-stage, and, while the solution of the crime is woven into the pattern of each story, it by no means constitutes the essence of the story. In fact, strip the crime from each book, and you still have a thrilling story, a test which the deductive type of mystery story could scarcely meet.

A London publisher wrote us that he recognized in our magazine a new school in writing, differing from anything else American, and unlike anything else English. He accredited the *Black Mask* group of writers with its inception and its accomplishment. We believe it was Mr. McKeogh, writing in the *New York World-Telegram*, who stated that all plots and props in detective stories had been used and abused, and there could be nothing new except treatment; and he, too, gave credit to the *Black Mask* writers for this innovation.

Such distinctive treatment comprises a hard, brittle style—which Raymond Chandler, one of its most brilliant exponents, declares belongs to everybody and to no one—a full employment of the functions of dialogue and authenticity in characterization and action.

To this may be added a very fast tempo, attained in part by typical economy of expression, probably, has had definite influence on writing in other fields. As Mrs. Harry Payne Burton said: "Hammett and his confrères have shown our authors how to attain the shortest distance between two points; and are we glad!"

The contributors of this brittle style were, notably, Hammett, Raymond Chandler, Raoul Whitfield, George Harmon Coxe, Roger Torrey, Forrest Rosaire, Paul Cain, Lester Dent, among others. It was rather extravagantly tagged as the "hard-boiled" school, and it was imitated throughout the "pulp" field. There is, however, this difference of distinction. While many *Black Mask* characters were admittedly "hard-boiled," the appellation belonged to the characters rather than to the school of writing. Style and treatment were something else again.

These writers observed the cardinal principle in creating the illusion of reality; they did not make their characters act and talk tough; they allowed them to. They gave their stories over to their characters, and kept themselves off the stage as every writer of fiction should. Otherwise, as Raymond Chandler puts it, that most powerful factor, melodrama, becomes "used as a bludgeon and not as an art"—and loses ten-fold its effectiveness.

They did not themselves state that a situation was dangerous or exciting; they did not describe their characters as giants, dead-shots, or infallible men. They permitted the actors in the story to demonstrate that to the extent of their particular and human capabilities. Moreover, as they attained their skill, they wrote with greater and greater restraint, careful of over-exaggeration in a word of their own where text demanded their descriptive contribution, adhering to the sound principle that whatever arouses the incredulity of a reader—no matter how true to life—has exactly the same effect as that which could not possibly happen. As a consequence, they wrote convincingly.

Long is the roster of the contributors to the magazine's individual type of crime fiction. Many who saw their first stories in print there have since risen to the heights in other fields of literature. It is often said, in that period, that their product, in its best examples, was several years ahead of its time. These writers were blazing new paths.

Most of the writers who together produced this magazine have since contributed the most skilled and successful crime novels written in the past decade, and have also contributed enormously to the best Hollywood has to offer in the mystery field. Hammett and Chandler are outstanding examples. There are a score of other writers who contributed their share to make the *Black Mask* group outstanding, writers who favored us with their first work and have since come into national recognition. We would like to mention them all individually, as we so clearly remember them. We would like to include in this volume examples of each one's work, but in both cases space forbids.

We make only one final point. We do not, and we cannot, claim credit for the original work of these *Black Mask* writers or for their success. It is our conviction that no one person can bring forth successful writing from another. A discerning editor may help toward skill and craftsmanship, but application of that skill and the thought behind it are the sole properties of the writer himself. And, so, without any further introduction from me, meet the artists who made *Black Mask* what it was, a unique magazine and a new influence in American literature.

Joseph T. Shaw [242]

This is a compelling introduction that clearly defines the Hard-Boiled School of Mystery Writing, how it evolved, and the impact

---

242   Shaw, *The Hard-Boiled Omnibus,* Introduction, pp.v–ix.

it has had on, not only the literature of telling mystery stories, but also on American literature in general. By selling this concept of the anthology to the Simon and Schuster Publishing Company, Cap Shaw had sown the seed of what was to flower into the most famous and best anthology of its kind ever published.[243]

As in all worthwhile endeavors there are going to be a fair share of trials and tribulations. Creating this anthology was no exception. For starters, the work of two of the several stalwart writers for *Black Mask* were included in the initial selection of stories; however, for reasons alluded to earlier, both Frederick Nebel and Erle Stanley Gardner elected not to have their stories republished in the anthology. In essence, they felt that their previous stories were out-dated and did not properly reflect their growth as writers that had taken place in the ensuing years. Another distraction was Dashiell Hammett, who had very "strong convictions about royalties to authors." As a consequence, he demanded more money for permission to use his story, a demand that, if accepted, would have upset the budgeted fee structure that had been established for stories used. In spite of a $1,000 limitation as a total for all royalties to the authors for the use of their stories, a compromise was finally reached with Hammett that made his fee contingent upon the number of anthologies sold. This mischievous behavior was particularly vexing recognizing Hammett's penchant for alcohol on one hand, and the fact that he was garnering $1,300 a week in royalties from three weekly radio shows on the other.[244] One of the burdens under which my father labored was the stipulation that any fees in excess of $1,000 had to be paid out of his pocket—so much for sentimentality, loyalty and friendship. The final tally for "permission to

---

243   Hagemann, "Cap Shaw and His 'Great and Regular Fellow's'," p. 143.

244   *Ibid.*, p. 147.

use" was $1,085.[245] Raymond Chandler, who graciously reduced his fee from $100 to ten dollars, became quite upset when he realized that the story he wanted in the anthology was different than the story actually used. Ultimately, he vented his anger for this breakdown in communications on Sydney Sanders, the owner of the literary agency for which my father was then working. There is another aspect to this incident that is not readily apparent. Sanders also represented Gardner as his literary agent, and Gardner had expressed previous dissatisfaction with Sander's performance in that role. The outburst over which story had been mistakenly used may have been another rationale as to why Gardner no longer wanted to be represented by the Sander's agency. In fact, shortly thereafter Gardner did sever the relationship.[246]

The meager budget allocated by Simon and Schuster for this project was a constant concern and definitely restricted the extent of the anthology. Thirty-five stories by thirty authors were initially proposed, with only fifteen stories written by fourteen authors actually used. The total word count of the thirty authors was over 310,000 words, two volumes worth, with approximately 148,000 words contained in the selections published. For some reason, four authors, William E. Barrett, W.T. Ballard, Dwight Babcock and Eric Taylor, were listed but with no stories associated with their names. "Either list was a veritable treasure chest of *Mask* fiction which is to say the best hard-boiled stories available."[247]

One anomaly is that only fourteen different authors are noted. Raoul Whitfield had two stories included in the anthology, one of which was written using the pen name of Ramon Decolta. What is intriguing about this is the fact that Whitfield had apparently

---

245   *Ibid.*, p. 146.

246   Mac Shane, *The Life of Raymond Chandler,* p. 145.

247   Hagemann, "Cap Shaw and His 'Great and Regular Fellow's,'" p. 146.

divorced in 1932, remarried in 1933, separated from his second wife in 1935, and, three months later, was a widower. As the sole heir to his wife's estate, he inherited a fortune, a fortune that he expended within a decade. He died of tuberculosis in January 1945, penniless. In an interview in May 1981 with E.R. Hagemann, Prudence Whitfield, Raoul's first wife, reminisced about my father, saying "that 'Joe was like a father to us all.' Born in 1874, he was a good twenty to thirty years older then 'his sons,' and those he liked he praised to the limit." His paternal concern is seen by his printing two Whitfield stories so as to give Prudence a helping hand. His check for $140 to her was not bad at all in 1946.[248]

Another challenge my father had to confront in creating the anthology was the utilization of an in-house editor the owners of Simon and Schuster appointed to oversee the project. The need for a liaison between my father and the publishing company is easily understood; however, it introduced another level of communications. Assisting in the selection of the fifteen stories was not a problem in that the editor's fictional and stylistic preferences were respected. The potential source of contention arose over the content and authorship of the Foreword and individual bio-critical essays to be written on each of the fourteen writers. The original plan was for Raymond Chandler to write the Foreword and my father to develop the bio-critical essays. The Simon and Schuster editor felt the individual introductory paragraphs sounded too much like "advertising blurbs" rather than the expected unique, intimate stories. The disagreements were resolved by my father writing an introduction for the whole volume, and by eliminating the individual paragraphs entirely. Fortunately, a number of these prefaces remain today in the Joseph T. Shaw collection of the UCLA Special Collections

---

248   *Ibid.*, p. 150.

Library. They are a part of his working file for the anthology, and in the words of Stephen Mertz "they make fascinating reading, especially in view of the fact that Shaw is considered by many to be the most important editor in the history of American detective fiction."[249] Seven of the fourteen are as follows:

*On Chandler:* He writes with authority. His characters are the sort of people who would do the things ascribed to them. His people are real people, given to you in all three dimensions.

*On Lester Dent:* A grand fellow, Lester Dent. Lester has preferred to expend his talents on the rough paper field. However, we believe there are elements and a treatment in the story presented here that point the way to more ambitious accomplishments, which we've an idea will be substantiated when Lester turns seriously to novels.

*Peter Ruric (Paul Cain)* is an aesthete in taste and ambition. Allied with his aesthetic moods is a grim sense of realism in its hardest texture, framed in his recollection of his boyhood experiences in Chicago where Peter saw something of life in its toughest phases. We suspect that Peter drew from some of these firsthand glimpses for his first published work, a book length *Black Mask* serial entitled *Fast One.* At the time of its writing, Peter was a close associate of Raoul Whitfield and Dashiell Hammett, who were in full stride, and found himself, indeed, in the matter of grim hardness, while Raoul and Dash paused on the threshold, Peter went all the way with *Fast One.* Published as a book both here and in England, while of a dated period, it is a story to be shuddered at and not easily forgotten.

*Norbert Davis* is a natural. If we were to pick anyone who, in spite of all human trials and tribulations, looks upon life resignedly and mostly all in fun, our nominee would be Bert. His sense of humor is prodigious. There is one thing that makes Bert Davis an individualist; he always

---

249  Stephen Mertz, "Captain Shaw's Hard-Boiled Boys," *American Detective,* Summer 1979, p. 264.

did and always will write just what he very well pleases; mostly what strikes him as "funny."

*On Hammett:* He has always seemed to us rather amazing. He was endowed with one of a writer's most valuable assets, a rare ability of observation and the gift to analyze character beneath its surface appearances.

*Raoul Whifield* was a hard, patient, determined worker. His style from the first was hard and brittle and over-inclined to staccato. Later, he became more fluent and went along, shoulder to shoulder, with the best of them. Earlier, a newspaperman, he wrote from knowledge of men, and women, and their ways. Personal tragedy in the midst of his career, and death this past year, cut off what might very well have been a brilliant future. Whit was ambitious. He wanted to invade other fields than that of crime detection and criminal conflict.

*Roger Torrey* stands high in the list of those who contributed most to *Black Mask's* distinctive style. His writing was hard and it was "brittle." His characters were hard and tough and so convincing as only to have been drawn from actual observations and experience. Yet, tough as they were, Roger always found some good beneath. The cause might be unlawful and even venal, but somewhere along the line or in the payoff, that good would come out in a way of loyalty or sense of decency. And perhaps it was the more effective because it would be unsuspected in the convincing reality of those all tough men.[250]

Perhaps these prefaces do sound like "advertising blurbs;" however, written some six decades ago, they cogently reflect Cap Shaw's personal views on seven of that genre's premier talents who appear in *The Hard-Boiled Omnibus* and who wrote for him in the pages of *Black Mask.*

In retrospect, all thirty writers should have been given the opportunity to contribute to what would have been a two-volume

---

250   *Ibid.,* pp. 264–265.

anthology. Will Murray stated that *Black Mask* produced quite a body of "tough guy" literature in its day and had an enormous influence upon not only the mystery field but also on American literature. Yet for all of its influence, comparatively little *Black Mask* fiction remains in print today.[251] A lost opportunity, especially in view of the fact that the other two anthologies in this area did not appear until 1965, with Ron Goulart's *Hardboiled Dicks,* and in 1977, with Herbert Ruhm's *Hard-Boiled Detective.*

As my father refocused his energies on being a literary agent, he still remained the editor. This was quite evident as he worked with those authors he represented, and it was also manifested in the form of an anthology of eleven Western stories written between 1935 and 1950. This literary collection, published in July 1951 under the title *Spurs West!* included, for the most part, the work of his clients. In the late 1940s and early 1950 many of my father's writers were primarily writing about the West; in fact, nine of the eleven stories reprinted were written in the time period 1948 to 1950. My father's introduction hits a responsive chord for all fiction storywriters. Under the heading of "A Challenge," it reads as follows:

> In the whole American scene there is no field so fruitful for the writer's craft, so diversified in human behavior, so resourceful in natural properties as our frontier West. Furthermore its traditions are indelibly stamped on almost world-wide consciousness.
>
> And notwithstanding its properties have been so used, abused and over-used as to become trite and stale, it is practically unexploited in a literary sense.
>
> That in itself is a challenge.
>
> From the first, the field of Western fiction has been a paradise for the

---

251    Murray, "Lester Dent: The Last of Joe Shaw's *Black Mask* Boys," p. 128.

beginning writer. Story plots were there for the taking; rustling, land and water squabbles, the legendary feats of cowboy and outlaw, of peace officer and gambler and stage robber. Using these properties alone meant only placer work, surface scraping. Missing the one essential element of all, it led to the "bang-bang" era, and monthly audiences of more than twenty million readers absorbed the too often fantastic tales that ignored credibility and the true principles of the craft.

Such stories were truly "pulp" in the real meaning of the term, but not because they were published for the most part in wood pulp paper magazines.

There appears to be a widespread, erroneous and uninformed impression of what is "pulp" and that everything published on pulp paper is unworthy of polite attention.

In our understanding, "pulp" is the sort of writing that ignores character, employs melodrama solely for what is hoped will be its shocking power and uses violent action as a substitute for story development and crucial solution. It is careless both in phraseology and structure. It gives no consideration to credibility and drama. It is largely the product of unskilled or beginning writers or laggards in their chosen profession.

Perhaps the distinction can be made clearer by the fact that Dashiell Hammett, appearing in a wood pulp magazine, did not write "pulp." Neither did Sabatini nor many others who employed the rough paper magazines as a stepping stone in their progress. *Blue Book,* printed on wood pulp paper, does not publish "pulps."

By the same token we have seen far too many "pulp" stories, especially in Western and crime fiction, appearing between the hard covers of book publishers.

In their better phases, the rough paper magazines have been what high schools are to colleges, to those writers who have the will to go on. Writers who have taken their work seriously and had the good fortune to deal with a knowing and ambitious editor in that field, have produced values which, with professional skill, would be very welcome in higher places. In the works of such writers you will find substance, authentic character and authentic action; values which would add both interest and strength to smooth paper pages and which, and in particular authentic action, are often beyond the experience and knowledge of writers trained solely in smooth paper circles.

The era of the "pulps" is closing. Periodicals of that type are becoming outmoded, while their substitutes on the stands reflect an encouragingly higher grade of perception and understanding by the same vast reading audience. And it is interesting to note that the magazines holding stubborn places in the changing scene carry the better Western stories.

The element missing from the great majority of Westerns is character, personality, the presentation by written word of real, credible human beings of flesh and blood, of recognizable characteristics.

In a similarly drugged situation in crime fiction, Dashiell Hammett introduced this element and revolutionized the age-old detection story pattern.

A two-dimensional figure, distinguished only by name, dress and occupation, is merely a symbol of a man without personal reality. "If you kill a symbol," Hammett once said, "you commit no crime." There is no impact in the happening. There is no literary value in the effort.

Oddly, since its vital importance to this fiction has so long escaped understanding, the one most responsible for the country's awareness of its pioneer West was an artist—Frederic Remington.

He personalized the West.

Charles Russell, Will James and other artists added to its factual luster. Writers, for the most part, have lagged far behind them in preserving the reality of the West. Except in rare instances, skilled craftsmen have ignored its truly great possibilities. Yet those few, rare works, attaining literary quality, have been so outstanding as to be hailed as novels and not by the unfortunate term of "another Western."

Quite recently, a series of those earlier stories were gathering dust of the forgotten until a man in reality personified their hero, and now Hopalong Cassidy is a household name throughout the land.

Other Screenland symbolic heroes are daily making clearer the realization that character alone is the mainspring and touchstone for public appreciation. Welcome the day when something good enough comes along to attract the craftsmanship of that well nigh peerless handler of melodrama for its dramatic effect alone, Alfred Hitchcock. As one of the shrewdest and most capable minds in the industry told us not long ago: "Above everything else, I would like character in a proper Western story."

And there you have it; a field as limitless as the infinite complexities of man, in which to expound the symbolism of the American spirit, later vivifying Alaska, as alive today on our battlefronts.

So far as material of the sort is available in short story form, this collection has been selected primarily for its character presentation, and with the hope that other writers, and editors as well, will heed the challenge and respond to it.[252]

## AS A LITERARY AGENT

IN THE late 1936 to early 1937 time period, my father joined the Wilson, Powell and Hayward Literary Agency. Lester Dent quickly signed on as one of the authors to be represented by him. Dwight Babcock, who was represented by the Jane Hardy Agency, also turned to my father for representation. With respect to Lester Dent, he dropped away quickly. As Dent had pointed out to Phil Durham in the letter dated October 27, 1958, he had lost the fire in his belly. My father tried to encourage and motivate Dent but the wind had gone out of his sails.[253] This was not the case with Dwight Babcock. He stayed with my father as his agent for the duration of his writing career, a career that ended in 1946. Even beyond that time my father continued to attempt

---

252   Joseph T. Shaw, ed., *Spurs West* (Garden City, New York: Doubleday & Company, Inc., 1951), Introduction.

253   Murray, "Lester Dent: The Last of Joe Shaw's *Black Mask* Boys," p. 132.

to move Babcock's work, selling one of his stories, in shortened form, to Avon in 1950.[254]

In deference to the authors he represented, my father also had many irons in the fire at that point in time. In all probability these activities worked against his being able to give full attention to functioning as a literary agent. In a letter to Dwight Babcock dated September 10, 1936, he related that *Blood on the Curb* had been sold to the films as an Edward G. Robinson vehicle, to be filmed under the title *Stiletto*.[255] In addition, as previously described, my father tried to establish a new mystery-detective magazine to take the place of what had been lost with the redefined *Black Mask* magazine; he attempted to establish Mark Harper an author of mystery/adventure stories; and he wrestled with ideas that would trumpet the great literary work done by *Black Mask* authors during the heyday of that magazine's fruitful years. Without clearly identifiable bench marks, the trail blazed by my father after his departure from *Black Mask* through 1945 lacks clear definition, although one senses extensive, creative activity having taken place during this period.

It was only after the signal achievement of the publication of *The Hard-Boiled Omnibus* in 1946 did my father turn his full energies to the task of being the facilitator between writer and publisher. In early 1943, he had become a part of the Sydney A. Sanders Literary Agency.[256] Sanders and my father developed a warm, supportive and satisfying relationship, one that persisted until Sanders' death in 1951. My father had a tremendous respect and admiration for Sydney Sanders both as a man and as a professional. While with the agency, my father functioned as an associate literary agent, having his own independent group of authors.

254   Traylor, "Murder Up His Sleeve," p. 73.

255   *Ibid.*, p. 66.

256   *Ibid.*, p. 71.

This group numbered between twelve and twenty, and, although my father would assist any writer who asked for help, by and large these authors were experienced and had been brought to the point where they were considered to be in the upper echelons of their respective fields.

Following Sydney Sanders' sickness in 1949, and untimely death in 1951, the control of the agency passed into the hands of Mrs. Sanders, creating an intolerable situation for my father. Poorly advised, unscrupulously influenced and unethically motivated, profits that had accrued from stories sold to publishing houses by my father were diverted to the agency. Undeterred, my father resigned his position and on April 15, 1951, a month shy of his seventy-seventh birthday, opened his own agency, Joseph T. Shaw Associates. An immediate problem was that many of the authors who elected to remain with my father had previously signed agreements with the agency stating that in the event of their departure from the agency, all subsidiary rights on their work would remain with the agency for twelve months after their departure. In essence, the Sanders agency would continue to reap the harvest from the work of these authors for the following twelve months.

The disruption necessitated by having to rebuild a new inventory of stories, finding and setting up new office accommodations, gathering supportive staff, and communicating the changes taking place with both writers and the story recipients were burdensome and time-consuming. Furthermore, not all the writers with whom my father was working chose to leave the agency. Thomas Walsh, a former contributor to the pages of *Black Mask,* who provided six stories between 1933 and 1935, elected to stay with the agency. This was a source of disappointment for my father. Correspondence between my father and Walsh is revealing.

*December 27, 1951, Tom to Joe:*

I had no intention of avoiding you these past few months; but being a little uncomfortable over the fact that you had left the Sanders agency, I suppose I did leave things ride a bit. I've been with the agency a long time—18 years, in fact; and it seems to me quite a serious matter to break off an association of that standing.

I hope you won't feel hurt or offended about this. Of course I have no complaint against you in any way at all. On the other hand, I have no complaint against the agency either, and in fairness to them have decided to see how things go with the next serial.

*January 4, 1952, Joe to Tom:*

Thanks for your letter. Makes me feel better. For outside of all business angles, I've always had a strong personal interest in your progress, and I think you know that.

Now, lest you think I have little conscience in withdrawing from Marde and my expectation that you would, sooner or later, come with all the others, I want to say that what she did and was planning to do with me, as she so often threatened, would never have been done by Syd. Nor would I have withdrawn from him. Bill Barrett, longer with Syd, I think, than even you, knew and understood that. And felt there was no other thing I could do.

I an not trying to argue, Tom. I just want you to know the facts so that you won't classify me with the majority in this profession, who know neither conscience nor loyalty.

With Marde taking over and breaking the arrangements I had when I first became associated with Syd, I was forced to look upon it as an entirely new association, as it actually was. Several of the smooth paper editors as well as many of my own writers told me more than once that I was stretching loyalty beyond reasonable lengths in staying on as long as I did, trying to give her the help she needed but consistently refused.

In your own case, she was willing enough to leave you to me, until you showed what you could do and became a real money earner.

In the last few weeks, before leaving and in spite of the help she had taken from me, I pushed sales to the utmost, somewhere around $50,000 to $60,000, on which she had the whole income. Just recently, she had $1,000 on one, hundreds of dollars on others. When a query comes to me on work placed while there, I refer it to them. I don't see how I could have done differently or more, and this is what I wanted you to know.[257]

These setbacks notwithstanding, first and foremost, my father's basic responsibility was to be a fruitful literary agent for those writers seeking his support. Recognizing that there was a vast gulf between an editor who dictated what was to be published, and a literary agent who was attempting to define a market that lacked clear definition, there still existed a common ground between the professions of editor and literary agent. That common ground was the continuing opportunity for my father to provide the same care and concern he had showered upon his *Black Mask* writers to those authors he now represented as agent.

The functions of an editor were clearly identified earlier; however, although one would expect a parallel set of criteria for the literary agent it was not so. Without the opportunity to accept or reject a story, the literary agent could only hope that a story he was handling could fill a niche in the demands of an editor. Authors have a propensity to feel that a finished story needs no further work, and he is, therefore, less prone to welcome changes or to gracefully accept criticism from an agent. On the other hand, an editor can reject a story and has the authority to dictate changes that could make it acceptable.

Whereas, an editor is concerned with sales to be made with a specific product to a specific market, a literary agent has to be

---

257   UCLA Library, Special Collections.

aware of a wide array of markets and then must attempt to match a specific story with the appropriate outlet in order to reach that market. The available markets were everchanging. From the mid-1940s to the early 1950s the pulps were disappearing from the scene, television opportunities were expanding rapidly, documentaries were very much in vogue, the radio had limited appeal, and movies were still the ultimate goal. Television, movies and documentaries were markets to be explored, but not necessarily by the author's literary agent. For the pulp writer, he had no alternative but to make his writing acceptable for the smooth paper magazines, or expand his stories to fullsize novels. This then led to several other opportunities such as serialization of potential full-length novels in magazines, softback novels, assembling several short stories into collections, and striving to get stories reprinted. Each alternative offered varying monetary returns and rewards.

To facilitate the process of tapping various markets, my father opened lines of communication with all of the potential magazines that would entertain the types of stories his authors were creating. This information was shared with his writers through a monthly publication entitled *De la Bouche du Cheval*. The first of these communication vehicles, dated April 15, 1951, is indicative of the clarity with which he spoke:

> In spite of all arguments to the contrary there is always a place for the written word. Observation of film, television, radio and even theater is fleeting. The written word stays with you, to be reviewed for recollection of first impressions and probed for new meaning.
>
> Without doubt it has lively competition for popular attention and when employed in fiction today it has an additional competitor in non-fiction stemming from the all-demanding interest in the national and world situation.
>
> Thus there has been no time in our history when there was such

demand for stories of commanding interest. Not so many years ago, a magazine circulation of a million was a prized achievement. Today a million is a mere mark of basic prosperity; consequently, the market is wide.

Too, time was when the story was the main consideration. Today, when competitive conditions have demanded keener analysis, it has been generally recognized that interest in a story is derived solely from interest in the personalities involved; without recognizable characters, there is no more interest than in a newspaper report.

Various editors have expressed this in different ways.

We like best the stories in which action is motivated by the nature of the people involved. Margaret Cousins—*Good Housekeeping.*

We visit you every Wednesday. We want you to like the people we bring along with us. Erdmann N. Brandt—*Saturday Evening Post.*

An editor was moved to keep on turning the pages; he got interested in the people the writer was dealing with. Knox Burger—*Collier's.*

The people we want to meet in our stories are the people we would want to invite into our homes. Robert Meskill—*American.*

Our novels, as well as our short fiction are judged... by reader identification (with the characters). Lilian Kastendike—*Redbook.*[258]

These words of wisdom, conveyed to his group of writers seeking to get published, are a mirror image of the very same words my father used to exhort his *Black Mask* writers from a time period two decades earlier. With the clarity of a bell ringing, the message was the same: "... interest in a story is derived solely from interest in the personalities involved." At age seventy-six, my father had not lost the edge—he was still the teacher.

The vagaries of this new challenge can best be seen as one examines the correspondence between my father and three of his authors. Although only a sample size of three, these authors

---

258   *Ibid.*

did have common concerns. Impatience was a dominating trait that manifested itself by a continual questioning as to why their individual stories had not been immediately accepted by editors, whether or not all avenues had been pursued as an outlet for their stories, whether or not my father was actually trying to move the stories, and why similar types of stories that had previously been sold were now being rejected. Successive rejections became a source of disappointment leading to discouragement and ultimately the cause for many writers choosing to move away from the writing profession. Most writers seemed to live only one step away from the poverty level; however, all were seeking the opportunity to generate a predictable outlet for their stories. Only a few found it.

## WILLIAM R. COX

WILLIAM COX was not a novice, having written for the pulps for an extended period of time and had been under my father's tutelage since 1945. The exchange of communications covers the period from July 30, 1945, until January 11, 1952, and represents the only available correspondence between the two men. During this nine-month period, there was a total of eighty-three pieces of correspondence exchanged between my father and Bill Cox, and fifty-six pieces between my father and editors on Bill Cox's behalf; further, within the letters quoted below, there was additional discussion on the particulars of individual stories and activities. In short, the dialogue was extensive.[259]

Essentially, Cox's field of writing was sports, generating fiction in football, baseball, basketball, golf, tennis, boxing and wrestling; he also had written Westerns, detective stories and adventure stories. The year 1948 was a fruitful year for him; unfortunately

---

259  *Ibid.*

the subsequent years did not bear the fruit he had anticipated. He was convinced that the writing profession was where he should be, and, yet, he was expending time, energy and creativity on television and films. He was considering going back into the newspaper field or as one who would solicit advertising for a large newspaper. He also considered concentrating his efforts on the slick magazines to which he had sold stories, and he toyed with the idea of writing novels

With respect to his writing, he apparently was a proficient professional, but was in a rut from which he could not extricate himself. He rejected criticism from editors who would not accept his material, he refused to follow up on suggestions to develop stories on ice hockey for which there was a market, he questioned my father as to his diligence in finding markets for his work, and he sensed that editorial changes did not bode well for him.

From a personal point of view, he was in a second marriage with a backlog of alimony payments. His new wife required hospitalization and surgery that necessitated his selling his automobile to meet the medical expenses, and in November of that year his beloved kid brother was killed in an explosion that left two young children fatherless. Compounding his problems was the fact that he could not help but notice that his peers in the writing field, to whom he felt superior as far as writing was concerned, were "hitting it off big."

Like a shade slowly being drawn, one could see the frustration building and the ardor for writing ebbing. In January 1952, Bill Cox called it quits on his career as a pulp writer and turned to writing full time for television and screenplay for his future endeavors. What precipitated this discouragement and disillusionment? Obviously circumstances, some of which he could have controlled, much of which he had could exercise no control over. Excerpts from the correspondence between the two is revealing.

*June 3, 1951—Bill to Joe:*

Of course I saved enough of that April flood to get through May and start us on June, but what am I supposed to do when it runs out? With no sales reported, it looks as if there will be no money for us through June! Milt Smith has offered me all the big accounts in time for his newspaper advertising expansion... if I will turn salesman for him and take a burden off his shoulders. Hank Kesler (television and movie contact) is trying to get me a job to prevent this, as we seem to work wonderfully together on screen things, and if he is, as expected, made a full producer at Columbia within the next few weeks, I have a job there at minimum of $500. He showed the treatment I wrote from his outline to Andrew Solt, a very fine writer who makes $2,000 per week, and Solt says that it was a crime I didn't make as much as he, that he knew professional writing when he saw it and what is the matter with the Hollywood's producers? This is all very fine, but as yet no one pays me any dough! I hope matters straighten out. If they do not, I am very soon quitting and going back to newspaper business as a sales manager and start working those big accounts.

*June 4, 1951—Bill to Joe:*

Received your check for $73.80, representing the sale of "No Hitter" to Popular Publications for the sum of $82.00, and this finds me as angry as I can ever get at anything. Since when do we accept cuts without notice? How low have we fallen? What use is there in remaining in this business where we have no bargaining power, no dignity, no hopes for improvement? If the Author's League had any guts it would get every writer in the country to stop writing and let them get the magazines out with nothing but reprints they so dearly love! But perhaps I shouldn't cavil at the League—pulp writers have never made enough money to gain any economical security upon which to base a firm stand! They have been exploited miserably through the years. And what makes me whopping, seeing red-mad is that "No Hitter" is a story which I carefully thought out, rewrote and rewrote again! It took time and effort and craftsmanship learned through long hard years. What price free enterprise, what price the American independent spirit, what price our birthright? The whole sorry mess is indicative of our position in the scheme of things. We, who were once proud to be free lance writers, are now unable to get credit at the corner store!

I am terribly sorry that this is the first check I received from your new set-up. I sincerely hope this is not an evil omen... I know they are buying from tyros and beaten veterans for whatever price they can gouge. If so, please let me know at once and allow me to wash out the vile taste of this outrage. I don't know why I am bothering to enclose this football story, "The Winner." It scarcely seems worthwhile. Thursday I hope that my friend offers me enough hope in the newspaper business to get out of this miserable puny racket! I'm sorry that I feel this way—but the publishers leave me no choice!

## June 7, 1951—Joe to Bill:

I don't have to tell you how it upsets me to have you worried and disturbed. It is something I never could and never can brush off in the manner I saw so much of in recent years. Jake [Ejler Jakobsson, sports editor, Popular Publications] called me on some pieces including "No Hitter," on which I had no record. He said he could take "Ball Boy" at your regular rate but could only take "No Hitter" at a compromise. I knew, from your letter, that you wanted any kind of money and as quickly as possible. How could I have done otherwise, Bill, under the circumstances? I felt I would really have done wrong if I told him to send it back. That check came through and was sent on at once. I expect the other one daily and will hurry that to you.

Although there seems to be improvement in the rough paper market, the change over from Jake to Widmer [Harry Widmer, Western, *Adventure* editor, Popular Publications] on one of the sports books with Harry working over Jake's inventory has been temporarily holding up things there. However, *Adventure*, with Jake running it, should be an improvement for us. Jake is writing you, although not yet sure of his full editorial wishes on *Adventure*. He thinks he will want some sports but says they will have to be somewhat different from those for the straight sports magazines; more story background. He wishes you would do a hockey story for *Sports Novels*, says its fast pace lends itself to your style of writing. And there is a wealth of material in hockey outside of the action.

"Revolt." I sent you *Collier's* letter on this to see if you wanted to change the opening a bit, since independently, we both had the same impression. Perhaps less mention of the others, in favor of the hero, might do the trick. Please let me know. If you agree, I think it advisable to wait a bit longer on Widmer. He has too many right now, because of the change. Of course, any of these that went to him first can still be sent to Jake who keeps only his *Sports Novels*.

P.S. I keep mentioning the intermediate markets: *Argosy, Toronto Star* and *Blue*, in order of rates. The editor of *Star*, on from Toronto, called on me this morning, wanting stories, particularly shorts up to 4,500 or 5,000, no longer. They pay me $300 to $400. No sex, light on drinking and too rough stuff, but want action, suspense, romantic setting, fast moving, well written.

## June 8, 1951—Bill to Joe:

Thanks for the letters. They take a lot of answering, so will get at it now. "Lawman," the first of my experimental Westerns dealing in character seems to be not what they want, doesn't it? The fact that none of them sold really sunk me. I used to do Westerns galore and sell them; was suddenly socked with a rejection saying "this is the old fashioned type story," and took a deep holt and tried to learn what they wanted. Reading the magazine taught me nothing, so I tried character stuff. Now it seems I have failed at it. What is left to me in this business?

I still think of "Revolt" as a character progression story. Warren

Brown's [associate fiction editor, *Collier's*] double talk is only further confusing. He should reread his criticisms... he says one thing, then ends up in parentheses with "(though it keeps it from being a predictably tough)" fight story. This is what I intended! His criticism is invalid by any logical standards! Brown mistakes realism for "sentimental happiness." Brown is like so many of them, a sugar coated cynic, a new type which has sprung up in our time! The story happens to be a good one. So I'm not surprised if no one buys it. Kennicott [sports editor, *Blue Book*] will!

Hockey I have never done. Haven't played since I was sixteen. Never look at it. Our league broke up out here for lack of customers. My opinion of modern sports is very low, believe me. Only professional football and wrestling and track and field seem to contain the old elements... and track and field was always dull to me! Well, I ramble. I get back to our desperate situation. I cannot exist, it seems in this market. *Toronto Star* and *Argosy* don't seem to like me. *Blue Book* cannot carry the load. Milt Smith made me an offer which entailed leg work, sweating it out on sales effort and frankly, although the money is there, it is neither quick nor certain. It involves no writing, only salesmanship. I fear I do not want this. I've been a writer too long. Kesler is working for me in pictures, I am going to try and stick it out awhile. But I shudder at the future as presently outlined. Surely you can see this.

... If you have other criticism, I'll appreciate it. If you see a story in here for magazines, or for Gold Medal Books, get me an okay to go ahead and I'll spend some time. I have two other ideas: Can't we sell the Neighborhood stories to Gold Medal? Can't we sell a "Joel Reeve" [Bill Cox's pen name] sports story collection? I say Gold Medal, I mean any of the pocket books which are ruining my business! How about the Dumb Dan Trout series? Kesler is reading two for pictures—they are surprisingly good and could be slightly rewritten for book publication if the price was right.

You see I am trying very hard to solve this problem of the new business of writing for a living. It's all very confusing, discouraging and wearisome. Movies and TV are just as bad. I'm reading *From Here to Eternity* and if you think Wolfe was wordy and vague, you got something coming!

This boy can't write to keep himself warm! Maybe I should write a dirty, long book, full of blasphemy, corruption, disease!

## June 11, 1951—Warren Brown to Captain Shaw:

Bill Cox has a nice idea in "The Winner" but he has reduced his characters and conflict to too simple a level so that the story reads more like The Rover Boys at Kings College than a *Collier's* story.

## June 18,1951—Joe to Bill:

How I would like to sit with you for a good long talk. There's always a way to beat a tough situation, and with the tools at your command it should be far from a discouraging job. Of course an author should write his own story. Every editor expects him to do so; but the editor has to judge its suitability for his own magazine, and we have to reckon with that, and what he tells us should be a guide. It doesn't do a damn bit of good to fight them, and at the same time we don't have to compromise on quality to please them. With your skill, you should not find it difficult to do what is wanted from their standpoint.

Frankly, I don't think you have tried enough for *Toronto Star*, and even *Argosy*, to say they don't like your work. Bill, several of these editors have found you uneven. They say when you are on the ball you are unbeatable. I wish you would think this over very, very carefully. But you can't judge an unbeatable story strictly from your own point of view. I am speaking of smooth paper, of course, but it goes all the way down the line. The lower range audience has a certain perception; the slick one has a different understanding. Sentiment suffices for the former; but not for the slicks. They want emotion subtly handled. If you could only get a break from your constant worries, you would judge all these things normally.

This is a long screed, Bill, but I'm hunching for you and fully confident of what you can do. I'll have to take "The Hard Way" to Wellfleet, leaving tomorrow, for a chance to study it.

*June 26, 1951—Joe to Bill:*

I hate to see you so discouraged, and I can't help thinking that you have misjudged the present situation. It is true that the lower market is much narrower than it used to be but it has not faded out. The point is that stories that were easily saleable a few years ago are now bought, when they are purchased, at a cent or a cent and a quarter. Generally speaking, you might say there is little or no market for them, and the writers who have stuck to the older style have found it tough sledding. Those stories, both Westerns and crime, were largely synthetic and depended mostly on action. There has been a radical change from that. Today the demand is for character and logical action stemming from the characteristics, and not thrown in just for actions sake. And by character I mean the self-determination of real personality.

I'm sure I have written this to you all of the last three years, for I knew it was bound to come. Bill, the question you should ask yourself frankly is, have you changed your type and quality of stories. You have said that Tilden [Mike Tilden, Detective and Adventure editor, Popular Publications], who used to buy freely from you, has taken very little the past two years or so. Tilden is fully alert to the changes. He has a limited budget and limited space, and he cannot pay his top of two cents except for a limited number of the new and better quality. Those of my writers who have made the change are in constant demand at his top, but they have less and less dependence on that market and often put aside other work through a sense of loyalty for him.

You might say that the same changes have come into the slick market, but you can observe this more from contact with editors than often from published stories. They want stories based on real, recognizable characters and they want logical, convincing action, but the writers are slow to respond.

That is why I feel that my group have a wonderful opportunity today. They faced a changed situation squarely, realizing that stories readily saleable a few years back have no worthwhile market today. With this realization, they have gone deeply and thoughtfully into it, have learned to understand the essential principles and elements and, as a consequence, are coming along nicely. In fact, that same group who, some years ago, depended solely on the lower market, are making more money than ever before.

I write all this thoughtfully, Bill, and solely with your interests in mind. And it is pointed up by just having read the script, "The Hard Way." And that is definitely the older type. When the market and editors change, a writer must change to meet it or be left behind. You will see many of the once big names in the slicks fading out. They either cannot or stubbornly will not meet the change. I can give you the name of a formerly famous writer in the slicks now scarcely selling one of her stories.

I sincerely hope this frank appraisal will change your kind of thoughts. Your really fine ability is just being used in the wrong direction, and that brings you nothing but disappointment and frustration. We didn't like the New Deal, but we had to adjust ourselves to it and make what we could out of it.

I am returning "The Hard Way" as you requested. I have the impression that the movies, generally speaking, are slower to be alert to change than editors. Just as reprint houses continued to buy the old bang-bangs when they could see the pulps fading, and only now are cooling toward them and demanding better.

## June 29, 1951—Bill to Joe:

Thanks for your long, explanatory letter and your kind interest and good words. But I still don't quite understand. What is a "old-type story"? Or, much more to the point, what is a "new-type story"? As you say, one cannot learn by reading the magazines. Would you say that Hemingway's stories are now "old-type stories"? F. Scott Fitzgerald's certainly must be! And poor old Maugham—Max Wilkinson told me in 1940 that he was old hat. And now can you define a short story? Surely you are not telling me the magazines want realism! If not realism, true to life characterizations, which you know damned well that cannot and will not print, then what sort of pseudo-realism are we now supposed to coin for them? What is their object? Are they out to entertain in their fiction? Or to instruct? Isn't it all just a wee bit silly? *Harper's, The Atlantic,* and *The New Yorker* publish the real short stories, don't they still? They don't pay any money because people want to read the pap which the flicks furnish them. You mean the slicks are now searching their own souls? I don't believe it. Suppose I wrote a story about a real prizefighter, do you think the *Post* would buy it? They would not. I'd really like to know.

Also I would like to know just in what way "The Hard Way" is old hat? Because our characters aren't dope addicts or nymphomaniacs nor cheaters at their studies, nor psychopaths, is the story out-moded? Maybe a gambling syndicate should approach the hero when he runs out of money? Hell, we don't even tell you who wins the ball game we show—this is old-hat? This was never done before in fiction or on the screen! I'm not defending "The Hard Way" as a magazine story. I had little hopes of selling, even with a magazine approach in rewrite—and right now I have little hope of ever selling a slick magazine story again. But I just do not understand what is old style in stories and what is new style. I am puzzled and very interested. Could you cite me examples?

Meantime I am making a fast buck with Telemount, doing Cowboy G Men scripts and loving it. Been on location, all very exciting, visualizing scenes before writing them. The merry westerns are so informal and yet tight and neat, like a good pulp, so that I feel at home. The producers love me, they are slightly underpaying me and I am learning. Cowboy G Men, I'll predict, will be a great success. The format is fine for the kids, the stories are historically correct, the format elastic and I am writing the dialogue! Wish I owned a piece of this show. Not so bad, though. I bat out a script in one day, rewrite in another, from their plot idea and with their characters and get $250 and there are twelve in all to do. It adds up to $500 per week and I've got a basketball started for Jake, and am awaiting word on what to do for *Blue Book,* when you learn that from Don.

Also, "The Hard Way" has an excellent chance to sell, as the picture people are beginning to realize you cannot make films for Los Angeles and New York audiences and keep alive. The sticks want the corn and the lighter things, with a good feeling in them. We have, I should tell you, rewritten extensively on the character of Mike, being careful to show that money is not his motivation, the he is a good boy with a few wrong ideas which get straightened out. Well, thanks again. Please explain further, so that I may know what you mean by the "new story" for the great slick mags. Maybe that's the kind of story I always wanted to write and they wouldn't buy!

*August 9, 1951—Erd (E.B. Brandt, Associate Editor,* The Saturday Evening Post) *to Joe:*

This Cox ["It Signifies"] is too rough for the characters to overcome. Thanks however, for letting me see it. [cc: to Bill Cox]

*August 16, 1951—Warren (Warren Brown, Associate Fiction Editor,* Collier's) *to Joe:*

"It Signifies" by William R. Cox is a bit too predictable and its characters run to types." [copy to Bill Cox: "This sort of comment doesn't make too much sense. Might have said, lads were too tough for the mag."]

*September 4, 1951—Joe to Bill:*

Thanks for your interesting letter. I sure hope you will make out with those ventures on T.V. and film. I think with the coaxial cable open to L.A., more programs will originate on the West Coast, particularly films rather than live ones, although the latter, with stars available, might do well in spite of the time handicap for East showing. Anyway, I'd like to see you stick away a solid backing and then I very much suspect you'd come back to your first love, creative writing. In any event, you'll never be satisfied with anything else.

I still can't go along with you in your feeling that the slicks are against you. You haven't been in position to follow the changing trend, since, necessarily you've had to concentrate your attention on other media. By changing trend, I mean a discernment by what competent editors there are, that synthetic characters and stories alone cannot possibly compete with the non-fiction stemming from the world situation which commands the attention of everyone. You can't judge this, Bill, from current magazines. The majority of writers either have failed to understand or are incapable of producing the needed values. James Hilton had an article on the situation, which is probably the toughest magazines and books have ever faced, but he failed to give the true cause or suggest the remedy.

It all rests with the writers; editors can't do it. It isn't their province. The older, name writers apparently can't or refuse to change their methods which brought them success in past years and, hence, are not helping. I have been pointing it out as the great opportunity for those serious writers who learned fundamental, authentic values in the lower markets and have since perfected their skills and either were born with the ability to present real human beings as their characters—like Tom Walsh for example—or have acquired that ability.

The situation today with fiction editors, generally, is one of great confusion. With fiction falling off, crowded by non-fiction, publishers first blame their editors, and as a consequence, editors don't dare to buy anything that won't please the publishers. And that is a hell of a situation. So it is only the sort of stories with striking and obvious appeal that have any kind of chance. And that appeal must emanate from interest in the character. I'll give you an example: in one month I sold three short stories by one writer for $2,000 each. In these stories, interest was carried entirely by interest in the character, his part in the story and the importance it was to him. Where he resorts to story interest predominating, that is, interest in the incidents per se, it is difficult to sell the story at all.

*October 1, 1951—Joe to Bill:*

Kennicott will not leave until April. Sold him a couple last week. His leaving is one of those damned things that happen to good guys who are too loyal. Widmer has been shaken out of Popular, Tilden taking over his magazine with Jake taking back the sports book. Temporary trouble is that Widmer bought too much and our stories held up until Jake can work some of them off. With coaxial working to the Coast, many programs are originating there, which should materially help you.

*October 9, 1951—Bill to Joe:*

Good news on Jake taking back the sports books. Widmer was never very strong for me, so his going won't matter. I wonder does anything matter in the pulps? I haven't had notice of a market in the field for several months now. My wife underwent surgery for hysterectomy last week and I'm another $1,000 behind—only it amounts to an automobile at the moment. I sold my car to pay her out! TV here is this way and that way. I'm seeing Wisbar or Fireside today about a couple of stories. I take it you are not involved in the field in NY. Perhaps it will all be out here in another year or so. I'm shocked to hear from you that Kennicott is not retiring but is being let out. Who is taking his place? I may have a story for him next week.

*October 16, 1951—Joe to Bill:*

Widmer left Popular before settling for the reprint story, and I have been after Al Norton [Alden Norton, Associate Publisher, Popular Publications] who said he would take care of it. Sorry that things have been so tough with you. About time you should have a real break. Seems to me you are on the right spot for T.V. work, but I'd be sorry to see you go into it altogether. I still wish you would try more often a sports story for the big magazines. Sold one yesterday to *Collier's* by William Heuman, and you will remember him as strictly a pulp writer. As a matter of fact, you and Heuman practically filled Jake's books. I wrote you about Widmer piling up that inventory, before he was let out, which obliged Jake to hold up everything until he can cut it down. And how about something for Don Kennicott? He's still buying.

## October 17, 1951—Bill to Joe:

My wife endured her hysterectomy, we found malignancy in the largest tumor, so we were fortunate indeed to have gone ahead with the operation. Now she is laid up for six weeks and how we will manage I shudder to contemplate. Her weekly stipend has been keeping us above water. I sold the car, so was able to pay for everything, doctor, hospital and so forth. It came high but we both hate debt. If any of the Popular editors are open for fiction you might let me know.

## October 29, 1951—Bill to Joe:

... So I chose the second "Duke" story, which you do not know, written in 1942, and will do as the boys suggested. The deal at U-I [Universal-International Pictures, Inc.] is in abeyance until they decide who will head the new regime there and there are no pulp markets according to your last market letter or any other advices and Kennicott has evidently too much boxing, and football is over for the year. So I'll try a book. Don't bother to guide me on it—I'll have it underway before you can cogitate on the matter. Let the chips fall where they may... and all that stuff... I wrote to Donald Kennicott.... He was always best to me, always my friend.... Am going at the book right now.... It'll be a lively one, in a style I have carefully considered since Friday.... I hope to have people in it.... More later.

*November 1, 1951—Joe to Bill:*

About the Western book. The best chance, and it's getting to be about the only one, is with Gold Medal Books who pay $2,000 advance on contract. They publish originals at 25 cents. However, they also are alert to the fact that the ordinary Western has practically faded from the picture. The washout of the pulps made that evident. Now the reprint houses are very, very reluctant about Westerns, won't take the ordinary ones of the old sort, and unless they do take one, the original, hard-cover publishers, also won't take them. In fact, they check first with the reprinters before acceptance. However, it won't be much of a gamble to do a few chapters on the "Duke," with brief outline of balance, and I will see what Gold Medal says. For them, the minimum length is 60,000.

*November 6, 1951—Bill to Joe:*

… I take it all the pulps are moribund and suppose the above yarns are dead so far as they are concerned. If this is so, please return these manuscripts to me for possible revision for better markets or for TV. It is necessary for me to take an occasional shot at slick paper and other markets yet unexplored and also eke out with occasional shots here—or to go back to driving a truck. I'm only sorry I didn't definitely catch on some months ago. I'll never understand the secrecy attending the slow death of pulp magazines, the indecision and phoney optimism of the process. Probably they died they way they lived! Don't hesitate to tell me, Joe, if your handling of me is not worth the postage. I can readily understand it—neither of us have made anything this year. Maybe a change would be good for us both—I don't know. I feel I have gone nowhere but backwards despite both our efforts.

I simply cannot understand why "It Signifies," a good story in my best vein, hasn't sold somewhere—anywhere. You have neglected to tell me anything about it except that the slicks rejected it. I did not write it for slick, but for *Blue Book* or *Adventure.* I surmise that Jake can't buy anything now... but nobody told me this. I am guessing. The boys at the Fictioneers bullied me into trying the book I am sending under separate cover. Jim Geller long ago sent "Willy Boulder" to Lengel at Gold Medal. It was rejected, but at least it was submitted there and Lengel admitted he liked it. He asked me for other things... and frankly I almost gave Jim the "Duke" book to handle, refraining only through my loyalty to you. I also assume—although I have no way of knowing—that you are busy with books and slick paper and whatever else you can sell. This is correct and natural, since there is no market for the old volume business. I had a brief chat with Bonham, who assures me all is well and going great guns and more power to him his fine serial and good work. A very nice guy, one of your best boosters.

Sitting out here, considering my future, I have many grave decisions to make. Pictures and TV are about as bad as pulps were in the early days—believe me, pictures are as uncertain as the weather. I've been waiting on a promised job at U-I since Labor Day with one of their best producers unable to squeeze me in. Fireside Theater is haggling with me. My sports series is being titillated by two outfits who are scared to spend the dough in making it. 20th Century still holds that wrestling story, with Jim Fisher trying to foist it on producers who all want to do another "All About Eve." Last month I made $125 from TV, last payment on my fourth Cowboy G Men show... then they hired someone else a la the usual TV method. My wife was in the hospital, it cost over a thousand, I sold my car to pay part of it, went into debt for the rest. Bless her, she is going back to work next week, having made a miraculous recovery after a complete hysterectomy. But I can't sit around with her paying the rent and food bills.

I'm detailing all this to make our understanding clear. It is vitally necessary that I choose a way of making money which includes very few short story sales—and I am, face it, essentially a pulp short story writer. Slick editors reject me vigorously, with no comment or encouragement, as though I were an outmoded, tired old hack, and I cannot blame them. I must find a new style of writing for them and intermediate markets or quit the business. I haven't found my niche out here. It's rather serious, isn't it?

Through a friend, I am even assaying a syndicated sports column! Samples are out now. There seems to be few alternatives in your markets, so far as I can gather. Women's magazines are not for me. The "true" mags are not for me. Articles are not for me. I'm a fiction writer with no markets and that's the truth. Therefore I must find markets or forever still my typewriter. Let me know if you have any ideas. I am not fault finding, as you know—that's not my dish of tea. I'm inquiring. Thanks for everything. I hope something happens with the "Duke" book. I have, as I said, other ideas about books. I also have the idea of changing Dumb Dan Trout's name and using him for *Blue Book* shorts. Further than that, not anything going your way at present. Maybe it's not worth the candle—I don't know. That's the trouble—sitting out here I don't know about New York.

### November 8, 1951—Joe to Bill:

I have yours of the 6th, and I guess you must have missed my letter, or its meaning, when I told you the discouraging news at Popular. For a long while, you and Bill Heuman had been supplying the majority of sports stories for Jakobsson's magazines, and he was asking for more of them. Then Jake was shifted to edit *Adventure* and Jake's magazines went over to Widmer, with still some of your stories, wanted by Jake, to be passed on. Widmer figured your stories, and Bill Heuman's, had appeared too frequently in the magazines and, ignoring those Jake had asked for, loaded up with other names. Before the latter could be run off, Widmer was dropped and Jake, handed back the magazines, was stuck with Widmer's inventory which put him out of the market for some time to come.

I'm sure I told you this, but perhaps not in such detail, and, since that was the only decent market for the stories, I probably didn't give you the details of the submissions. In fact, there seems the only thing to do is hold yours and Bill Heuman's until Jake can buy again. For example, Jake had every intention of buying the revised "You'll Never Make the Club," which he asked to have revised, until he was prohibited from doing so. I've tried the one-cent market on some but without success on this general type. As you say, that was a story laid against a Carney background but it did employ a fight and the future of the Negro and manager was the prize ring, so according to Kennicott's dictum, he didn't have more room for the genre for some time ahead. But he was looking, as I wrote you more than once, for something to take the place of the Murphy-Neighborhood series. In view of the foregoing, let me know which, if not all, you want back. One or more of these should go again to Jake when he's ready.

I'm sure I don't have to tell you that I've always been watchful of your interests. It's not always been easy to take advantage of spots, such, for example, *Blue Book,* or when I've urged you to try for more slicks. You've had to watch out for every advantage out there, and I judge that, at these times, you had something in hand that seemed more advantageous to follow-up. And you'll have to admit, Bill, that I've never complained. And I've never reneged on my attention to you.

Judas Priest, when I've so often heard the word, "Don't waste time on this one or that, he isn't making money," I wonder if I'm really an agent. I can't see it that way. When a guy is serious, I stick with him no matter what his luck is. And now, why-in-hell, don't you do a baseball story for the slick boys, making character the thing, on which Frank O'Rourke has no exclusive patent. I always liked the "Duke" stories, as you know, and hope this will have luck with Gold Medal. It's not in the usual run, so it will be up to Lengel, Carroll et al, as you also are aware.

### November 15, 1951—Bill to Joe:

Having tried so many things, we now try this little piece. A good bit of work has gone into it. I have not aimed it at a market, although I will make a TV piece of it in script form. It is a story, it is well written, it was suggested to me by one of Ray Stark's (footnote: Vice President of the Feldman organization, Famous Artists Corporation—had been handling some of my father's West Coast activities for an approximate two-year period) clients of whom I spoke before, B. Slatkin. He shares in it with me, although he wants no mag credit. *Collier's,* of all fiction magazines in smooth paper bracket, might possibly read it. Then *Esquire,* I suppose. Then *This Week,* then so on down the line. Try it, anyway. We'll try a *Blue Book* character, a private eye. Will try a baseball next, if nothing here intervenes. They still promise weekly to send me to work at U-I, but nothing happens. TV is equally coy, praising effusively, buying cheap stuff from bad writers.

Now to your letter: No, I wasn't sure of the particulars of the situation at Popular. My ideas were confused. Widmer certainly kicked over the apple cart, such as it was, didn't he? The bastard never did like paying a writer more than ½ cent, not since his days with Wynn. In 1937–38 he used to promise 1 cent per word if I'd give him a short one at ½ cent. Then he would find fault with the penny story and buy the other! Phil Conroy subsequently sold every one of these Widmer rejects to *DFW* and the Popular editors for well over 1 cent. However, you still do not particularize about the other pulp markets, detectives etc. Are all shut down? What about *Zane Grey Western,* of which I hear glowing reports as to word rate? And *Ranch Romances*—have they quit buying? I have a story in the current (January 1952) *New Western* and noted only one reprint in the book.

About the stories still "alive" with you: Evidently the pulps might still, according to you, absorb the sports and westerns. But I intended "It Signifies" for either *Blue Book* or *Adventure.* Hasn't Jake still got *Adventure?* He asked for a carney story. The whole situation is messy, of course… I'll let you know if any particular story should be withdrawn.

I can see one thing: If I am to go back to magazines, at any time, it is necessary to change my style of story telling. As you know I am dropping "Joel Reeve" except for *Blue Book* where it is so firmly established. If I can get a new slant at things, perhaps I might come up with something. It will certainly not be that which formerly sold. This postulates no unsurmountable problem, it is difficult but feasible.

Hope we have luck with the Duke.

*November 20, 1951—Joe to Bill:*

There are practically no other worthwhile markets outside of Popular. One cent is their rate and at that they favor their favorite writers who have been giving them what they want.

You speak of changing your style of story telling. Isn't that good enough! The whole is that in this time of fiction pushed by non-fiction, more editors are finally working up to the fact that character and not story alone carries the mail. Wouk's *Caine Mutiny* so obviously illustrates that man the who reads when he runs should see.

*November 26, 1951—Bill to Joe:*

Well I landed over here (U-I) for treatment—about a month. It's a musical with comedy and drama called *Universal Girl* and I'm getting a chance at a nominal sum, to work into screenplay on it. It'll be Technicolor, with stars and just between you and me, Jimmy Durante, for whom I have already sketched a great character part.

Joe, my kid brother Ray was killed the other day. You remember him— you exchanged correspondence. He was getting out ore in the mine they own and a premature explosion got him and wiped him out. He leaves a sixteen year old girl and a seven year old boy and I'm frantic with worriment about them, of course. I couldn't even make the funeral—Bayard is extremely inaccessible and I had to sell my car to pay doctors, as you know. I ought to be feeling great about my chance here, but Ray was the good boy—and my only family. Everyone is gone now except my worthless sister and myself and I feel very much alone in a world I do not like.

However, we must go on—and on. My wife is wonderful, working again three days per week and maybe we'll come out with some peace and happiness somewhere. I do hope all is well with you. Am waiting to hear on the "Duke" and on the weird short story with interest.

## November 30, 1951—Joe to Bill:

I am shocked to hear your bad news. You know my sympathy for you. The only thing we can do, Bill, is to keep on fighting, and surely the break for you is long overdue. When it comes, you will be amazed how quickly the hard past is forgotten.

I am sorry I haven't a good report to give you on the "Duke." As I wrote you, the general Western market has faded very badly, and the only safe venture into that field is with outstanding character or great historical significance. Gold Medal found the "Duke" story too light in emotional impact and with too familiar action. They have cut their Western list away down. In fact, just rejected a second Western from a writer whose first book, a while back, they acclaimed highly. The weird story has been turned back from first submission and, while out again, I can't feel too optimistic about it because it is definitely outré in a very selective market. Incidentally, the new editors of *Blue Book* are paying better than of old. We should have some of the Joel Reeve quality for them as well as a try for higher up. I hope the new work turns out well for you.

## December 5, 1951—Bill to Joe:

Too bad about the "Duke" at Gold Medal. I take it you are trying another market? Would you mind telling us who rejected the short story "Meeting at Hondo"? I am anxious to know the reaction to such a story—a new thing from me, as you are aware.

I'll be here for three weeks, possibly much longer... if I make good. Musical comedy is new to me also—but a man has to jump through hoops to stay alive these days. We seem to getting a good treatment, with a story for a change. The producer is a very nice guy. We have a Cinderella tale— what else? This studio hasn't made a musical since *Up in Central Park* put them in the hands of receivers. It is necessary to make one economically and sure fire to restore the confidence of the studio executives. We will have color, comedy, songs, dancing—and Durante. It should be a success and if it is I ride the train, of course. Meantime I'm on a flat deal with no dough forthcoming until I turn in a story. This, of course, is to refrain from establishing salary until we can demand and get a decent wage. Have a *Blue Book* crime character started and will try to squeeze it in. Is he in market for any sport? Let me know.

### December 11, 1951—Joe to Bill:

So far *Esquire* has rejected "Meeting at Hondo." Believe me, Bill, it's not a story I would want to send to *Post* or *Collier's* over your name. You stand too well in both places now. Gold Medal has not yet sent a final rejection of the "Duke" story. I sent you the report of only one man there. I'll keep you advised.

### December (sometime between the 13th and 23rd), 1951—Bill to Joe:

I was somewhat shocked at your negative reaction to "Meeting at Hondo." I did not suggest that you submit it to the *Post.* It is definitely not for *Ladies Home Journal,* either. But *Collier's* has published many off-trail stories lately, or haven't you noticed? I submit that this is a well-written fantasy with a good theme—that evil can carry a man a good way, and then when discovered in him lets him down.

Joe, in the past few months I feel that we are not seeing eye to eye. I mentioned it before. Perhaps the fault is entirely mine, I know that you have my best interests at heart and that you are sympathetic and earnest in all your dealings. But face it—we're not getting anywhere together. Perhaps, while I am temporarily removed from the magazine market both by its refusal to buy and my inability to write for it, we should call a halt. I think you had better withdraw "Meeting at Hondo," inform me as to what other rejections it may have had and return it to me. If any of my other material is out for sale, wait until it is returned or bought—then let's settle up.

Comes the time when even the best of friends should consider their mutual welfare. I am making you no money and have no feeling of good things in the future. I have no other agency in mind at present and indeed shall probably follow Ketchum's example for a while and deal directly in any such cases as I deem there may be a chance for sales. Actually, no agent would care about handling me right now. What profit? Put it this way: I am dissatisfied with myself and would like to get a clean start. Your ideas and mine don't jibe of late. It's healthier for us both to part good friends and for reasons not too unselfish—but not selfish either.

I may never write another magazine story, you know. Al Cohen, who is my producer here, swears he'll not let me go. My deal here is not a good one—but it is a start and I know many writers around the country who are truck-driving or mail-carrying or just plain starving, so I'm lucky. I may get the Neighborhood on film soon with Wayne Morris, a personal friend. This would keep me out of magazines indefinitely. Meantime, I want to experiment and you, my good friend, are against this sort of thing, although you may not realize it. I know the editors and publishers have the jitters, witness they way they chop and change in policy. The boys at the Fictioneers' Christmas party tell me they have folded the sports magazines at Popular for good... formerly they thought the sports were next to love westerns in circulation. Magazines are enduring a trying period—with writers taking the lumps.

Well, Joe it's been a snow-ride lately, but we had it good once, not so long ago. We never appreciated those pulps until they died. Bread and butter is so necessary. Let's call it quits for now. Keep in touch with me. I'd appreciate the return of "Hondo" at once—there's a collaborator involved, you know…. Thanks a million for everything—all your goodness and kindness through the years. All the best wishes for happy holidays—and forgive your errant pal….

*December 28, 1951—Joe to Bill:*

Of course I can't take exception to your decision and you know I wish
you every success. The fact that you mention, that we do not see eye
to eye in many bits of writing, has bothered and worried me for a long
while. As a matter of fact I cannot recall where you have agreed with me
during the past several years when your major magazine market faded
completely and it became necessary to adapt to other media. Believe me,
I mention this only for the interest I still have in you and your progress. I
have never set myself up as a know-it-all, but the men who faced exactly
the same situation as you and who listened to me have come through
grandly in the different order in their work.

You mention Ketchum who decided to change to another agency or try
on his own. A mutual friend tells me that Ketch is now making good on
what I tried for years to get him to do, and I am pleased that he is. When
Ketch wouldn't take it from me, I even got this friend to try to persuade
Ketch into those lines. Naturally this is confidential to you, and I speak
of it because I think it could be of advantage to you, when you return to
magazine writing, as you will, if you would reconsider some of those
points we discussed at length. I might mention that a book, now first
on the best seller list for months, exactly confirms the principles I have
tried so long to explain to you. The interesting point about this book's
tremendous success is that it wasn't made by commercial publicity but
by word of mouth by readers, the most talked about book today and the
best lesson ever given writers.

*January 7, 1952—Bill to Joe:*

Hope the holidays left you feeling fine. They sure can be rough! We
were very quiet, from lack of money, but U-I paid off soon after Christmas and I've done two Fireside Theater shows—the highest price they
ever paid—and am submitting another outline to U-I tomorrow, with
the backing of my producer friend, so all is going well at present, thank

you. Expect to go onscreen play in a short time on the Durante musical I did there, they like it very much, I hear.

You say "when your major magazine market faded completely and it became necessary to adopt other media" and Joe, for your own benefit, you are way off the beam. In fifteen years of writing for a living I was never a major magazine writer. I was always a pulpster, selling never more than four slicks per year. When the pulps faded, my markets evaporated. I don't want you to have the idea in your head that I was a smooth paper writer. True I have failed to sell them since 1949—but that's another matter all together. They also changed. Am I the only writer who has failed to find their new screwball system of buying? I know better. I also know that some of the old pulpsters who never sold them before are now doing very well. It's their innings and God bless them! I'll take mine out of TV and pictures until the day comes when I get another, fresh slant on magazines.

I'm sorry that you feel your advice was good and my performance bad. I never did take instruction very well. The best to you always. The greatest success in all your endeavors! Thanks again for everything!

*January 10, 1952—Joe to Bill:*

Golly, Bill, we still don't seem to speak the same language. By "your major market" of course I meant the pulps. How could I mean otherwise, after all our work together?

Unfortunately, William Cox was not able to bridge the gap between that which had previously allowed him to realize success in the pulps and the current higher expectations demanded by the editors of the so-called slick magazines. The loss of William Cox as a client must have been a bitter pill for my father to swallow. Bill Cox was only one writer of many; however, the fact that my father was not able to pull Cox out of the doldrums, in spite of repeated words of encouragement and recommended directional changes, must have been a source of frustration and sadness.

# NORMAN A. FOX

NORMAN FOX'S genre was Western short stories, serializations and novels. He had been a client of my father's for the better part of six years although the correspondence examined only covers the period from January 10, 1952, until August 1, 1952.[260]

My father was always delighted with the opportunity to work with both husband and wife as a team, recognizing how beneficial it was for the writer to have a support system. Not only was this important for emotional support, but it also provided the writer with assistance in interpreting what was requested by my father, critiquing the stories written, and proof-reading and editing the finished work. All of these activities enhanced the communications between author and agent. Often times my father would engage in separate correspondence with the writer's wife just to ensure her awareness of the importance of the role she was performing. Two letters exchanged between Rosalea, Norman Fox's wife, and my father are representative of the flavor of these communications.

January 19, 1952

Dear Cap,

Do you remember our pondering at lunch whether there was any word to take the place of the rather clumsy "know-how"? What do you think of "capability"?

Says the Winston dictionary (American): "The quality of being able to do; ability to accomplish; especially, the possession of mental power; used in the plural for mental attainments."

And according to the Shorter Oxford English: (I like this one better because it gets down to bedrock fast.) "The quality of being 1) able to take in (dating from 1775); 2) roomy or comprehensive (about 1650);

---

260  *Ibid.*

the quality of having power, or fitness for (1597); the quality of being qualified, gifted, able (1606). When used in the plural, *capabilities:* an undeveloped faculty or property; a condition capable of being turned to use (1778)."

Pardon me if this little fling into words has been something that you wish you knew less about, as the little girl said in reviewing the book on penguins.

We think very fondly of the time we spent with you, Cap. And believe me, I shall be very careful about saying "funny"! We hope to see you before another two years go by.

Why not at Virginia City? Something to hope for!

Love,

Rosalea

And the response:

January 24, 1952

Dear Rosalea:

Capability—yes, but hmm—Oi polloi tend to take new bait. Savvy is even closer but that takes us to savior faire which is foreign and even broader in full interpretation with other implications. Doggone interesting anyway. Wonder if it would help to go to Latin, capere.

And Mike says, "Nan" had a wonderful letter from you. Grand people says Mike, to which I heartily subscribe. My only regret I saw too little of you two.

Best regards,

Joseph T. Shaw

Perhaps this is superficial talk; however, it was essential in establishing and maintaining strong lines of communications; it also made the spouse an essential partner in the writing game. In much of the correspondence between the two men, references are made to Rosalea and the role she played.

Story rejection is a way of life in the writing profession, as is frustration and disappointment. In general, writers initially blame themselves for rejections, so the resulting disappointment is expected; however, repeated rejections can give cause to discouragement and ultimately to lashing out against those who are not able to see the beauty and strength of their artistic creation. Recognizing the reality of this transition in moods, gave my father the awareness of when and how to intercede.

One of Norman Fox's work's in progress was a novel entitled *Long Lightning*. Fox was not a novice as a writer, rather, he was a highly respected author of Western fiction. Regularly he had been authoring and selling two novels a year. All rights for ten novels had been sold to Dodd, Mead Publishing Company; he had sold movie rights for twelve of his novels; he had sold many short stories to an array of magazines; his work was appearing in hardback covers, softback covers and as serials; and he had been requested to write two books, one pertaining to the cavalry and its development, and the second one to be a novel on the history of Montana. In effect, he was a successful writer; however, he was also in transition. Expectations from both magazine editors and novel editors were becoming more demanding and selective as to what they would publish. It was my father's responsibility to prepare Fox to meet this challenge of change.

*January 14, 1952—Norman to Cap:*

... I also found time to meditate on a new approach to the opening chapters of *Long Lightning,* and I'll be sending the new treatment off to you soon, as per your suggestion while I was in New York. Then full steam ahead to finish the book.

*January 16, 1952—Norman to Cap:*

The changes in the version enclosed will be self-evident, and I think you will agree that I've improved the first chapter greatly. Since this is only one chapter from one book, it seems to me that the treatment I employed in making the changes is the important thing, for if my reasoning was correct, than the improvement should serve in good stead in all future work.

It seems to me now, Cap, that the trouble with the original version was that it was too static by virtue of being narrative rather than having real physical and mental and emotional feel for the character in which the reader could participate. The idea was sound—a man trapped in the rocks and in danger of his life—and I've not forgotten that Erd [Erd Brandt, associate editor, *Saturday Evening Post*] was much enthused over the action opening of *Tall Man Riding*—but the trouble in *Long Lightening*, originally, was that the situation was merely *stated*. Now I've got my man feeling the heat and hearing the whine of bullets and longing for the shade and coolness of the unattainable mountains. Without yet truly knowing the man, the reader, can put himself in the man's place and so sympathize with the man.

I've also taken care of that matter of quick identification of the man, as per the Erd Brandt dictum which you pointed out. And the Negro is now a big man, rather than a seven foot-freak, and many other minor changes have been made, most of them designed to make the hero more understandable and sympathetic.

I've learned a lot from this re-do, and I thank you for your discernment. I'd known that the first chapter was wrong, but seeing it through your eyes helped greatly to clarify the weaknesses. I hope you'll agree that the premises upon which I made the revision are valid, for thus the lesson learned will carry into the future.

*January 21, 1952—Cap to Norman:*

This version of first *Long Lightning* chapter is infinitely better, particularly in style. There are still a few minor points we can discuss when the story is in. You've put more life into it and is much more readable. I'm anxious to see the rest of it.

*January 29, 1952—Norman to Cap:*

I have your two letters about *Long Lightning* and am immensely pleased that you consider my re-do of the first chapter a great improvement. I decided, after a second look, to give the second chapter a thorough work-over, too. The present situation of the work rather precludes my showing you the whole job in rough draft, as your letter suggests. This week I'll finish the entire writing on the book. In the meantime, Rosalea and I are busy at editing the earlier chapters and passing these along to my typist.

... it appears that we may be up against a time element condition on *Long Lightning*. According to the latest *Publishers Weekly*, *Ghostly Hoofbeats* will be released by Dodd, Mead on March 10th. Undoubtedly they'll be showing active interest in a new manuscript. We'll have an extra copy of *Long Lightning* for them, of course, and it will take a few weeks for them to read the script and get around to drawing up a contract. But we'll have to make the interim count in securing a magazine sale.

As for the magazine market possibilities of *Long Lightning*—to Brandt or not to Brandt, that is the question—we can discuss them when I shoot in the finished script. Your reaction to the product will be the prime guidepost. I wonder if Don Ward's [editor of *Zane Grey's Western* magazine, as well as editor of Dell Books] market has loosened up so that he might be interested, if it comes to that.

*February 1, 1952—Cap to Norman:*

What I am hoping we will capture, and in *Long Lightning*, if possible, is that immediate character interest so urgent with Erd, and which other editors are coming to realize also. Might tell that clever partner of yours to watch out for it.

What a lot of writers do is know a character thoroughly and like him but keep those like-inspiring qualities to themselves and fail to have them shown to the reader. They take for granted if they like a character, you will too, but that ain't just enough.

## February 16, 1952—Norman to Cap:

*Long Lightning* goes forward to you today. I am sending the script by air express so that it will reach you that much earlier, for as you know, we are going to be up against a problem of time in getting a magazine sale, since Dodd, Mead will soon want a book script. I have a carbon for them, of course, but will hold it here in the meantime.

I hope you'll consider *Long Lightning* worth showing to Brandt. I feel that it has a number of things in its favor. Single viewpoint is maintained throughout—the story is a departure from the usual ranch imbroglio, of which Brandt may have had more than enough—and moreover I am confident that I have done a finer job on characterization than in any previous book. I think that in this one I've discovered an angle on characterization that will serve me well hereafter. In fact, we have a high enthusiasm for this book, which remains undimmed, even though we've lived with the story constantly these last few weeks.

Enough of an author's bragging. Should Brandt like the story well enough to perhaps suggest revision, we'll be up against the problem of Dodd, Mead, but I say let's not worry about that till the time comes. It is possible that I may be able to produce an ace-in-the-hole, if necessary.

In the event that the *Post* turns down *Long Lightning,* I am confident it is the kind of copy Don Ward likes, if I may judge from his vociferous enthusiasm for certain of my books he took for reprinting. A sale to *Zane Grey Western*, while not as fat a check as a *Post* sale, would nevertheless make a nice bonus prior to book publication.

Now let's hear what you think, capitan mio.

                                    Tired but hopeful.


## February 18, 1952—Cap to Norm:


Four times Erd Brandt has said: "knew after the first 20 pages this
wasn't for us, but___." Once he said to us, "Any one of those four stories
you have sent me would have been adequate if they had had the elements
we insist on."

Now I fully believe *Long Lightning* in the bulk is going to be adequate
to show him. However, I've been giving a lot of thought to what Brandt
looks for and insists on having. Hence I've scrutinized the first twenty-four pages to see if they hold it. And now I want to ask you if you will
be willing to take a look with me and, if you agree, endeavor to insert the
elements where they are missing. I grant you there's good writing in it,
but I'm thinking now of what Brandt will hope to be in it which hasn't
a great deal to do with quality of writing, as we've often seen.

I can mention two of his demanded elements: First, recognizable
human qualities of a man that appeal to one's interest and sympathy for
whatever situation he may be in. It was missing from the four, any one
of which would have been adequate! It is missing here. Let's see if we
can't get it Norman. In fact, if it's to be worthwhile to show to Brandt,
we jolly well have to. You've given a splendid description of someone
caught in such a jam, a description you mustn't lose. But that someone
could be anyone. If Brandon were to be shot there, no one would give a
hoot. No doubt you like him well enough; no doubt we'll come to like
him as we go along. But not from the first pages. Because we don't see
the human qualities. He has not shown enough of himself, of his appealing characteristics to catch us, to arouse our interest in him personally.

He suffers from heat; he has bullets whistling around him. The only
thing you develop of the man is that he has a philosophy that keeps his
thoughts from giving up or the end. You stay too aloof from him. Can't
you get close to him? Let him look at his hand, with the pistol, test its

steadiness; look at the lichen on the boulder before him, see where a bullet had streaked it white; feel the strength in his fisted left hand, and feel its impotence in that situation. All that is physical but it brings you closer to him, as would a gesture to ease his collar, or the stiffness in his crouched position. Then the thought of what he might be leaving behind him; the provision for someone dependent upon him; something good and unselfish that he has done that makes him fight with any conscience and good mind.

You tell what he has done in years past, but that also is aloof from the man, the individual personality. The intimate gestures bring one close to him; now let's see inside him. The good traits, not through your description but what he discloses of himself. The fact that he has had this job or that doesn't do it, or falls far short of doing it. Does he think of something or someone good and wholesome to which or whom he may not return; of some good deed he wishes he had completed? Then how does he feel toward the man he shoots at? Does he want to kill?

These may not be good suggestions, but I want you to get right inside his shirt and trousers and show the reader what a hell of a good guy you are and make us think how sorry we would feel if you got shot. That's what Brandt has been hammering at. You can't put a wooden man, any more than a wooden Indian, behind that boulder and expect Brandt would go for it.

Second, immediate identification. Where was he going? Where had he come from? Was it important or urgent that he get to Salish? If so, why? Where was his crew? How come he was alone? What was he doing there anyway? His calling name of Lucas, a man he'd never seen and only vaguely heard of, not only too abrupt but not rationalized. He doesn't figure the reason of the attack, but all of a sudden calls a man's name and hits it right the very first time.

Hope you understand my purpose in all this.

Now, Don Ward couldn't publish before November issue, on stands in October. Dodd, Mead want a title in April, manuscript sometime in May for an October publication; in June for November publication but consider October better. They will also postpone for Spring if for any reason, but I believe you want two a year with them. Also Don Ward is thinking of 25,000 to 35,000 in place of long ones, but not decided yet. If *Post* took it, they might postpone for several months before scheduling and running.

So have this to decide: If you favor submission to *Post* and will do this extra, but not momentous work on the opening, we might be faced with getting a quickie to Dodd, Mead in mid-May. However, if *Post* should take it, it would be worth any postponement and they still may run it before October. If you want to skip *Post* submission, although I hope you won't, then we'll see if Ward will take it out and tell us what he would pay for it.

### February 21, 1952—Norman to Cap:

I greatly appreciate your lengthy letter of February 18th regarding the opening pages of *Long Lightning* and the necessity to get the things Erd wants into those pages before we submit to him. I'm 100% in accord with your thoughts, and I shall get at the revision at once and hope to have said revision on its way in a few days.

Admittedly we may be up against an awkward situation if the *Post* should take the serial and not be able to run it before October, at which time Dodd, Mead wants to bring out the book. But I believe, with you, that we should have our chance at the *Post*. Possibly other phases of the situation will resolve themselves.

I am very grateful to you, Cap, both for your promptness in giving Long Lightning immediate consideration and for your careful thought as what it needs in the way of bolstering.

### February 24, 1952—Norman to Cap:

... Enclosed is the revised first chapter. The tangible items, pertaining to identification, etc., have all been taken care of, for I checked these off one by one with your letter of the 18th. The intangibles I've tried to remedy also, making Brandon's human qualities recognizable and so turning him into an individual man. Your mentioning that he might stare at his hand suggested to me the gimmick wherein he considers his own character in terms of his hand. I thank you. Whether I've yet raised the opening to the level of acceptability by Brandt is, of course, a matter of conjecture, but I feel that you will agree that the chapter is improved in many respects.

I'll await your further reaction with considerable interest. If we don't hit with the post and if Don Ward favors 25,000 to 35,000 words in place of long ones, what about Mal Reiss? There is the *Toronto Star* too, but I'm afraid the realistic man-woman relationships throughout the story might be a bit strong for that market.

### *February 26, 1952—Cap to Norman:*

... I really think this new opening does tell more. Also it gives approximate suggestion of the period, so please disregard my letter of yesterday.

This will go to Brandt. I have already asked Miss Cowley, of *Toronto Star*, her status on Westerns. As for Fiction House, I question if they could publish it in time for Dodd, Mead.

### *February 28, 1952—Joe to Erd:*

I am sending a new story by Norman A. Fox, *Long Lightning.*

### *March 4, 1952—Erd* (Saturday Evening Post) *to Joe:*

This Fox *(Long Lightning)* is a competently done story, but he just doesn't give the characters the polish that would make it a possibility for us. It is too bad because it is a good background he is using, and while he has very little plot he has a well-paced narrative. I would be glad to see his next one.

*March 5, 1952—Joe to Norm:*

I know this will be a disappointment to you, which I share keenly, yet it is the closet we have come to the *Post.*

What, I feel, will bother you more is why the characters didn't grip as Erd hoped they would. I realize that I didn't explain fully or clearly enough, but if you will look at your first and the typed draft, of the opening, then at what I tried to express in the letter on which you made further revision, I think you will see what I was endeavoring to explain.

Please don't mind if I go into some details on it, because it is the only thing that keeps you out of *Post* pages.

Let's start with the premise that we must see and feel the personalities of all the main characters and in a way that instills more than a passing impression; nay, a strong liking, reminding us of the character of some-one we admire or of the characteristics of our ideal of the best manhood, which, inevitably human and no superman, at least suggests the we'd like to be ourselves. Such, for example, John Ridd in *Lorna Doone.*

Now to get the full impact of such impression, we have to have the man, or woman, come close to us in familiar little things, but that is only one part of it.

One cannot give the desired impression by narrative description. The man's looks and appearance won't do it; neither will telling of his occu-pation. All of that is helpful, but if one stops at that there is no register-ing of individual personality.

One has to have him talk in a way, act in a way that will show what is mind is that determines his speech and action, that displays what his character is.

To get it all, one has to visualize the man, or woman, in person. Short has a way of doing it, with little, homely things familiar to everyone and, by so doing, brings the man in person before your mind's eye. One of such things I recall. I think it was in the opening of his *Vengeance Valley,* if that's the title. He mentioned the button missing from the man's coat as he gets ready to ride to the girl's house. I tried to suggest the same thing in having him see the streak left by the bullet, looking at his hand, his sweating face and easing his collar.

Here is what I think has tended to keep you away from this sort of treatment. I think your early work was concerned chiefly with story and incident, with characters, or actors, in the story secondary in your thought. I am fully confident that if you will set your mind right on the matter of having your reader visualize your characters in person and feeling their personality you will accomplish it.

Frankly, I wasn't confident that you had accomplished it in that last revision but I judged it was the best that could be done at the moment. It certainly was a big improvement, but we see now it wasn't far enough.

You can still concentrate on story and incident but it is evident we must have equal concentration on the visualization and feel of personal character.

Of course you can do it, Norman, if you will consciously set your mind on it. And this should extend not only on your hero or main character but on the others as well. When you come to the woman, than those familiar feminine touches.

It is amazing how just a little unexpected turn will bring out this impression of distinctive personality. I recall one in a story yet unfinished in acceptable form as a whole.

A big fellow, a fisherman, leads his companions, also of the fisherman type, into a shack, the home of the suspected murderer who we happen to know is innocent. The big fellow and his friends are intent, perhaps even to so-called lynch justice.

In the crowd are one or two determined on the lynching and apparently the big fellow and the others will go with them on it.

The big fellow ties the suspect with wire. Then the suspect, given the chance to talk, tells how and where the murdered man's body was found, as had been told by those who had discovered it, but with respect to the tides and to the big fellow's understanding. At once he cuts the wire, and knowing the attitude of the other men, he turns to their intended victim and says, "Well, there're only two of us, but I guess we can take this crowd."

Do you see how that demonstrates what sort of a human being the big fellow is, how at once you visualize him and how just that little thing remains unforgettable in the whole story whatever it is?

It is this sort of visualizing distinctive, individual personality makes a story, and whose absence at least keeps us out of the *Post*.

So, Norman, please let's work out this sort of thing to the last touch in the big one coming up, *Badlands Beyond.* As I said, I believe you can do it competently once you set your clear mind on it. But let's not be satisfied with any compromise this time. Let's be absolutely sure of it.

### *March 7, 1952—Norman to Cap:*

I have yours enclosing Brandt's rejection of *Long Lightning*. Frankly, I'm not too disappointed. I can now see that somehow I got off on the wrong foot at the start of the story, and while subsequent revision came under the heading of improvement, it just didn't shore it up sufficiently. I'm pleased that Brandt found so much that he did like about the yarn, and I'm grateful to you for your continued efforts to help me. We have definitely isolated the bug, which is characterization. On to the next job.

In the meantime, though, there is still the question as to whether we'll be able to make some magazine money on this one before we have to sign contract with Dodd, Mead. I note with considerable interest that Mal Reiss (editor, Fiction House) could publish on October 1st. This would certainly clear our skirts, for Dodd, Mead would not be bringing out the book until October or November. However, since a Don Ward check would likely be twice what Mal would pay, I certainly hope we can do business with Don. He has displayed considerable fondness for me, so perhaps if the circumstances were explained to him, he might be willing to juggle his schedule a bit in our favor.

### *March 10,1952—Cap to Norman:*

Thanks for yours of the 7th. I am today sending *Long Lightning* to Don Ward, after talking with him.

*April 24, 1952—Cap to Norman:*

> Don Ward wants *Long Lightning* for $1,000, cutting it about 30 percent
> to fit his space. He can't publish it before December. I talked with Tom
> Dodd [Vice President, Dodd, Mead] and he said he would really prefer to
> let his publication go over to January and thinks it would be in your inter-
> est to do it, then pick up the two a year after that on the regular periods.
>
> I judge this will allow you to take your time to complete *Badlands
> Beyond* carefully and have another one on hand for Dodd, Mead.

In this foregoing exchange of letters, note the several variables
at work. First, my father's constant theme concerning character
development over plot; second, the responsiveness of the author
to receive instruction and remedy areas needing strengthening;
third, the changing expectations from the reading public, and,
consequently, the changing markets and demands of editors on
the work of authors; fourth, the alternate routes a manuscript
can follow depending on its length and content, and the timing
of its submission; and, fifth, whether or not electing one course
of action precludes the use of other avenues.

All of these observations are exemplified in the one hundred
day cycle for *Long Lightning,* a cycle initiated by the submission
of a rough draft from Norman Cox to my father. The cycle then
flowed through successive structural changes in the opening
chapters, through rejection from an elite magazine, to continued
guidance from my father, resubmission to a lesser market, and,
finally, acceptance. While the *Long Lightning* project was in progress there was also extensive dialogue with an array of editors as
my father sought buyers for other stories that Fox had developed
or was in the process of developing.

In perusing the full body of correspondence between my father
and Norman Fox, several other factors become evident. It is obvious that Fox was a successful writer in that, for the most part, his

stories sold, albeit through any one of several different outlets. In spite of many successes, he never assumed an air of superiority, but always one of humility. When rejections came he never expressed disdain for the editors or criticized their decisions; indeed, he placed the burden for rejection on his own shoulders, acknowledging that somehow he had failed to properly present the material. He took seriously the instruction and guidance provided by my father, and he never dwelt on failure, always looking beyond a "no sale" to alternate opportunities.

With this very positive attitude he and my father developed a very fine working relationship. As stories were passed from one editor to another, they incessantly shared ideas as to the best approach to follow, and would not make commitments unless there was mutual agreement. My father had no qualms about allowing and even encouraging Norman Fox to be in contact with editors and movie and television agents; however, both, understanding the importance of communications, ensured that copies of all correspondence were shared.

My father and Norman Fox had great trust in each other, each was sensitive to the other's reputation in the literary field, and, on delicate matters, they would consult closely to avoid running afoul of ethics, another agent, or publisher. They were responsive to each other and to the markets they were attempting to reach.

In spite of the several potential market opportunities available for the literary work of Fox, reaching any one of them could be a tortuous and frustrating process. In the center of this ebb and flow of correspondence was my father, the literary agent, who had the responsibility of keeping in balance the many different forces at work while at the same time ensuring that Norman Fox's best interests were being served.

My father was more than a catalyst for the many transactions taking place. By nature, he was deeply concerned about the individual growth of each of his clients, pushing them to aspire toward bigger and better markets. This is the area in which he was supreme. Not content to allow them to remain at a fixed level, he pushed them to continue their growth; moreover, this emphasis on growth was not at the expense of his responsibility to sell the work that was being produced. The push was in the form of instruction, examples of which are threaded throughout his letters. A letter from my father to Norman Fox dated May 1, 1952, shares the approach used.

Dear Norman:

I've been thinking over *Long Lightning* and speculating on *Badlands Beyond,* feeling that there are some impressions aroused by the former that might be avoided in the latter to advantage.

Of course you realize this is my viewpoint and apparently not Don Ward's, for example. At least he did not speak of it. But it didn't make the *Post* this time and I have found that Erd's views and my own are consistently more in accord than often Don's and mine.

I think we can say that Don holds closer to the older effects of Westerns in exciting incidents as compared with emotional effects arising from character; the physical rather than the mental or spiritual. At least in his editorial policy for his magazine, for Don is a competent judge and appreciative of good writing.

You have this same comparison, Norman, between *Feathered Sombrero* and *Thirsty Land.* And now I guess you know what I'm driving at.

While there are some excellent characters in *Long Lightning,* characters you feel as real people, particularly the old construction boss, at the same time there are several things that give me an impression of unreality; as if conjured up from beyond ordinary human happenings and logical human behavior; things more of imagination than of convincing fact. And I think the latter is sufficient where the story is based on character and the emotional effects produced on character.

I doubt if it is necessary to enumerate these things for I'm sure you recognize them. However, I might mention one or two. I first felt the sense of unreality in the opening situation; the fortuitous arrangement of the terrain. Isn't it true, Norman, that close to the sheer break of the rim there would be no boulders, where from erosion or glacial action they would be scattered partly on the slope yet practically all on more level ground as a talus on the bottom? Then the silent dropping of the riata without warning, its lucky catching in the dusk, the mysterious girl, the fabulous black. Then the extraordinary set-up in the valley where one mustn't enter even with friendly purpose although the outlaw and his gang seemed not unwelcome.

How much more convincing and effective in its impact the scene in the logical surroundings of the boss' private car.

There is another point too. In the opening, the hero and the outlaw are in deadly combat. Later they meet in town. Tell me, Norman, exactly what you would have done meeting a man who had been trying to kill you. You are as square as they make them, but I doubt much if your generosity would have gone that far, or if it should. I'll admit the hero hasn't your stature as a man, but this is too close to the time when so many writers treated this sort of thing as a game of tag. One wanted to kill another but a second one got the drop on the first; then they would turn their backs on each other and nothing would be done.

I have emphasized these things, possibly exaggerated them. This is no intention to revise *Long Lightning*. It pleased Don and no doubt will please Dodd, Mead. However, I am quite sure they influenced *Post's* decision, and, if so, we sure don't want them to militate against *Badlands*.

Had a good talk with Bob Murphy Tuesday, who has been pitch hitting for Erd while Erd is on the Coast. Bob was speaking of a short story by Peggy Curry they had recently bought, praising the emotions she had put into the story, which he said was distressingly rare with writers. He asked me how I got emotion into the story, and I told him it was by creating a situation where the presence of emotional feeling was obvious and having the characters show, with restraint, the effect of that emotion on them but, I will add, more by how they act than what they say.

We talked further of the present trend. To my gratification, he emphasized a point Erd had stressed before; that a whole lot of writers once popular with the *Post* were not so popular now. And we agreed on the reason. As Bob put it, those writers continue to put story and story manipulation first and lack the ability to demonstrate character and human emotion.

In the same vein, additional insight and guidance was provided in excerpts from a letter dated July 12, 1952.

Dear Norman:

... *The Long Lightning* will be published in the December issue, on stands in November and off in December.

I haven't wanted to push you, Norman, but at the same time I can't help feeling that a steady rate of income, whether greatly needed or not, provides a satisfaction that makes any writer more at ease on long work. And a long, serious work—such as *Badlands Beyond*—is a time consumer. Thus if you come to a pause at any time, where you want a new perspective look at the big one, why not do something, say in the way of shorts or short novelettes. Don would welcome it, I can assure you, and anything of yours that comes in gets sized up for far higher up.

And while I'm on your work, I want to gall you that Don Ward sincerely believes that if you keep steadily on in the way you are now writing, doing your story, that you are heading for Number One spot of all Western writers. And I don't have to tell you my opinion.

Neither Don nor I think you should mould your work especially to please anyone; for example, the *Post*. And on this, I want to make my feeling clear to you. It is this; I want your own story as you write it. At the same time I believe that there will be no compromise and no deterrent to what you put into it, if we shape the opening, the presentation of characters, in a way that would make a *Post* sale. That is all I favor. I don't want you to follow any *Post* pattern. Only so far as to get true character impact and character interest right off. And that is entirely regardless of the *Post* or if Erd had never spoken of it.

Don feels, and I agree with him, that if you carry in mind too much what *Post* wants, it will impair and not improve your own individual style. So, I wish you would forget *Post*.

I believe, in the work over and our discussion of the first chapter of *Long Lightning,* you saw for yourself the greater effectiveness in opening with a convincing scene which would allow the hero to show at once the sort of man he is. Believe me, Norman. Once that strong liking and personal interest are established, the story is well on its way to success.

Please tell me if I've made my position clear. I don't want you to think I'm trying to squander your natural talent to fit into anyone's mould. Since you wrote *Thirsty Land* we've been aiming for big things. Don still swears *Tall Man Riding* is one of the best Westerns he's ever read.

Norman Fox was an apt student as can be seen in a letter of response to my father on July 19, 1952.

Dear Cap:

Exploring some further aspects of your letter of July 12th, relative to your conversation with Don Ward about my future, I'm pleased indeed that Don believes I'm on my way to a high spot among Western writers, especially if I keep going in the manner I've been pursuing in recent years.

Don says, and you concur, that I should not mould my work especially to please anyone; for example, the *Post*. Actually I have felt all along that whereas the *Post* requirement of impact of character at the opening is definitely worth considering, to go beyond that in a planned effort to hit the *Post* would be to produce a tailored story rather than one written free of market inhibitions. Thus when you wanted me to revise the opening of *Long Lightning* I did so, not necessarily to please Erd Brandt but because I felt, with you, that the new opening would be stronger and therefore the whole story would be better—from anybody's viewpoint.

I'm back at work on *Badlands* but I've not yet sent you the opening simply because I'm not sure that I've yet got it set the way I want it. This work, Cap, has got to be a novel of the West, rather than a commercial Western novel, and I think that it is going to run at least 75,00 words. So much the better, for if it were only 60,000 and were published as another Dodd, Mead Silver Star Western, I feel it would be foredoomed to failure. It hasn't the super-heated action or the torrential pace that readers of commercial Westerns expect, and its appeal is to a different plane of readers. Whether it will qualify as the historical Western that Tom Dodd had hoped I would write, I do not know, but it is a story of a definite place and time—Montana, 1885—and the hero's problem is not to lift the mortgage or push the railroad through in time, or any of the standard problems of the commercial Westerns. The hero's problem is a simple character problem—to find his place in a frontier civilization and so find himself.

The work is painstakingly slow and has so far involved many revisions and much research. I can say that nothing I have so far written has given me greater satisfaction in the writing.

Continuing the flow of communications was my father's response dated August 1, 1952.

Dear Norman:

Quite regularly I go over the properties given to Ray Stark and Ben Benjamin believing the reminders will do no harm. In this connection I wrote Ben specifically about one of yours and quoted, without name, Don Ward's appraisal of you. I think Ben's reply will please you: "Many thanks for your note on *Tall Man Riding* by Norman Fox. You may recall from some of my previous correspondence my enthusiasm for this particular story. I keep trying it all the time. As a matter of fact, I just purchased some more copies the other day in an effort to renew the interest. I think the publisher is absolutely right, and I do appreciate your writing to me about it."

I've read and reread your good letters analyzing both your work and the economic situation.

This may not be a good way to express it, but I feel sure you will understand what I am trying to say; and that is there can be no doubt that you have been steadily reaching a maturity in writing, without which one cannot find a worthy vehicle for the greater thoughts which have been the inspiration for his progress all the way.

By maturity I mean both understanding and the acquisition and firm establishment of habits that automatically encompass proper care for plausibility in all things, small and large, the authentic presentation of personalities, the authentic action and reaction from the specific characteristics of the distinctive and different individuals rather than the author's assumption of what they should be.

All this progress stems definitely from the time when you came to look upon the book as the best and proper medium toward your success as a writer. And it is inevitable that some of the earlier habits of a less careful attitude should from time to time intrude until finally automatically recognized and avoided. Thus, for example, in *Long Lightning*, an action story, we found a few in the opening.

Then, again, the old method was to attain the solution by the physical defeat of the opposition.

Now *Badlands Beyond,* as I visualize it from your description, while against physical and human obstacles, is more along psychological lines than pure action, and, therefore is less apt to admit those earlier and less mature discrepancies.

At the same time, Norman, I believe it will require a full knowledge of the personality of your main character and essentially the expression of his characteristics by himself with the author quite aloof from any attempt by him to interpret them for the reader.

I know. With all the good thoughts and philosophies you have been building around this big story, the temptation is so strong to get in there yourself and loose them in your own language. But you must resist that temptation. Otherwise you will make it an essay by Norman A. Fox, and this is a story, not an essay. You must put those high thoughts and philosophies into the mind of your character and let him find his own way to express them.

The latter is maturity in writing.

As to the economic situation, the wiser course seems to me some work for Don Ward. If any of this falls into the 5,000 word length, there are several higher markets. With G.M. [Gold Medal], who are really fussy over their Westerns now, you might run into a situation of wanted revisions that would take more time than you would want to spare.

I haven't yet found good opportunity to talk with Dodd over the collection but will do so shortly.

Best wishes,

Joseph T. Shaw

This letter, written on the morning of August first, was so characteristic of my father's inter-relationships with others. First, the words of praise and affirmation of the value of the work they do, followed by concern over the individual's economic situation and future career opportunities, then the ubiquitous instruction and guidance, and, finally, words of encouragement. In the early afternoon my Dad was gone, having died of "Coronary Arteriosclerosis with Occlusion."

In the seven-month period from early January through the first of August, there were ninety-three pieces of correspondence available in the UCLA Library Special Collections files pertaining to the working relationship between Norman Fox and my father. These letters represent a treasure trove of information shared, problems confronted and problems solved. It was a tapestry of concern and gentleness between two men; and it was a tapestry that expanded to embrace many others. This correspondence represented a business endeavor in a business environment, achieved within an atmosphere of integrity and concern for ethical standards.

Now the voice, that meant so much to so many, was silenced. Norman Fox's condolences were expressed in a letter to my brother, Joseph T. Shaw, Jr., dated August 18, 1952...."And now I would like to convey to you and to the rest of Cap's family my deep sympathy in your recent loss. Be assured my own sense of loss is great, for it was my pleasure to have known your father personally as well as to have had him as my representative. Cap was a gallant, courageous gentleman with a sense of integrity that is all too rare in this crass, commercial age, and he had a faith that could move mountains. We who knew him well and loved him deeply will miss him very much, and as another of his clients pointed out, there will be a day when all of us will wear a special badge of distinction, for we were Cap's boys. He was far more than an agent to us, I assure you."

## THOMAS THOMPSON

THOMAS THOMPSON'S genre, like Norman Fox's, was Western stories, short stories, novelettes and novels. He was my father's client from 1945 until August 1, 1952. The correspondence available, of which there are 387 letters, covers the period from January 13, 1949, until my father's death on August 1, 1952. [261] Like Fox, Thompson too was considered to be in the upper echelon of Western writers, but, as was true of many authors, it was a feast or famine existence. Fortunately, because of subsidiary rights and royalties, income, limited as it was, came from several different sources. Movie rights for one of his stories were sold, and, although he had written several novels within this period of time he never hit that "big one" he was hoping for.

Although a highly effective and prolific author, and a much sought after lecturer on the history of the Pacific Northwest, he

---

261   *Ibid.*

was burdened by a lack of confidence in his ability to write. Tracing the correspondence over the course of three years, Tommy Thompson was unduly harsh on himself and on his ability to write; consequently, even in the face of success, he would find reason to become depressed. Quite predictably, within days of hitting bottom, my father was always there for him encouraging, guiding and directing his renewed efforts. When success came to Thompson, the success realized was accompanied by a visible exultation of work well done. Further, through the ups and downs, one could sense the growth of trust and affection between the two, reflected in the spoofing of each other through loose language, word play, and chiding. The following letter and its accompanying responses demonstrate this emotional swing:

*April 20, 1949—Tommy to Cap:*

I hate to do this to you, knowing how busy you are, but I'm seriously in need of some help. As I think I've told you, I've been working harder than ever before, but one look at the number of stories I've mailed will show you that the work never gets completed. I'm accumulating a growing file of stories that are either unfinished or finished and so far wrong that I can't see a way to save them. It becomes a very frustrating thing and is responsible for both my lack of income and my current crop of ulcers.

A few days ago I told you I was working on a short novelette of the Mike Tilden type. It started out all right—it seemed to me—was going along fine. And all of a sudden it fell apart at the seams, just as everything else is doing.

Enclosed is that so-called novelette. It is approximately 7,500 words long, I guess, neither a short nor a novelette. It is a dead duck, just as so many others are dead ducks, stuck here in my file.

My reason for sending this along is this. This is directly out of my machine, no editing, except for the editing I sometimes do as I go along.

It is an accurate first draft of a story—or what once started out to be a story. In this perhaps you can see where I'm going so far off the beam, for I think it is pretty typical. Right at this point it seems to me it is completely without pace, without direction, without life, and yet when I started it I was all steamed up about it.

I know you are busy as hell, and as I say, I hate to ask you, but I really do feel we could save some time, perhaps, if you'd look this thing over and tell me what's wrong with my thinking. Remember, now, that this was supposed to be a pulp story. Where in hell is it that I've lost the old touch? What am I thinking about that makes a story wander like this one does, winding up nowhere? Can you read between the lines of this thing and perhaps discover what's wrong with my conception of a story? We used to get a fairly good yarn out now and then, it seems to me, and here lately I've given you a bunch of crap that seems to miss everyone.

What I'd like to do is get back on the footing I was on last spring, where I was writing twenty or thirty thousand words of good, above average pulp copy every month and taking time to play with a short now and then. At present I am doing neither, and I seem to have lost the touch completely.

This is a hell of a big order for you, I realize, but I need to sit down and discuss it with someone and I think that someone should be you, for you have seen what I can do and have done and you know what my limitations and abilities are.

I don't have another copy of this one, so I would appreciate it if you would send it back, along with any comments you wish to make. I'm not particularly concerned with saving this as a story—although that would be nice if it could be done. I would just like to have your idea on what is wrong with the thing—why it is dead, incomplete, neither a short nor a novelette.

Meanwhile I'll move along to something else and I'll be sending you the first of *Lost Valley* soon. I hope to hell it isn't screwed up in the same way this is.

## April 27, 1949—Cap to Tommy:

Watcha mean busy, when you don't call on me for medicine? Perhaps I am filling prescriptions and selling 'em over the counter all day but it's up to you to put yours in the bunch. So I was very damn glad to get yours of the 20th with the first draft of a new one.

I haven't read three pages of *Shadow of the Noose*—and most of the trouble with this one is in the half dozen opening pages—before I could see what was wrong. It's too loose in all its joints. It's all surface stuff. A thing mentioned here another there, all going a little wild because nothing is rationalized or complete in its thought.

All right; let's forget that for a moment. There's a good story here some-where in the scrub, but we'll get to that later.

Let's call the draft the effect.

Now let's see if we can ferret out the cause.

Of course you realize it all lies with you, so we'll have to see what's wrong with you right now.

I'll give you my idea, frankly, and you see how it fits.

Obviously, there is no concentration here, which accounts for the disjointed, incomplete and unreal details.

So why isn't there the vitally essential concentration that would make the whole seam-proof and sound and right all the way?

Well, just now, you don't think its worth a damn, not worth doing, but you've got to do something so you just force yourself to put words down and let them run and feeling, when you've finished the chore, it won't be worth a damn.

And you're sore as hell with yourself for feeling that way and you don't know what you are going to do about it.

But I reckon we got to do something about it, Tommy, for you're a hell of a good writer when you are friends with yourself and feel that confi-dence that everything you do is good.

Now with many other writers, name writers, I believe the reason their current stuff is so much off quality (a complaint from all editors) is that subconsciously the general atmosphere of insecurity, the war menace constantly dangled before us, the spendthrift spending of government, the continued call for more taxes, all these things are in their minds all the time, preventing the necessary, complete concentration on their work.

I do not think this is the true reason behind your wobbling concentration. I believe if you could see a sufficient, dependable income flowing in you wouldn't give a damn about the rest.

Well we got to get that dependable income and the only way we can get it is by concentrating full-heartedly, enthusiastically, on every bit of work you do. You didn't like this piece a bit while you were doing it. You hated its guts, didn't have a damn bit of fun.

So, we'll have to find the exact cause—which we haven't so far—before we can affect the cure.

I think it is because you are thinking of gathering the harvest while you are doing the hoeing, and if you think that way there's no fun hoeing and, hating it, you make a hell of a job of it. Now there's lots of fun hoeing, if you look at it right, seeing what nice hills you are making, how you are getting stronger when you put some effort into it and don't just drag the hoe along scuffing your heels and kicking the rocks and swearing at the sweat trickling down your neck and belly and wishing you could go sit in the shade with the guys who've finished their hoeing.

The odd thing about it, you ask any of those guys and they'll tell you they were happiest out there in the hot sun hoeing and have known nothing like it since.

You're happier when accomplishing then after you have accomplished. If it weren't so, we'd never get anything done.

It would be no sense picking this thing to pieces. You can do this better than I. It is the effect, a careless piece of hoeing. I'm sending it back to be hoed over again. You've got the characters; the seed is in. Now you get to hoeing and like it. Be confident of it; be enthusiastic about it. Hell's bells, Tommy, there's nothing wrong with you. You aren't in any slump.

And not so much wrong with the story in that a little work won't fix. Don Ward should grab it.

Funny thing about that thing slump. It's infectious as hell. One guy thinks he has it so a lot more think they have it. Like shell shock, battle fatigue, occupational disease and all those damned things psychiatrists have wished on us and which, when our intestinal fortitude is low, we fall for like a pack of ninnies.

Look, I met Ray Stark here, had a good talk with him and like him better than anyone I've seen from Hollywood. Says he's a salesman; doesn't try to tell any writer what might be wrong with his stuff; isn't trained or qualified too, although he can tell why it didn't sell here or there. Sold fifty-four stories last year, about a fourth of all he bought; won't take publisher's accounts; doesn't want much more from agents than he already has—since he works on the quality rather than the quantity method as Ned Brown, Swanson and others do. Guess that explains why we haven't had luck with Ned.

But, he says he believes he can get from me material that has value and will handle what I send him. That is, he apparently looks upon me as a judge and helper toward better quality of material and that is what he wants in order to do his selling job.

Sounds like a hell of a promising combination if we can make a go of it.

Several stories and considerable correspondence later, and in response to a partial draft of *Lost River,* submitted by Tommy, was the following:

*July 6, 1949—Cap to Tommy:*

I have yours of June 29th with pages 45 and 45a, 57 to 79 inclusive. And I wished they ran to whatever the whole will make because the darned thing is so interesting.

I spoke about maintenance of tension. You not only have carried it into the Gil-Elaine scene but it's just plain damned terrific from there on.

I'm wondering if you haven't done a pretty clever thing in incapacitating the Senator a bit. I mean in this way. So far Rod has not predominated the scene, and I think that is probably the way you wanted to bring him on, slowly and then with increasing stature. But, as Segundo, he couldn't very well be the big man so far as the Senator is concerned.

His coming encounter with Mayhew is very promising; the fact that without consulting anyone he is going to go in and call Mayhew to account. And I sort of hope you won't let Mayhew lick him, a la Luke Short. No, I don't think for a moment you will. Probably you'll have the thing interrupted, undecided, so the question will hang between them and make the reader even more anxious to read on.

You may not be much shucks as a fisherman, but I'll tell you in all seriousness, Tommy, you are doing one hell of a fine job here. I'm tickled pink over it. I can't recall many things I've read before that brings you closer to the feeling of close contact with Indians than this last section. Most every other writer merely says "Indians" and lets it go at that. Here you not only smell them but you also feel them for what they are.

I don't want to make you too cocky so you'll ease up at all on the rest, but I can't help mentioning the things that are really swell, just as I jump on you when you dangle a five inch thing and call it a fish.

This lack of confidence is understandable when one becomes aware of Tommy Thompson's background as revealed in a letter to my father.

*July 30, 1951—Tommy to Cap:*

It is now four AM of a Monday morning, my favorite time of the day, and I am out in the shed thinking seriously of you and of me and of the business we are in. Outside my window the dark blue redwood covered hills are just shaping up. There is a smell of dry grass and dew in the air, my coffee pot is steaming. Strange, but I am right back to those days in

Topanga Canyon when all I wanted in the world was a chance to write. It is hard to believe that so much water has gone under the dam; it is even harder to believe that I am better equipped than I was then, but I have deliberately piled a stack of magazines and novels here in front of me and I am trying to make myself realize that I did the work. One hundred seventy-five stories; three novels published, one in the works, a new one here on my desk ready to be polished up.

The new one, of course, is *The Girl From Philadelphia,* for I have decided to get in and clean that one up. But before starting it I wanted to take this time to go back through the files and read a couple dozen of your wonderful, oh so patient, letters. They are a constant inspiration and the finest course in writing a man could have. Which reminds me—. In your spare time why don't you write a book on writing?

Over my desk, just typed in caps and thumb tacked where I have to look at it all the time, is a summary of everything we have talked about—the three point requirements of a story.

I'm not modest, Cap. I'm a conceited poop, really, and I hate conceit. Sometimes I feel so damned confident—feel like I really have something on the ball. But I'm so afraid somebody will think I have the swell-head that I don't like to express my confidence. Well, I reckon you and I are good enough pals now that you would take me even with my faults.

So I'll tell you how I feel. I do think I've done pretty well in the past five years. Some of the boys who started when I did haven't done as well and I'm sorry for them. Also I'm damn anxious that they don't think I'm crowing over their grave, because that isn't so. I have a real concern for people; I love people (and sometimes I get too damned involved with people) but I dry up if I'm not around them. I find that people are more interesting than anyone.

But on to me—my favorite subject. There are times, it seems to me, when I have a real perception of human problems, and, after all, what the hell else is there to write about? The cows being stole and the dam being blown up is just so much who shot John unless John himself is concerned. Frankly—and I'm not complaining, I'm very, very grateful for it, in fact—I've seen a peck of trouble in my time. It not only seasons a man a bit, it mellows him to the point where you can see a bit of good in the worst. It has been said of me that I am "a man of great good will," or, as John Hawkins once put it, "if there are bastards in the world, Tommy never met one." Well that isn't entirely so, but I am more interested in finding out what makes a bastard than I am in the mere fact that he is one.

My father and mother were divorced when I was two years old. My mother had a little money which she spent in a couple of months of hell raising in San Francisco. Broke, she headed for the lumber camps just north of here in a logging camp. During that time, and until I started school, I had four or five "dads." It left my older brother and older sister pretty bitter. I was too young, and besides I can see how it could happen. War I over my mother married a guy by correspondence. He was a complete bastard. My brother left home at fourteen to work in the lumber camps; my sister married at sixteen in self defense. That marriage smashed, of course. She was left with a couple of kids. She married again and that smashed. My step-dad had only one claim to fame. He didn't work for thirty five years. We moved from place to place, dodging bill collectors, and when I was in the fourth grade we moved back into the high Sierras where we lived in a cabin with a dirt floor and cooked on an open fireplace. I had no shoes and used to wrap gunny sacks around my feet to walk in the snow. There was no school for me. In all I got in six years of grade school, but I got a diploma. We moved to the lowlands and I went to high school where I was very popular, vice president of the student body, editor of the school paper, all that. My step-dad thought that was fine. He started shipping fish in and I sold it to my school friends, house to house out of an old Willys Knight touring car. That was the only time I can remember being bitter. My step-dad went on one of his wild rages and tried to burn the house down. He had a can of kerosene in his hand, coming toward the house. I took a gun and shot the can out of his hand. He was surprised. Another time he took off after my mother with a butcher knife and as he came through the door I laid him out with a stick of stove wood. A man falls mighty hard.

So I left home—I was sixteen and after a little more than two years of high school I had my diploma. I had a dime in my pocket and the shirt on my back I got a job fighting forest fires near this area. I worked with a bunch of waterfront bums and as the fire would go out we would start another one. I'm not proud of it, but it was depression time and we were hungry. Then I got a job on a ship and went to sea and when I was in France my dad passed away and left me a thousand dollars. I came ashore in San Francisco, got taken and was broke, but I had paid up a year's tuition in a business college where I learned to type and started my first novel. (It didn't get finished and the world can be glad). I sang in night clubs to put myself through school, those dives where you went from table to table and sang for tips. An O'Farrel Street hooker got me the job and she was a wonderful gal, too.

In time I went to work for Heywood Wakefield Company as a male stenographer, $65.00 a month, was transferred to Los Angeles, met June on a blind date and proposed to her that night. In a short time I was the third highest salesman in the company, making $10,000 a year, which wasn't bad in those days. Had I stayed with the job—and they still tell me my job is waiting—I would now be assistant Pacific Coast manager at $25,000 a year. But I have no regrets and June and I have had a love affair that has lasted sixteen years and is still going strong. June's background is damn near as hectic as mine—her mother died when June was nine and June had to go to work doing housework to get what education she could.

None of this is intended to shock nor is it told with any bitterness. The step-dad is dead and I was the only one who went to see him, making a trip from Los Angeles to Oakland to tell the old boy so-long. He taught me a lot of things; he always respected me. He keeps wandering into a story every now and then and so do a lot of other people I knew.

Which maybe explains what you call my modesty or lack of confidence, Cap. It's a hell of a long way down there, Cap. I know. That's why the real estate manipulations. The one thing June and I prize above all else is security. So we chose a profession that has the least of it, I reckon, and it sometimes sets up quite a conflict. But damn it, I just couldn't do anything else if I wanted to. If there was just the two of us it might be different—though I'd rather die than have it just the two of us. There's Judy, who we adopted when she was three years old. She is June's niece and it was a case of not enough food in the house for everyone so we took one. Judy looks like June and has my personality and no one would ever believe she was adopted. She plays a piano beautifully and at fourteen is so refreshingly unsophisticated it makes me cry. The three of us, along with Meathead, have one hell of a time together. We under stand each other pretty darn well, I can tell you, and all three of us know what it means to scrape bottom.

Which brings us now to the present and the future. Cap, I do believe that I have reached the point where we can reach out for a few of the big ones. I hope *The Preacher* was a step in that direction—that it is at least one that could be shown to Meskill so that he would know we are thinking of him and working toward him. As far as selecting markets, that is your job. From here, though, it looks as if we would be ahead to concentrate on Meskill. By that I mean, if after a long spell of not show-ing him one we come up with one that is both a possibility for *Post* and for Meskill I would almost rather see it go to Bob to get those rates up where we want them. But, as I say, you know a lot more about that than I do. Funny thing, *Post* doesn't awe me the way it does some writers. Cosmo, on the other hand, is to me the highth of good reading—and I realize it will be hard to sell them a western.

Cap, I want to sell a *Post* serial. I want to sell American one novel a year and I want to sell them a couple of shorts. My *Post* serial will become a book, of course, and backing that up we'll do another book for Don Ward, maybe, or we'll blow up one of those American novels or one of those Country Gentleman short serials, so we'll have a couple of books a year. Of course, we want to give dear old Mike a Frosty and Brownie and a

Windy McCloud now and then and we can always be darned proud to be seen in *Zane Grey's Western*. I wish I could be a little more confident and a little more ambitious, but that's the way I am. Conservative as hell.

At five AM in the morning, all alone in my little shack and now it's getting red in the east and the prune trees in the orchard outside my window are taking shape. Beautifully clear this morning; usually the fog comes in from the beach during the night, cooling things off. We are twenty miles from the ocean by road, about sixteen as the crow flies. Like the Preacher says, "It's a hell of a big world, ain't it?" Let's open it up, you and me.

It was good talking to you, Cap. I've been wanting to for some time. Now you talk back, and believe me, you've never had anyone who would listen more closely.

## August 2, 1951—Cap to Tommy:

You and I are sure psychic, or mutuo-telepathic.

But first let me tell you I've scarcely ever received such a wonderful letter and such a compliment for its confidence. What moved you to let me share your thoughts, Tommy, at such an hour when the mind is clear and untrammeled by the considerations of every day, I do not know, but I welcome it much more than I can tell you.

As I see it, the game is to make of yourself the best you can, and the greater the handicaps a fellow comes through to his accomplishment, the greater the praise to him. And you win all the accolade.

You have moments, of course, when you deeply regret all those early stages you came through, but let me tell you it has endowed you with a rare wealth of understanding and not underestimating human kind.

And everything you have told me fits into the pattern of the serious and ambitious plan I have for you. I mentioned it nebulously, but you must have thought out what was behind it and you have come up with exactly what was needed to help put it into shape—your firm, first-hand, intimate knowledge of the vagaries in human character and human behavior.

Now, Clarkson Potter and I had quite a session over you. I didn't want to go into it with you until the *Girl From Philadelphia*—retitled *Something Else*—was in shape in your mind if not on paper. Young Potter is a keen thinking chap and is backed by Karen, a bright mind now elevated to the editorial council of Doubleday. It may be Karen's thought—she's a modest gal—or Potter's. At any rate, he brought forward what I have long thought for you when the time was right.

We conclude that your skill is too great, your thought too deep for the restricted field of Westerns. We want one of your next works to be a novel, a novel of human relations. You have too much to tell, and the skill now to tell it.

Now do you see how every word you have told me fits into this? This will take lots of thought, lots of conjecturing, possibly some trial and error. But that's the idea, Tommy. Just where we will make a beginning, I do not at the moment know. You will have to come most largely into that. Its theme may be what I've referred to as the game. It should have pin-point focus, and what you have done in *The Preacher* shows we don't have to worry about that. Another thing will be to decide on the vehicle of the story, and here I would say don't choose it outside of the knowledge and familiarity you have demonstrated in the details of your letter.

The same would apply to the characters. Your attitude toward it will be your attitude toward life and fellowmen. An attitude that shows no criticism; the goodness of your nature. It will be a simple story, rich in its simplicity, simply told, understandable by everyone. It can't be hurried, although once you have the idea, your inspiration will rush it through. Yet it will take time to complete.

Meanwhile, we'll do one for Meskill, for the *Post*, in the Western field. One for Mike, or more; for Don Ward; so that the novel will have a chance to grow on you. In *The Preacher*, you get "A" in all three counts, plus the guts and feeling. And this was written after Clark and I had our little talk.

This is ambitious, Tommy; as great an ambition as you have dreamed up for yourself. I feel a sense of humility should go along with a great ambition; a feeling that you have the means and ability to do a service to others and that is what this will be. And you have that humility which has nothing to do with confidence or lack of confidence. On the contrary, it is knowledge that you have the means.

And now we'll be practical about it. Also we'll earn our way to it. Short stories, novelettes, a serial, that will have good work in all of them and make the weightier task easier.

I've given you lots to think of, Tommy, but we'll take it in our stride.

Tommy Thompson depended on the support provided by my father, respected him deeply as an agent and a gentleman, and often expressed his gratitude for my father's influence on his work. Tommy Thompson was an apt pupil responding quickly to suggestions made, and seriously attempting to master the elements of writing to which my father exposed him. The ebb and flow between author and agent was impressive. The frequency of letters over the years, their length and depth were inspiring, especially in view of the fact that the two men had never met personally nor had they shared more than a handful of telephone calls over the years.

AS INDICATED earlier, my father worked with a group of any where from twelve to twenty authors, most of whom were in the upper echelons of writing ability in their respective fields. He treated each writer individually and the problems of each as unique; however, he was absolutely consistent in emphasizing those elements that were essential to good story telling, i.e., the role of narrative as opposed to dialogue, and character building as the driving force dictating the plot. He also declared that critical to character development was the effective use of dialogue, not just the spoken word but communication through movement and action that functioned in the absence of unspoken words.

Unfortunately, by selectively citing some letters while ignoring others does not do justice to the entire body of expressed words, thoughts and emotions between teacher and student. Further, the preponderance of the correspondence is of the action-reaction type; however, insightful nuggets of wisdom, instruction, and expressions of warmth and gratitude abound.

In a letter dated January 13, 1949, my father set the stage with Tommy as to his expectations from Tommy with respect to character development. Subsequent correspondence over the course of the next three and a half years further defined and reinforced this basic theme, and the subtleties involved. In this letter, my father addressed Tommy's struggle to portray the character traits of the hero in his story the *Lost River,* a story being developed for magazine serialization and then to be consolidated into hardcover, book format:

> Our frontier West, our traditional West, demonstrated a unique character of terrific impact when one gets its full effect. I do not say that it produced that unique character even though it is now indelibly associated with that locale and period. For example, I have seen on the streets of Prague, Czechoslovakia, a man who in looks, carriage, appearance, bearing, could have immediately stepped from a group of Remington's. And you know how faithfully he reproduced, in appearance and bearing, that typically unique character. The clothes did not matter a damn. It was the man, the personality, that was unmistakable. I saw the same thing in Chicago, and it wasn't his Stetson, his mincing high-heeled, springy step, his gear. It was again the personality that looked forth from his bearing. That's all surface, video.
>
> I'll give you roughly my impression of his character and then how he is most effectively reproduced through the written word: First and above everything else a reticent guy. You can't tell a damn thing about him except by summing up what he himself does. You don't know him at all

until he himself does something. You don't know if he will face danger until you see him do it. You don't know if he is ambitious or content with what he finds, until he shows you. He is sensitive, easily hurt in his pride of his personality. When you think of it, he is the acme type of individual freedom. He is a respecter of other people, and he demands that respect for himself and would die in defending it.

We have looked (1) at his appearance and bearing and (2) his manner of showing what he is only through his action. He does not tell you a fact outright. He leaves it to you to tag the truth correctly. And he doesn't show that he gives a damn if you do or don't. There you have a rough, crude portrait of the type, the character, the man, the only sort that has made a story of the West outstanding. And those writers, a very few, who have succeeded in giving a faithful portrayal of this character stand out above all the rest. Their works alone will live, along with the art of Remington.

I think the foregoing expresses, in a way, how those few writers have achieved a faithful portrayal, and it follows right along with what we've been discussing recently. They permit the character to portray himself.

## And Tommy's response in a letter dated January 17, 1949:

I've read and re-read your letter of January 13, trying to give it the careful evaluation it deserves. I'm quite sure I got the point you were making and it has started me on a line of thinking that will eventually break down some of my difficulties, I know.

In the first place, here is the main thing I got from the letter. For some time now I have had the feeling that writing—just the mere stringing together of words—was not the thing standing in my way. The trouble has been, and continues to be, story. I've felt that I have never hit a story that was big enough. There's been a lack of importance, the missing of "the broad canvas," or perhaps a lack of epic sweep. I've been so completely aware of this that until you letter arrived I'm afraid I couldn't see the forest for the trees. Every time I considered a story my first worry was how to make it big. I thought of railroads smashing across the trackless empire; hordes of Indians; millions of buffalo; billions of acres of land. The big canvas—. Now suddenly, after reading your letter, I've come to the conclusion that that is a back door approach to the problem. The character that you have set up, I believe, is the epic in himself. Properly developed, his character becomes so all important that anything he does becomes the epic thereby. I've thought a lot about *The Virginian*—. In that book there is no struggle of empire, no clash of hundreds of armed men against thousands of blood letting Apaches. And yet the book still stands as a western "epic," and the only reason it does is because of the epic proportions of the character himself. Now that to me is the point of your letter as I see it, and I sincerely hope that that is the point you wanted me to see.

The character I am now attempting to develop is a composite of all the things that made the west great. He, in himself, is the western epic. He is the expanse of the land, the struggle for survival, the bad, the good, the conflict of society against nature, the wind swept freedom that comes to a man who knows he is great. He does not have to tell anyone that he is great, nor does he have to deny it. He himself, is the big canvas.

### *June 9, 1949—Cap to Tommy:*

There's a thing I've noted in some of your dialogue and if it's a tendency I want to get it to your notice immediately. In effect, that dialogue should be self-sufficient, should be qualified to convey all essential meaning and impression. If the spoken words were modified by author's explanation of why they were said, what they were intended to express and the effect, the dialogue would also be the author's own admission that it was insufficient and needed his bolstering.

Good dialogue needs no interpretation. Neither should action, for, like dialogue, action expresses a man's character.

## July 24, 1949—Cap to Tommy:

Here's something I've learned recently, or at least I've not given it top rating in the various points we've been stressing. And that is, it is dangerous to ignore any single character in a big story like *Lost River* or any book length. Perhaps I can put it this way; every actor should be perfect for his role whether that role is big or very small. This came to me in a certain work where the main actors were right but certain supporting ones were neglected. Also there were one or two, having the possibility for more important contribution were overlooked.

## July 27, 1949—Tommy to Cap:

I hope this is clear, Cap—as clear, that is, as it is to me at this point. Keep in mind that I fully expect to do some heavy re-casting of material when the entire thing is finished. The thing I want to accomplish in the first draft is a "feeling" for the people. After that, we can make them do the things that will bring off the story, I think. The "plot" part is a bit of mechanics that should be put in and made secondary to the characters, for it has to grow out of the characters. Stop me if I'm wrong.

## August 4, 1949—Cap to Tommy:

Rod should be the instigator and manipulator of every move or action. If not, he doesn't rate the chief role and you have lost your one holding thread of interest. Please consider this carefully, Tommy. I assure you it is most important. You must tell all of the story you possibly can through the hero's eyes.

Recently I had a major disappointment—and the author too of course—where the *Post* came down on exactly this thing; the hero just stood back and other characters divided his role. We don't want that to happen to *Lost River*. But just now you are headed that way and the letter of the 2nd goes even further in that direction. I think that sums up my objection to changed viewpoints; where they detract from the hero's importance I would avoid them like poison. Where those parts of the story can be told through the hero, I'd let him do it. Any story has importance ONLY as it is important to the hero.

### August 10, 1949—Cap to Tommy:

Your background theme, as you plan it now, sounds very good. The harder and tougher the fight, the more he grows. And that's the whole story; a matter of character developing. Yes; the Senator's partner, and bigger and stronger in his way. Rod is the lead actor. Even the Senator, secondary and supporting in the cast. I don't think I have to add more just now, but let me know.

### August 25, 1949—Tommy to Cap:

And here's a funny thing. Just last night June and I were talking about story heroes in connection with our friend Rod Buckley. I said, "I spent learning how to sell furniture and I've suddenly come to the conclusion that writing a story is a bit of salesmanship. You don't go into a store and say: You don't want anything today, do you? You walk in there and you are completely positive about everything you do and say. When you write a story you are 'selling' the hero, and the same rules should apply. You don't use a negative approach. You've got a big piece of merchandise—a good one—and you are positive about it. You get in there and you sell him every inch of the way. The incidental characters are devices you use to show your pet pieces of merchandise to the best advantage—." The idea intrigued me, and although it may be poorly put, I think you know what I mean and what I am beginning to see.

To me, Danny in the *Price of Bananas* story was not a negative character. So if he was not to me, why does he appear so to the editor? Simply because I did a NEGATIVE job of selling instead of a POSITIVE job. The same things apply to Rod Buckley in *Lost River*.

Funny how all these things start to fall in place, one by one. One of these times we're going to turn out a story where I remember to put all these things into their proper place and we're going to have something. You know, I'm beginning to have fun.

## August 31, 1949—Cap to Tommy:

However, I find quite a few interpolated explanations after dialogue and some long explanatory pages, and I would like to weigh these pretty carefully. I have made a few marginal notes, very lightly so that they can be easily erased but it seems the best way to call points to your attention for you to pass on.

The overall trouble, I find with subjective treatment is that, while it is an easy way to convey the reason for a man's stand or action, it makes you study him less intently—as you would if it were more objective—hence the result is you don't begin to know him so well as if you had to reason out yourself why he said this or that or did this or that. But it is a pretty sound rule that interpolated explanations after dialogue are both an admission that the dialogue is inadequate and that the author is taking a shortcut to make plain the effect.

If you follow the objective, it is well to keep in mind what Hammett once said to me about it. "There are no short cuts in objective treatment." He knew that and stuck to it, and I believe that is why his work hits with such impact. You know he hasn't taken the easy way to get it across to you.

It's a great story, Tommy, and it's coming fine.

## September 14, 1949—Tommy to Cap:

Just received your long and carefully thought out letter on *Lost River*.

I'm glad the suggestions were not given didactically—. That's a hell of a good word. Had to look it up though—. At first glance I figured you wanted me to start with Page one and write it over, but on more somber reflection I can see that it is not that.

Rest assured I'll consider all angles carefully and do everything I can to build Rod. But at the moment I can't see changing the "story line" much.

## September 15, 1949, morning—Tommy to Cap:

I didn't sleep a wink last night, thinking about *Lost River*, so at five this morning I came down to the office and I've been sitting here in complete quiet thinking it over. I'm afraid I did just what you asked me not to do in your letter—that is, I made a snap decision in the heat of keen disappointment. When I received your letter I felt as if the whole damn story had crashed around my ears. I wanted it to be perfect. It's not, so leave us face it and take it from there.

In the first place, your criticism of Rod is a hundred percent justified. He's not the man he should be or you wouldn't be worried about him— nor would I. And after sober consideration, I am worried about him. But, and this is what scares hell out of me at the moment, can we fix him by patching him up? I rather doubt it. He would always be a vulcanized inner tube at best, I fear. I see the guy; I believe in him; I think he is perfectly capable of doing the things you want him to do. So why don't you see it the way I do? Simply because I haven't given the guy a job—a job big enough to bring out the best in him, with you, the reader, sitting on the side lines watching him do it. So if that's so, Cap, it isn't the fault of the writing or of Rod. It's the fault of the story conception.

## September 15, 1949, afternoon—Tommy to Cap:

The more I think of building Rod up by making him the power behind the Senator, the way you suggested, the better I like it. However, we don't want to do it by patching up a few spots here and there. I think we should give a very careful evaluation to both the Senator and Rod and that can't be done on the spur of the moment.

### September 19, 1949—Cap to Tommy:

I don't know when anything has pleased me more than your two letters which I found at Scarsdale on my arrival last evening. It's this way, Tommy. I have great regard for your writing, but you are too damned honest in your thinking to do your best in something in which you cannot believe in, and I want your best. That is why my immediate reply was to do him as you see him even against my own conviction that a more important Rod would make a more effective story. I wouldn't for a moment want you to do a thing a certain way on just my say-so. You have to believe in it yourself.

Now that you do tend toward the same impression, it will be easy sailing. And I don't visualize too much trouble by a damn sight. You will be surprised to see what a few significant insertions will accomplish in the impression created. Nor do I think you have to tear the Senator down in order to build up Rod.

### September 27, 1949—Tommy to Cap:

But best of all, I just this minute finished *Lost River* and I am tickled to death that you suggested the re-work. It makes all the difference in the world, Cap, and I just know you're going to be pleased with it. Rod Buckley is the real he-coon, all the way, and he's still a long ways from being a superman. So help me, pal, it's the best damn job of rewriting I ever did, and you were sure right when you said it would be fun. And I've just run plum out of words to express my appreciation to you. All I can say is thanks a million for a swell time.

*October 1, 1949—Tommy to Cap:*

Sure I feel good. My brow is wet with honest sweat and I owe everybody—. No, seriously, I feel I did an honest job of work—whether it's right or wrong, I did the best I knew how. And I learned so damn much, thanks to you, and it's going to keep showing up in everything we do from now on. Why shouldn't I feel good? And wait until you see this novelette I'm doing for Mike (or one of the others). You'll see the work on *Lost River* showing up in every line, I think.

Tommy's growth as an author is clearly visible; however, even two years later the pushing and pulling between teacher and student continued to persist as it pertained to character development. In the following notes, the primary story under consideration was *Shadow of the Butte.*

*August 17, 1951—Cap to Tommy:*

Hell, Tommy, I'm learning more in working these things out with you than you yourself. I've come to know that certain things are right. Such as, where interest in character and character's part and outcome is greater than interest in the story itself, you've got something for the best of them. Where story submerges character interest, might as well knock off and go feed the chickens.

*August 27, 1951—Tommy to Cap:*

Which brings us right back to where we always wind up. Character. And I think you said a mouthful when you said the character part should actually submerge the story. That is why (when a guy is looking for excuses for his own stuff) it is so easy to say, "My gosh, that's the stalest story in the world." Well, maybe it is if you take it all apart and expose its bones. But it is the handling and the characters that are the important things. The bones, I am beginning to discover, are all about the same.

But the important thing is, the story always has people in it. Wonderful, real, sympathetic people. The "plot" never changes. The people actually do. Or at least, which is just as good, the reader gets the impression they are fresh and different. Ah me. Not too much to it, really. Funny how it takes a man yars and yars to be able to do it. But we'll do her!! And I ain't the least bit ashamed of all the work that's gone into *Shadow of the Butte*. I think it shows.

## *August 30, 1951—Cap to Tommy:*

So you gone and done it. *Shadow of the Butte* runs like oil. Also, it has a depth, spread and scope in human feeling greater than you have produced before. If I were to criticize, I would have liked a little less narrative treatment, yet the tension, the intensity of feeling and situation goes a long way to offset that.

I must add a further word on *Shadow*. It is this. In forming your own opinion of others in real life, you do not take that of another person to make your own judgment. And I believe this is the soundest principle in writing and you have done this excellently with Ellen who, despite the opinion of everyone close around her, forms her own judgment of Rombeck from what he shows her of himself. Well done, Tommy.

## *September 4, 1951—Cap to Tommy:*

Tommy, there is more in this new book [*Shadow of the Butte*] than a smooth story. In fact, there is in it considerable of what both Potter and I are confident you can put into a novelette. It's odd, but I do not think this is a story for the ordinary Western reader. Plot and action are at a minimum. The whole quality of the book lies in the progressive demonstration of the two characters and Ellen's reluctant but steadily growing realization and appreciation of Hank's character. I am awfully proud of it, Tommy.

## *November 16, 1951—Tommy to Cap:*

You give me the willies. Reading my mind, I mean. The mail just came and caught me taking time out from a western novelette to just peek at *Caine Mutiny.* Damn it, I can't leave it alone!

I have never in my life been so impressed by a book and I have never in my life met such terrific characters. Do you realize that this guy Wouk never resorts to profanity and yet has the saltiest bunch of dirty talking cussers ever assembled in the crew of the original *Caine?* And the underplayed seduction scene between May and Willie at Yosemite, ending with the line, "But the deed was done." I have never had so many belly laughs and yet it is a serious book. So help me this guy is a genius.

Those are little things. His characters living through self expression I caught quick. Little bits of dialog, little tags, little human failings in all of them. The original captain—DeVreis—for example. What a hell of a swell guy and yet Willie couldn't stomach him. And what a swell bit of constant characterization that sets up for both of them. This is a book.

## *December 20, 1951—Cap to Tommy:*

Still, as far as you have gone, it is far and away beyond the figures of earlier days, taking its place along with Hamp and Ellen and the Preacher [from the story entitled *The Preacher*]. It shows that you are now definitely on that plane where you search for the mind which inspires the various acts and speech, rather than scheming them and then attributing them to the several characters.

And you can put it in your book, Tommy, that this sets you among the top flight authors no matter what is produced. I've checked with Mike on this story, saying nothing whatever of what I had written you, and find that his opinion is exactly the same, and he greatly applauds what he calls a tremendous advance in character expression over all the work you did for him.

If the next *American* novelette is going to be the embryonic novel, that will take time. But if you want a sooner shot at *American,* and Bob wants you to make it, a short would be good or a novelette that's not a Western and not the novel. A story of human conflict and emotion is where you find it. Just set it where character and background are familiar to you.

### February 5, 1952—Cap to Tommy:

The older writers, those who had attained "names" in the field, either cannot or won't deliver the stuff that is most wanted today; the character predominant sort. They worked and made their successes at the time when the majority of editors consider story as everything. Now more and more of the editors are coming to realize that all story interest is derived solely from the interest in the characters, the personalities involved. That's our slogan; what our crowd has been trained to do. And the old-time name writers are just not doing it.

### March 28, 1952—Cap to Tommy:

A writer who did very well in pulps, has now a book in hardcovers with a call for two more. I've got him to do pretty well in character expression, but his whole attitude toward the aim of the story was from the wrong slant. He was trying *directly* to impress the reader; to shock him with some success; to show him a lot of people doing things to each other. That is wrong; the pulp way; the newspaper way.

Your true purpose, as an author, is to impress your characters. You cannot control the impression of a reader. You can control the impression wrought on a character because he is entirely in your hands. You can make him interested; you can make him feel. But first you must regard him as a real human person capable of interest, of feeling and emotion.

No one can possibly draw more interest and feeling from a story than the author puts into it.

That interest and feeling are shown and measured entirely by their presence in the minds and hearts of the characters in the story. Unless the characters show their interest and reflect the emotion they feel, there is utterly no interest and feeling that a reader can draw from the story.

With respect to plot, my father stayed close to his authors as their stories were being developed. He not only served as a sounding board for each story, but also offered broad guidance and words of wisdom.

*September 24, 1951—Cap to Tommy:*

You know, Tommy, I've had a lot of interest in tracing the various steps to the best work you have done to date; the masterly development of "character" and attitude change in *Shadow of the Butte,* the result of a hell a lot of sweating, of dissatisfaction from time to time in its progress; the whittling down to novelette length so that the real values in the story stood starkly clear before you, and their retention to the exclusion of a lot of movement, side gestures and so on to the final conclusion. I think it would help to solidify your own recognition of the true course of any story if you would retrace these steps yourself. It exemplifies what we have spoken about before.

Let me repeat some of these points:

A single, easily understood thread of a story throughout.

A recognition that any long story should have one main achievement or conclusion and that everything in the story should be a build-up toward that conclusion. That is, the accomplishment of the underlying theme, in this instance the realization of the true values in the West and a Western reared character by another character alien by environment and association.

I wish you would assure me that you understand this fully. It is a major accomplishment whether or not you realize it. So many stories have been spoiled by too much plotting, too many incidents that in some instances lead away from the single track, as this did in its first long version; such as the over-emphasis of Hank's sister Sue's intrigue with the lawyer. In *Shadow,* all these side matters were directed solely to the development of the theme. I want you to understand it so that it will be the pattern for all your future work.

## *November 12, 1951—Cap to Tommy:*

It is going to take time and a lot off and on thinking on your part to assemble a plan that seems right to you. And in this process, I suggest you do what a famous teacher advised. If you suggested some thought to him, he would always demand that you write it out for him to see. He held that in no other way could you get it so clear in your own mind. So, as you think along, why don't you jot this or that down, for yourself, until it shapes up into something you would like to put up to us.

## *December 17, 1951—Cap to Tommy:*

You and I have learned and know, Tommy, that both beauty and strength are to be found in the simplest and most familiar things in life…. It is only because you have attained this high level of skill and understanding that you are now qualified to return to the simple and familiar and wring from them the true values which all people immediately recognize and still are always amazed at their source. Think how diamonds appear when first found. Back to your strength in simplicity now. The biggest thoughts, the noblest purposes come from that source, as well as their true effectiveness.

Frustratingly, yet predictably, Tommy's bouts with being disappointed and then discouraged came frequently. In many respects he was his own worst enemy. He was an extremely talented author who only periodically realized his strengths. Perhaps the growth and maturation process between the two is best embodied in the partial text of the next pair of letters.

*October 10, 1951—Tommy to Cap:*

You ask about my thoughts. I am very glad for you, Cap, that you can't know them. They are very dark these past few weeks. Just a passing spell, I'm sure, but, I have never been so discouraged, so completely unsure of myself. I have read *Post* until I am black in the face and I can't seem to learn anything. I have gone back and read half the pulps I have written and I wish to God I could write half as good as I used to write. I have also decided that if I try to stick to westerns I am going to starve to death sooner or later and I haven't got what it takes to write modern stories, so where do I go from here?

*October 16, 1951—Cap to Tommy:*

Yes, sir, that last thing I would expect to hear is that T.T. has been having a spell of the dumps. No, sir, that I cannot understand a-tall. Gee whiz, I would think that the mere thought of work in this field, with the masterly touch you have acquired, would fill your ardent soul with pure joy. Pretty poetic, that. But what the hell, Tommy. You are no blunderer with unfamiliar tools. The fields to be cultivated are wide open for you. You have discarded the hoe for a motored tractor, and you got plenty gas. You are now in the upper reaches of the Western which will always hold its place. You are no longer digging trenches in the common Western which has served its time. Who the hell said you should put the bigger Western behind you? Not I; not Clarkson Potter; not June or Meathead. And I'll wager you a little bet right now, solely on my own opinion; that the not-to-be-mentioned-again *Shadow of the Butte* will bring us movie money and take the blinders from your doubting eyes.

And I'm taking time off to set off a little T.N.T. under our Hollywood friends, if they need it. Anyway they are going to get it. So, to work, Tommy, me lad, or should I say doubting Thomas.

These few pages show only a fleeting glimpse of a good and caring man, a compassionate and responsible friend, and a very capable author; however, he did need the constant presence of a father figure to lean on. In spite of these emotional set backs and momentary work stoppages, Tommy never turned his back on his writing career. Further, my father's exhortations were starting to bear fruit. Tommy finally was able to step back and acknowledge his strengths and weaknesses and use the resulting conclusions to lay his plans for the future.

*December 31, 1951—Tommy to Cap:*

And now to more disagreeable things. In the first place, let me hasten to assure you that there was no disappointment whatsoever in having "Three Riders From Texas" go to Mike Tilden. My only concern at all was that you would not show it any place and I did feel rather strongly that Mike would take it. My hope was that Don Ward might take it, simply because there was a little more money involved. But never once did I consider you showing it higher up the ladder. It was an experimental piece of work from the first and I believe in a letter before I sent the mss in that it was a 'queer' one. However, it was one of those ideas that come along now and then and need to be worked out. It was a struggle; it took much more time than it was worth from a dollar and cents standpoint, and yet, to me, it was time well spent, and I see by your letter of Dec. 20th that you are inclined to agree with this theory. Your criticism—and praise—of the story is very clear. I appreciate it and agree with it fully.

Which, I think, brings us to the big problem now at hand. I see very little use in looking over the past year, which, to me, has been a disappointment in one respect only. And that is that I did not produce enough. There is no one to blame for this but myself, and I might as well admit that the past three months have been very hectic ones for me. Poor old Giff Cheshire now and then used to say he was in a "soul state." I guess that's what's the matter with me. I've been in a "soul state," what the hell ever that is!

Oh I've manufactured all sorts of excuses for myself. There was the nearly three months period which I deliberately took off to buy and sell houses. And then there is the past three weeks in which June and I both have been laid pretty low with the flu bug. But there is still quite a gap in between, Cap, and damn little production to show for it. That is bad and has worried me no end.

Let's take a look at what's happened and then see if there isn't some way out of the woods.

During this period there has been a definite fight against the typewriter. I would write two or three pages and suddenly be physically and mentally tired. The next morning I would get up bright and early, fired with ambition, go down and look at the two pages, edit them for a couple of hours, then throw them away and start over and this way complete as much as three pages. It seems to me that I have made every excuse to stay away from the typewriter. I doubt that this is plain laziness. Actually I feel at my very best when I am working hard. Long hours give me a lift. The actual typing of *Shadow of the Butte*, for example. I would be at work by six in the morning and I would work straight through until perhaps four in the afternoon and just be bustling with energy. And now, suddenly, I find a period where I am doing absolutely nothing and I feel physically beaten. I do not think there is anything organically wrong with me. I know myself too well for that. I believe, without asking any doctor or any one else, just being honest with myself, that I have had about three months of complete nervous exhaustion.

Now why and what brought this on, and most important, what to do about it? Perhaps the moving, the rather hectic summer had a lot to do with it. But I think more than that I felt an actual guilt toward the very thing you mention on the second page of your letter. Advantage stages. Definitely there should have been a fast follow-up after the *Philadelphia Girl;* perhaps too after *Shadow of the Butte;* and perhaps it's not too late to take advantage of *The Preacher.*

So why didn't I do it? I've gone carefully back through your letters and mine, checking the dates, and I think here's what I've found. And when laid out and looked at this way it looks very silly, so perhaps it won't be too hard to whip.

*The Girl from Philadelphia* was my first major sale. I know a lot of writers. I've seen many of them make an accidental slick sale and suddenly decide they were slick writers, too good to write pulp anymore. I believe right at that point I was pretty much obsessed with that idea. So I forced myself to prove that I could still do pulp and like it. Actually, perhaps, I should have taken advantage of the wind-fall and let Pegasus fly a bit.

*Shadow of the Butte*—we immediately started talking about a serious novel, which is still the most exciting thing of all to me. But, I am not so constructed, unfortunately, that I could immediately pick a subject out of the air and sit down and write a serious novel and have it in within a month or so. We did, however, follow immediately with *The Preacher.* So why didn't I come back with another as good as *The Preacher?*

Here's what happened there, and I am certainly not blaming you. I am blaming myself. But you will find, I think, that there is where Mike needed a novelette; Don Ward needed this; Mike needed that; Don Ward wanted *Loudmouth Jones.* All right, I have given Mike his novelette; three of them, in fact. And I am trying hard to give Don Ward his *Loudmouth Jones.* And the sad, sad, truth is that I want to write *Loudmouth Jones* just about like I want a hole in the head. I'll admit the first *Loudmouth Jones* story was a good one, but I do not share Don's enthusiasm for that Loudmouth gentleman. But, Don has been exceptional nice to us; I like nice people. And I feel sincerely that I owe Don Ward a lot. So for three solid weeks I have been battling with *Loudmouth Jones* and I am now on page five.

Now this, Cap, has got to stop and damn well soon. Not just for my precious peace of mind but for my precious pocket book and for yours as well. Something here somewhere has gone off the trolley. Something is wrong and we can't continue this way. I have to turn out more copy. Oh of course I can find excuses of some sort, I suppose. I am working so slowly and carefully so I will do so much finer work. That is the easiest excuse to use. But that too, Cap, can reach a point where it a bunch of damn poppy-cock. I am reminded of when I had my office next to Don James in Portland. Actually Don used to drive me nuts because every time I saw him in the elevator he was mailing another story while I was laboring away on the same one. I consoled myself with the fact that the ones I wrote sold for perhaps a higher rate than Don was selling and perhaps none of Don's sold at all. I believe one Thomas Thompson has now reached the silly stage.

I'm trying to bare my soul here, Cap, because I don't like what's happening to one of your clients. The main thing is to find a solution. And I suppose the first step is determination. And let's say I have that. But that by itself is about like sitting down and writing out a bunch of New Year's resolutions. I had determination last year, and, although it was a satisfactory year in many respects and did show advancement, I'm sure, it does leave me with this great sense of guilt that I could have done so much more had I only applied my efforts in the right direction and used my time to full advantage. So there'll have to be a sort of a plan beyond that and yet you and I have seen time and again that working to a fixed pattern is perhaps the worst thing I can do.

I've given this a lot of thought, Cap, because it's a very serious thing with me and with you and with the future. Going back to when I first started full time writing—first went with you. There was a terrific enthusiasm there. I was literally kicking ideas out of the way, there were so many of them. And every idea I got was a fresh idea. Going back beyond that to the short time I was with Gus Lenniger. I wrote stories like mad. He sold three or four, one of which was a nice little marriage problem story which went to *Every Woman*. But Gus—for whom I have nothing but the highest regards—was not my agent. Every time I got a letter from him I felt like sitting down and blowing my brains out. He was beating me into a pattern and I wasn't ready to be beaten into any pattern. So in time I came with you and from the very first your suggestions and criticisms have been exactly what I've wanted and what I've needed. It has been a wonderful experience working with you and even though I've kicked and howled a bit along the way I've enjoyed the hoeing.

Now here, Cap, is what I think, and I do not think this because you are trying to force me into any pattern that doesn't suit me. But it is the way I sincerely feel. I may be entirely wrong, but I want you to know about it. I believe the time has come when I need that original freedom of expression that just seems to charge a man with fire and vitality. By that I mean simply that for the next few months I think I should write, to a great extent, just about what I damn well please. I'll do some for Mike and I'll do some for Don and I'll do some western shorts with the hope they hit Bob Meskill and Erd Brandt. But I'm also damn well apt to do a story about two kids singing their hearts out in a night club; or a young wife worried because her college GI husband is taking too long taking the baby sitter home. I think I could write them with that old speed— that old enthusiasm. But I'm not fooling myself, Cap. Half or two thirds or maybe all of them will be duds. But the time has come, I think, when I've got to fire a few duds and you and I together will maybe figure out how to put the primer in a couple of them. But let's don't, damn it, saddle ourselves with "two novelettes and a short for Don" each and every month before we can cut loose "into the blue" as my Danish neighbor puts it. I'm going to have to go into free wheeling for a couple of months, I think. Maybe I'm nuttier than a fruit cake. And if you think I'm going "arty" on you I'll come back there and make you eat oyster shells. I'm hoping, Cap, that this is what you meant by trial and error, and I think very probably that it is.

Now, let's go one step further, and that's the matter of Clark Potter. I want you to assure me—and it is probably silly for me to even ask—but I want you to assure me that Clark Potter is still anxious to receive WESTERN novels from me. I would like very much to have a couple of western books in the mill each year for the next two or three years. That would be my backlog. You know and I know that nobody is making it entirely on shorts for the big boys. Now you know as well as I do that those western novels will be an attempt at *Post* serials. You know as well as I do that I will try to equal *Shadow of the Butte* or better it. And you know better than I do that a writer doesn't always hit the target. Maybe one, two or three of them won't be as good as we want them to be. Maybe they will be like *Gunman Brand.* But I'd like to know that an honest, sincere attempt, the best I can do at the time, will always be welcome. And should there be some flaws I won't be penalized just because my advance is higher than someone else's advance and just because I once wrote an exceptionally good western novel.

Putting this down on paper it almost sound silly, but I think, Cap, that by now you know me well enough that you see that a thing like this can form almost a mental bloc. With a little more freedom of thought and freedom of expression I think you and Potter will find that the serious novel will come along much sooner than you expect. For the time being, let's forget it completely, because if we don't it will continue to get into the way. For example—the novelette for Meskill with a modern setting. You and I both thought of it immediately as part of the "novel." Approaching it form that standpoint don't you see how I am immediately limited? Of course you do see it, because in your letter of Dec. 20 you have suggested that the novelette for Meskill not be a part of the novel at all. Which I should have had brains enough to see in the first place. But I didn't.

I've dictated this letter, Cap, and I've been sitting here and talking for quite a while. But then, when you meet me, you'll be surprised at the volume of guff that pours forth from me in a rather steady stream. I wish you could have been here today across the desk to argue back with me once in awhile. I hope that this is not too clobbered. I don't believe it is. You and I seem to have that rare faculty of understanding each other pretty thoroughly. There are a few things about myself, Cap, that I don't like worth a damn. I'm a little touchy, a little over sensitive, a little over sentimental. Sometimes I'm quite sure that the entire world is against me. Nobody loves me. I'm going out in the garden and eat worms. But fortunately, a day or so later I can sit back and look back at the other self and have a dog gone good belly laugh at his expense. These things, these quirks of disposition, go back a long ways as I'm sure you understand. I do often think that these very things that I dislike in myself are the things that made me want to be a writer in the first place. And I do believe that if I can ever free my ideas—get them out on paper—these shades of personality which so often seem to be weaknesses are the very things that will make me perhaps a better than average writer.

I hope so, and I know that you do. A whale of a Happy New Year to you, Cap. Dog gone it, I know as well as you do that we can do it in 1952. So what's holding us up? Well, after getting all this off my chest I doubt seriously if there is much of anything holding us up. Let's hear what you think.

### January 1, 1952—Cap to Tommy:

Been thinking of you a lot and wishing you all a happy and prosperous New Year. Also been thinking of all the various phases and vagaries of work of you and all our associates. Seems to me I'm becoming a sort of combination of (1) so-called agent, (2) an exchange of information, tips and what have you, plus (3) an attempt at an efficiency expert.

Is essentially is my job.

In dealing with each separate work of each writer something new is bound to come up that might apply to another's problem, and I try to see where this new bit would fit in.

Automatically the writers arrange themselves on different levels of progress, and that has to be taken into consideration so that a suggestion may not precede too much their respective stages of advance. These stages are (a) degree of understanding; (b) ability to utilize that understanding effectively.

Now, I rate you as close to tops in (a) and (b). At the moment I can think of only one more thought to give you that, with your own grasp and execution will mean absolute tops.

Let's review for a moment. Although your financial returns for the past year were regrettably less than for the preceding period, due most largely to causes that had nothing to do with writing, you have advanced immeasurably over any other similar period. You have come to complete understanding of the essential values and have acquired the ability to apply them effectively.

You now realize that incident is insignificant in comparison with demonstration of mind and character (which are really synonymous). In fact, incident is merely the vehicle for such demonstration. And realizing that, Tommy, puts you into the very top flight of authors. It not only makes your work of highest potential value but also, if fitted into your habit of thinking and planning, will save you countless waste of time and lessen the activity of my third department, as efficiency expert. Before I take up the latter, I want to give you that additional thought.

Very briefly, it is this: In Wouk's latest writing, *Caine Mutiny,* you see and are conscious of the mind of his character so that each appears as a distinctive individual apart from all other characters and so aloof from the author that it never occurs to you that some writer is doing this work and telling the tale.

That Tommy is the ultimate. See the mind of your character, that determines and controls his speech and actions, and you have it all. This is a step beyond saying let your character show what he is by what he does and says, although the effect is the same. Seeing clearly and understanding that mind gives you complete and utter control and you don't have to bother about "should he do this or should he say that." Tell me if, in my manner of stating it, this is clear to you?

Perhaps the most amazing thing Wouk has done in that work, is the slow, gradual development of the character Willie Keith. He is not a finished character when you first see him; it is progressive; he is at first embryonic of what he finally becomes. And this is a thought I want to give you in case you have not seen the book. In fact, if this is all clear to you, you don't need to read the darned book.

So now we go to (3) Efficiency of work. And in this department I include June as a most important assistant. She will know what I mean without explanation. She and I share our confidence and faith in your ability, in our mission for you. Neither of us have to tell you what to write or to prod you to work. Possibly we both have to restrain you at times if you should become impatient. For you have now reached the level where you make haste slowly.

So June is drafted, and I know she has long since drafted herself. But I want her to go at it consciously now. The wife of every writer, Tommy, as you well know, is a definite part of his enterprise as a writer without entering in to the details of his work, a definite, if not always recognized, contributor to his success or failure. And I want her to report from time to time, as she did so helpfully when you and I were learning to understand each other. You can't escape us, Tommy. Between us, we are going to put you on the top rungs whether you like it or not.

Going back to an earlier statement. I want to repeat that realization that incident is merely the vehicle for mind, and character and demonstration, that reaching into the mind of your character will save you countless hours' and days' waste of time in your thinking and planning, save you that bore-some frustration of devising incident and theme, and will bring your work to utmost efficiency. So now to work, Tommy, me lad, to great work. But take her slow and easy, although it should come continuously now off the assembly line for every sort of market.

June was a tremendous helpmate for Tommy. In fact, just during the six-month period from February through July 1952, at least six pieces of correspondence were shared between the two of them; and, as my father had hoped, she was instrumental in helping to keep Tommy "on task" and away from the self-pitying moods that could be so debilitating.

*January 3, 1952—Cap to Tommy:*

Seems to me you have all the answers to your wonderful letter of December 31st, in my letter to you of January 1st. Only one little post-script to add to it. If you are in any way fearful of being considered not coming up to what is expected of you, in any story, by anyone, at any time, forget it completely. It cannot possibly be in anyone's mind, except perchance your own. And if it is, throw the thought out.

So now put to work all these ideas of yours that are bustin' for expression. The time for indecision and hesitation is past. Keep 'em coming. Any and all of them. Freedom, for that is what you have. Write anything you damn please, anyway you damn please. That's the thing now. Shouldn't tell you this, but I know what you can do even if you don't so long as you have a free hand, and I'm not a bit worried over a wasted story or wasted time. Just turn your wolf loose. And if you don't think I'm more confident and enthusiastic than I've ever been, well, I'll have to show you.

*January 5, 1952—Tommy to Cap:*

I don't know why in hell we bother writing to each other. As you say, your letter of January 1st gave all the answers to my letter of December 31st. The fact that you answered the questions before you heard the questions is no longer any surprise to me.

Seriously, though, I am glad to have all my say off my chest and have your reactions be just the way I wanted them to be. It's a sort of a cold plunge, I think. I've done my interning and now the patient is there on the table and it's up to me. Scares me a little, makes me bite my nails, and at the same time puts stars back in my eyes and that, damn it, is necessary if a man wants to put some life into a printed word.

I'm not asking for comments (on work that he had tentatively discussed in a previous letter). Let me finish it. It may be haywire as a pet coon but I'm having more fun than I've had for ages. Read *Caine Mutiny*—thought I told you I loved it. Heard it advertised on the air the other day by a lady as the *Cainine Mutiny*. A damn doggy book. So maybe I'll spring loose, Cap. Your partner just swatted me and told me to get to work.

*February 13, 1952—Cap to Tommy:*

I told a writer not long ago that the successful men were those who could determine their true métier and concentrate upon it; the doctors, lawyers and so on; the frustrated ones those who were uncertain of their talents and themselves. So, just settle down to your work, Tommy, happily, contentedly, confidently. No more rainbow chasing; no more fussing and ulcer worry. You know what you do best and want to do. I know it too.

As Tommy searched for the level of self-confidence that would match his writing skills, it was still with a series of "fits and starts." When he went through periods where no creativity was forthcoming and his stories were not selling as he felt they should, he would be particularly hard on himself. However, because of my father's nurturing he was realizing growth and maturity. The letters Tommy received from my father always hit a responsive chord and served to help him regain his balance.

The only reason that the correspondence shared pertaining to Tommy Thompson is far more voluminous than that shared concerning William Cox and Norman Fox, is the fact that much more was available through the UCLA Special Collections Library. That situation notwithstanding, the manner in which my father dealt with all of his authors was similar. Even those who were not a part of his group were recipients of his counsel; in fact, never did he turn his back on those who sought him out.

As my father indicated in his letter of January 1, 1952, he was far more than a literary agent just plying his clients' stories from one market to another. He wanted his authors to continue to grow as writers, and to have visions of all that they could be. He recognized their different levels of growth and their inherent capacities to grow, encouraging each to stay within his limits until he was ready to move beyond.

The next letter from Tommy to my father sounds very familiar; however, there is, beneath the surface, a recognizable sense that he is truly putting the pieces together and preparing himself for the next level.

*April 29, 1952—Tommy to Cap:*

Sometimes I get to thinking over the past six months and all the hell raising I've done and all the production I haven't done and it makes me wonder why in the devil you bother with me. All I can say is, I appreciate your sincere effort to help a guy along. Some place in this bumpy road there are a few bog holes, I reckon, and I hit one of them. I can learn something from it or I can cuss my fate and stay at the bottom of it. Believe me, Cap, I never had any intention of doing the latter.

I have poured and re-poured over your letters during my "black days" and at times they made me mad and at times they made sense and at other times they meant nothing at all. Character, character, character, he says, until I would blow my top, screaming madly, "Show me just one character in the *Sat Eve Post* and I'll eat the whole damn magazine!"

Well, maybe I'd still make that bet, but I want you to know that I know you're right—always have known it—and know damn well I won't get any place until I learn to approach a story that way.

That other things—the guts—the willingness to shoot the moon—the confidence—a certain cockiness—that I'm going to have to find for myself. Dog gone it, I've seen it in every business. One guy—maybe he hasn't got any more than the next one—is on top because he pushes himself there. That little extra effort with a cheerfulness about it. A certain little swagger and cockiness that says "you better give me the job because I'm just a little bit better than the next one"—. A writer ought to have some of that, too. A writer ought to have guts enough to believe in himself—and I think damn few of them do. Then he would grab every idea that comes along, slap it down on paper where he could get a look at it, and lo and behold a lot of such ideas would be stories, I do believe. This I have to fight out with myself.

Comes a time when a writer has learned his bare fundamentals. He then reaches an awareness of what makes a story. I sincerely believe I have reached that awareness. Then comes the time for a little striking out right and left with real enjoyment in the striking, and out of such striking have come some pretty startling sales, I think.

I tell you all this, Cap, because the last few months have been so very unproductive and because tomorrow or the next day I will be starting the Wayne Hardisty in earnest. I have a short here on my desk—an odd little number—but one I want to get in to you. Then I will give my very best to Wayne Hardisty, and I want you to know I'm enthused about it and have faith in it.

So here we go, and I have another long one in mind for this fall—one I'm itching to do—one that needs to be told. But more of that much later. The main thing you need to know about me is that I consider $10,000 a year a good substantial operating base. Together we want to shoot for that, and if that means Ballantine or Gold Medal or whatever, we will have to consider it in time. But I should be free to write 'em, you should be free to market 'em, and I think you and I can agree now one hundred percent on that basis of operation. Maybe I need six months of pause and reflection. But now comes the time to put up or shut up, and we ain't about to shut up.

The 'arm wrestling' between Tommy and my father continued throughout the duration of their relationship. Tommy needed the pat on the back, the words of encouragement, and the willingness of someone to listen to his cries for help. This Dad gave to him with patience, concern and good humor. Yes, my father was far more than a literary agent for Tommy. He was his friend, as he was to each of his writers as they looked to him for his wisdom and guidance.

Some excerpts from several pieces of correspondence in the final days of my father's tenure follow:

*July 24, 1952—Tommy to Cap:*

Afraid it was a case of trying to please Cap Shaw and Erd Brandt without pleasing Tommy Thompson. Silly, of course, because that is the last thing on earth you intended—and you repeatedly warned me to do it my own way. Ah well, it ain't no life and death matter and it will come out all right, I know. A good knock on the head never hurt anyone, and in this particular case I think it probably did a lot of good.

Hey! What happened to Wellfleet? Fully expected you to be up there by now. Don't you miss that, dog gone you. A little whiff of that salt air now and then is good for a man. Of course, if you'd come to Santa Rosa we could drive over to the beach any afternoon and let the horse neck clams squirt up our pants legs.

*July 28, 1952—Cap to Tommy:*

Got a great kick out of *Loudmouth;* a well told piece all the way. Believe me, Tommy, you have not cause to envy the Messrs. Hawkins, Jackland Marmur and all and sundry. You have command of your craft now, and I mean craftsmanship. You can write what you want and write it well. Your attitude toward all you do should be both happy and confident. And I mean all of that. Hell, ask me what I think of Tommy Thompson's work. Of course, as you know, I am quite in the dark regarding the Wayne Hardisty opus, but am content to leave its workings and progress to you.

Gee, Tommy, all I can do so far is to think of Wellfleet. Well, perhaps I can get down for a bit later on.

*August 1, 1952—Cap to Tommy:*

I am very glad to say that Don Ward likes the Loudmouth story as well as I.

And then the response to the report of my father's death:

*August 2, 1952—Tommy to Mike Tilden (Managing Editor, Popular Publications):*

Just received a wire telling of Cap's death and you can imagine how shocked and upset June and I both were. Cap was part of the family. He was a damn sight more than an editor—he was a pillar of strength, a whipping boy who never whimpered and a guy who would stroke your head by mail. We're going to miss him, and I know a lot of editors are, but as I just wrote Norman Fox, a select few of us will always have a little claim to fame: "We were one of Cap Shaw's boys."

*August 8, 1952—Tommy to Mal Reiss (Editor, Fiction House, a*

*close friend to my father, and one who worked closely with my*
*brother in dissolving the agency):*

> Thank you very much for your letter of August 5th giving me more
> details on Joe's passing. I can appreciate how you all feel, but, like you,
> as long as it had to happen I am positive that this is the way Joe would
> have wanted it. The man seemed to thrive on work and activity, and I
> am sure this last year, with the agency, was one of his happiest ones. The
> work combined his natural "teaching" ability with editorial ability, and
> those of us who were fortunate enough to work with him will always
> owe him a great debt.

*August 10, 1952—Tommy to Mal Reiss:*

> Thank you for your very fine letter of August 7. I hope I wasn't the
> only one of the "stable" who was all up in the air, but I assure you the
> picture is much clearer now. For example, I knew nothing about Joe
> Jr., for although Cap and I shared many confidences Cap's family was
> his own personal affair, of course. He did mention once that a son—or
> daughter—got married, and that is about as far as it went. Once I wanted
> to send a Christmas gift and I had to write Frank Bonham to find out if
> there was a Mrs. Cap! So, you can see that I, by the same token, did not
> know much about the business or arrangement of the agency itself. As
> Cap would probably say, "we were too busy with business."

## IN SUMMARY

THUS THE journey came to a close; however, the legacy lives on:
  "As Ernest Borneman has pointed out, the *Black Mask* not only
was the training ground for such writers as Hammett and Chandler, but also contributed to the development of what Mencken
called 'the American language—a prose style which, by tran-

scending the limits of the crime story, has become part and parcel of the serious American novel.' "[262]

My father was a member of Mystery Writers of America. Upon his death his fellow members, Ellery Queen and Thomas Walsh among others, gave him a fine two-page send-off. Said Walsh:

> He was... almost jealously concerned for the professional dignity and standing of authors he represented. He would not tolerate a cheapjack or condescending attitude in regard to the job at hand, and he understood much better than more noted literary names that the important thing was to work with the means at hand—to raise in the only possible way, patiently and gradually, the general level of fiction writing in his time and field.[263]

As Hagemann observed, these were fitting words for the man who believed that detective fiction was "the most absorbing of all literature," for the man whom Ellery Queen called one of "the truly great editorial pioneers in the detective field."[264]

Eugene Cunningham, literary editor of the *El Paso Times,* stated that: "One of these days, a 'non-literary' history of American writing is due to be written. And it will give names of those editors who had vision and enough courage to depart from the rutted old roads and demand of writers realism and fidelity to life. When that history is written, Cap Shaw will be given his place as the Apostle of the New Mystery Tale, as Arthur Sullivan Hoffman of

---

262   Thomas Sturak, "Horace McCoy, Captain Shaw, and *The Black Mask,*" p. 140.

263   E.R. Hagemann, "Cap Shaw and His Great and Regular Fellows," p. 151.

264   *Ibid.*

the old Adventure Story field." [265]

As John Quincy Adams said: "If your actions inspire others to dream more, learn more, do more and become more, you are a leader." Henry Clay, great statesman and Senator from Kentucky in the early 1800s, was quoted as saying that; "Of all the properties that belong to honorable men, not one is so highly prized as that of character." My father was a visionary, he was a leader, he was indomitable, he was steadfast, and his strength of character was a beacon of light and hope to those he served.

Robert K. Greenleaf, founder of the Greenleaf Center for Servant Leadership in Indianapolis, said, "The great leader is seen as a servant first, and that simple fact is the key to his greatness." [266] This leadership model is radically different than what is apparent in today's world. It is one of humility and unselfish service to others. Service that cares for others is the basis of true greatness. My father's contributions to the field of mystery fiction literature were profound; however, these contributions diminish in significance when placed side by side with who he was as a man.

That which has been recorded as my father's professional journey says nothing about who he was as the head of a family as a husband and as a father, in effect, his personal life. In the hundreds of letters between my father and authors, publishers, and all others, only once does he mention his family and that only in reference to a graduation and subsequent marriage of one of his children. In some respects my father's personal life adds another dimension to who he was; on the other hand, the traits evident in his professional life are remarkably similar to those that can be seen and sensed in his personal life.

---

265   Eugene Cunningham, "Clearing the Desk." *El Paso Times,* Sunday, June 4, 1933.

266   Robert K. Greenleaf, *The Servant as Leader* (Indianapolis, Ind.: Robert K. Greenleaf Center for Servant Leadership, 1970, 1991). p. 2.

Joe holding Sandy, Milton and Joe Jr., Cape Cod, 1932.

# 10
# Husband, Father, Friend

TO KNOW my mother is to better understand my father. Her very advent to life was marked by controversy when one parent insisted she was born at midnight on December 1897, thus making the birth date December 25th on Christmas Day, the other parent argued that midnight made her birth date on the 26th. Whichever, the birth occurred in Prague, Czechoslovakia. Her father, Karl Muschak, was a well-known character actor with the National Theater and was one of its directors; he was also noted for translating and introducing the plays of George Bernard Shaw to Czech audiences. Her mother, Alice Hillstead, British born, was an English teacher who came to Czechoslovakia where she met and married her husband Karl; subsequently, Czechoslovakia became her adopted country. They had only one child, my mother, Hana Otilie Muskova, who attended private and public schools in Prague, and received her bachelor's degree in English language, history and literature from Charles University.

Czechoslovakia has had a long, illustrious, yet tumultuous history. "Whoever is master of Bohemia is master of Europe," said Germany's "Iron Chancellor," Bismarck, in 1886. "Europe must never allow any nation except the Czechs to rule it, since the nation does not lust for domination. The boundaries of Bohemia are the safeguard of European security, and he who moves them will plunge Europe into misery"—a prophecy that tragically came true. Since the end of the Thirty Years' War (1618 to 1648) Bohemia was dominated by Austria and deeply influenced by Germany. It was not until 1918, during the closing months of World War I, that Bohemia regained its independence. This new republic of Czechoslovakia was comprised of Bohemia, Moravia, Slovakia and Carpathian Ruthenia.[267]

My mother and her parents were deeply involved in the political activities leading up to and continuing through the creation of this new country. My grandfather was an unabashed patriot who early on taught my mother to be loyal to and willing to fight for freedom for Czechoslovakia. My grandmother taught English to Thomas Masaryk, the first president of Czechoslovakia (the one who many called the George Washington of this new republic), as well as to his successor, Dr. Edward Beneus. My mother was a courier, carrying documents to and from the leaders of the several factions involved with the revolutionary coalition.

After the Armistice, several American missions came to Prague to assist the Czechs in their transition to a new political system. Because of my mother's language skills, she was pressed into service as a translator for the different missions, one of which was the Child Relief Mission initiated by Herbert Hoover and directed by my father. It was here that Mom and Dad met and started a courtship that lasted for the next thirty-three years.

Although the Child Relief Mission had successfully completed its work in September 1919, my father remained in Czechoslovakia until 1924. The reasons were several-fold: He was recovering from an illness contracted while in the Chemical Warfare Service; he enjoyed being in Czechoslovakia, and had the opportunity to do some freelance writing; and he recognized the need in this new nation for one with his business acumen. Also, one cannot help but feel that staying there kept him in close proximity to my mother.

Returning with my mother to America, the two were married on

---

267  *Book of Knowledge,* Vol. 17–18, pp. 6342–6343.

February 14, 1925, in Brooklyn, New York. Initially they lived in New York City until after the births of my brother, Joseph Thompson Shaw, Jr., on March 26, 1926, and me on June 27, 1927. The family of four then moved to Forest Hills, Long Island. Eleven months later we moved to Scarsdale, New York. On July 25, 1929, my mother became a naturalized citizen of America, a glorious moment in her life. On July 16, 1931, my sister Sandra was born, an event that completed our family of five.

With my mother's lineage, and her background of having been raised in a crucible of fire, harshness, suppression and rebellion, it only takes two words to describe her: "fiercely independent." On her own she broke away from the Catholic Church, and, against her parents' wishes, came to America with a man twenty-three years her senior. This occurred at a time when her father was gravely ill; in fact, this parting was the last time she ever saw her father. It was not lack of love and respect for her father, but something she felt compelled to do. Upon leaving Czechoslovakia, my mother never returned.

In the development of this biography, and while concentrating on my father's *Black Mask* authors, certain comments by W.T. Ballard were noted. It was after my father had accepted Ballard's first story, and, in the process, requested that certain changes be made. Although overjoyed about the acceptance, but not all that happy about making changes, Ballard said "…but it was not a time to argue with an editor. No one with any sense argued with Shaw."[268] I had to smile and say to myself "obviously he had never met my mother."

Fiercely independent yes, but my mother was a lot more than that. Upon gaining citizenship in this country, she did not consider herself a Czech-American; rather, she was an American. Extremely proud of her country of origin, she never lost her love

---

268   Mertz, "W.T. Ballard Interview," p. 3.

of Czechoslovakia; however, she deeply loved her new country and what it stood for. Her allegiance to this country and its rule by law was profound, and, when we became embroiled in World War II, there was no question in her mind as to whether or not her sons would serve in the military—they would and they did.

My mother had the willpower to move mountains. Because of the disparity in age with my father, she realized he would be passing out of the picture well before she. Her goal was to get the children through high school before this happened—and this she did. As a result of Mom's pushing and pulling, both the school officials and me, I graduated from high school at age sixteen, only a year behind my brother. Our sister followed closely behind.

Education was important. My mother was fluent in at least five languages, an accomplished pianist, a writer, and a translator of children's books from another language into English. She decreed that her children would realize education beyond high school with the pronouncement that: "There is not a penny in this house to support you to go on to higher education, but you will go on." This we did: My brother was educated at Williams College and Yale University, courtesy of the Navy Reserve Officers Training Commissioning Program and Veterans' benefits. My undergraduate degree was from the United States Naval Academy, and my sister received a certificate in secretarial science from the Berkley School in White Plains, New York.

My mother was haughty and proud, her children were blue-blooded, the best that children could be. Little wonder that she didn't bat an eye when I enlisted in the Marine Corps at age seventeen just as World War II was coming to a climax, and contrary to the wishes of my father. My mother claimed to have never seen the inside of a kitchen before marrying my father, a statement I accepted as true because I remember clearly that Dad did most of the cooking.

As my father was gregarious in meeting people and building bridges to others, my mother was the opposite, being very reticent about opening up to those outside her family. She was reluctant to extend trust to others until she was assured that the recipient was worthy of that trust. My mother's love was confined to her family, and she would fight if anyone or anything infringed upon the well being of any member of the family.

In the same breath, my mother was both rebellious and naughty. As a youngster she was constantly in trouble with whomever was charged with overseeing her activities. This was obvious by watching her interact with a rebellious grandchild whom she would aid and abet with a wink of the eye and a pat on the back. Never in public, but in private she would enjoy an off-color story or joke even though she would never tell one herself. When she would allow herself, my mother had a prodigious sense of humor and, at the most inopportune time, would get an uncontrollable laughing spell. My mother also had a heart for those who were knocked down by life, the underdog, those who were being exploited by others.

When my father and mother had a difference of opinion on matters about which she felt strongly, she was defiant. With arms crossed and expletives flowing followed by "Joe," she would fire shot after shot. With respect to my father's driving, this too would bring forth the expletives as she sought divine intervention. After an eight-hour trip behind the wheel, with my mother beside him writhing and braking at every twist or turn in the road, my father, upon arrival at our destination would seek to regain his composure by washing the car.

But my mother and father had a beautiful love affair. There was not only genuine affection expressed between the two but also concern and respect for each other's needs. Dad would regularly send Mom notes expressing his great love for her, and she would gratefully and graciously accept them. One of the more memorable scenarios that my siblings and I enjoyed occurred when Dad had to leave the Cape for a short period of time to attend a meeting in New York City with either an editor or author of the opposite sex. For some reason, my mother became insanely jealous and then angry. Poor Dad, dragging back to the Cape after a grueling trip, was confronted with the words "the plot thickens." We had seen it coming when, prior to Dad's return, Mom had been stomping around the cottage muttering those same words. Once Dad was able to regain his balance, he was able to mollify Mom and the crisis passed in both her heart and mind. My mother, being the more emotional of the two, could get upset over the most minute matters; however, when the big issues occurred she was as solid as a rock. On the other hand, my father, regardless of the severity of the situation, just took things in stride and was always the steadying hand to bring the issues back into focus. An example of this occurred on August 12, 1941, the day one of my father's two brothers died. At the time my father received the news of his beloved brother's death, a critical business meeting had been scheduled that required his presence. As difficult as the decision was, and in spite of the grief he was suffering, my father felt he had no alternative other than to go ahead with this meeting. It was not easy, but it was something he had to do. A big issue gracefully handled. Whereas, Mom wouldn't hesitate to yell at her children, I can never remember my father ever raising his voice to us. Temperamentally, Dad was very stable.

As parents, they were supportive of each other and worked as a team. Mom took care of the minutia such as what the kids would wear, their schoolwork, and their whereabouts when not in school. A familiar refrain after one of the children invoked a severe infraction would be: "Wait until your father gets home." At that time, we knew that the sky was about to fall. On the other hand, my mother meted out the punishment where minor disciplinary infractions were involved—clearly I can remember more than once having a wooden spoon broken across my backside. My father would never beat or spank us regardless of the severity of our offense. What he would do was talk to us about the implications of what we had done, his disappointment in our actions, and what his future expectations were. This would be followed by the removal of certain privileges for a period of time.

Although Mom could get angry with us with a blink of the eye, I can remember Dad getting angry at us only twice. The first was when he got upset with me over my reluctance to embrace his fencing lessons. I don't remember what was said, but clearly I remember flying up the steps to find the sanctuary of my mother, with the flailing of a foil at my backside as my father followed close behind. The other time was when my brother found a two-dollar bill and, without seeking its owner or remanding it to a higher authority, made the mistake of spending it. Judiciously he spent some of that two-dollar bill on an ashtray for my father but it was for naught. To find something belonging to another and then spending it on one's self was intolerable. My brother received the brunt of Dad's anger, but it was a lesson we both never forgot.

Joe, Sandy and I were blessed to have had the parents we did, and to be enfolded in their love, concern and compassion. We were never without food, clothing or shelter even though there were many times when there was no money in the till. Mom and Dad always stressed that we stay close together as a family. Consequently, our parents never took vacations away from the children.

In 1932, we started to take summer vacations in Wellfleet, on Cape Cod. In 1935, my father purchased, unseen, a parcel of land from a friend who was having financial difficulties. The cost was $250. This was followed in the next year by the construction of a cottage at a cost of $3,000. It was an unpretentious cottage, a home that consisted of a bunkroom, a combination family and dining area, kitchen, bathroom and outside porch. There was no running water and electricity thus necessitating a hand-pump for water, a kerosene stove, kerosene lights and an ice box for the refrigerator. This cottage became our family retreat, one that has been enjoyed not only by the initial family of five but also by grandchildren and great grandchildren. Sixty-seven years later this cottage still stands as testimony to the foresight and vision of our mother and father.

One of the family's unwritten rules was that this cottage would never be rented, nor could friends use it without the presence of a family member. There was a time when funds were short—so short that the mortgage on the Scarsdale home was foreclosed thus necessitating the family to move elsewhere. Yet, not once did the issue arise of either selling or renting the cottage. It still remains our sanctuary. Even today, when entering the cottage after a long winter of having it closed down, one readily senses the presence of my father and mother. By God's grace we are still family.

My brother and sister have been asked to reminisce about their memories of Dad, and those activities and incidents they still recall in their hearts and minds. Memories do blur, but, fortunately, much remains. To my father's delight, Joe was the natural athlete participating in the entire gamut of athletic competition available to a young man growing up. Track, ice hockey, basketball, football and golf all received a fair share of his attention. To foster this love of sports, my father would take the two of us to sporting venues throughout the greater New York City area. I was not the athlete my brother was, but I still had a love for sports. For this reason, I willingly tagged along on these outings, whether it was to Madison Square Garden for the annual Sportsmen Show, track meets (the IC4A strikes a familiar bell, as does Gene Cunningham running the Wanamaker Mile), and one of the two professional ice hockey teams; or to the New York Athletic Club meets at Travers Island. Fortunately, professional baseball and football teams abounded in New York City; as a result, we frequently witnessed these events. Even local baseball games were a delight and, more often than not, when a game was played, Dad and one or more members of the family was there with him.

Dad presented Joe with his first pair of track shoes, introduced him to a Native American Indian guide from Maine whom he had befriended, impressed him into service as his caddy, and taught him how to hold and swing a golf club. Joe still recalls golf balls being hit from our backyard in Scarsdale into a vacant lot, as well as his indoctrination into the fine art of fencing at the dinner table through the use of a table knife to understand what a parry and a thrust were all about.

Joe still vividly remembers vacations, including trips of a week's duration to a private club at Tupper Lake in the Adirondacks where they had Indian guides; or the pre-cottage days when we stayed at one of the two Taylor Hill cottages in Wellfleet enjoying the beautiful weather as well as weathering the raging storms. There was one storm in particular where Dad inscribed a chalk mark on the bedroom floor before the storm was upon us; after the storm had passed we could see that the beds had moved eight inches.

Although the automobile trips to the Cape held lasting memories, each of us had different perceptions of the details. Joe remembered the trips being taken in an old Hudson—actually, it was a Packard. We both remember luggage being tied to the running boards. Many times we traveled at night to avoid Boston Post Road and Providence, Rhode Island traffic; unfortunately, this plan often back-fired when we would get hung up with cargo-laden, hundred-railroad-car trains trundling across road intersections in the vicinity of Taunton. Sandy's memories of the trips concentrated on the picnic table rest stops when our favorite fare was deviled ham sandwiches. That doesn't jog my memory; what does though, is that fifteen minutes into the trip, Joe and I were already nagging our parents to allow us to start eating lunch.

In our favor, there were not more than one or two of these trips each summer when Dad would try to stretch out each vacation as far as he could. Each trip was memorable, not only the going and coming but the joy of being there and storing up enough memories to last until the following summer. One of those memories we still talk about is when Dad took a fragile cloth-coated kayak and paddled across two miles of open water. In Joe's words, "he thought Mom was going to kill Dad."

In truth, the family squabbles were few and far between with the more contentious outbursts between my brother and me as we struggled for sibling recognition and rights. With respect to Cape Cod, it was and continues to be so much a part of the family that both my mother and brother retired to the Cape.

One of the traits that I inherited from my father was the attitude toward anything physical: "is it functional, does it do its job?" This explains why Joe and I were nonplussed when the major pieces of furniture in the living room of our Scarsdale home were a grand piano and a full-sized pool table: The piano to satisfy Mom's love of music, the pool table, in all probability, to satisfy Dad's need for a competitive sport. With proper decorum, the cue sticks were placed, out of sight, in a rack mounted on the dining room wall. Of course, after pushing the furniture out of the way, there was also enough space to spread a mat for fencing lessons. Sandy and I were not adept enough to get our lessons at the dinner table with a piece of silverware; no, we had to have the foils and masks, the whole works. Unfortunately, we were both duds. An obvious question is: Why not fencing lessons in the basement? Well, that is where we had our roller-skating hockey rink in the space not consumed by a furnace and a coal bin. Yes, that old house provided many cherished memories.

All three of us recall the monkey, Major Bowes by name, bestowed on us by one of Dad's authors who had been keeping him in the bathroom of his New York City apartment, until the landlord ran out of patience or the author ran out of funds. I don't remember how long he stayed with us, but each of us had an interesting "Show and Tell" activity for school while he lasted. And what about the little boy Michael who came to live with us for a period of time while his parents worked out their problems? Nor could we ever forget the two or three visits from our grandmother in Czechoslovakia whom my father graciously addressed as Lady Alice. She was a dear soul, proper to the nth degree and completely mystified that her daughter could even drive a car. Knowing our grandmother, who was the only grandparent we had ever met, we could readily believe that our mother had never seen the inside of a kitchen before coming to America—the home-made cookies Grandma brought with her left a lot to be desired with a taste that was not enhanced by the long journey from Czechoslovakia. In some way our grandmother was involved with our first dog, a beautiful German shepherd named Boagi, but I never knew or don't remember the circumstances. He became a faithful member of our family.

Lady Alice was a gallant, gracious and courageous woman, living through the German-Austrian domination, the very few years of freedom, the tyrannical years of Nazism, and then the Russian occupation. She continued to teach English to the Czechs in Prague even though, for the last few years of her life, she was totally blind. For years I would communicate with her, allowing her students to read my letters to her. We had a warm and affectionate relationship.

Sandy was the "fair-haired" child. Most vexing for Joe and me was that he and I had the kitchen duty after dinner, cleaning up, washing the dishes, and putting things away. We felt it was reverse, unfair discrimination, but we also recognized she was the apple of our parents eyes. Her memories of Dad, for the most part, are at a level above Joe's and mine. We were both gone from home and, in our absence, she was a great source of comfort to Mom and Dad. When my brother moved with his own family to Scarsdale, it again brought the major elements of the family together again. Both Sandy and Joe relish the story of the first television set in the family and the impact it had. It was in the infancy of television and sets were not only black and white but also large and unwieldy. As Joe told me, he almost got a hernia lugging this monster on the train from New York City to home. Dad was enthralled with it, and had it set up on a cabinet in the dining room of our Nelson Road home in Scarsdale. Most fascinating for my father was that he now had the opportunity to watch professional boxing bouts. When Dad stayed home to watch a Rocky Graziano championship fight instead of attending Sandy's high school graduation, he incurred the wrath of hell. Sandy remembers the incident a little differently. She said Dad did attend the graduation but was getting bored with the long-winded ceremonial speaker. It was at this point he got up and walked home to watch his fight. From the report I received, the championship fight was nothing more than the preliminary bout for the fight that followed. Nevertheless, Dad enjoyed his television and would make it a point to listen to his favorite singer, Dinah Shore, for fifteen minutes every evening.

Sandy lovingly remembers that, no matter how much Mom may have railed at Dad, he always kept his cool. She never remembers Dad swearing or raising his voice, using the expression "Judas

Priest" as an alternative way of venting emotion. Although Sandy was not inclined toward athletics, Dad often took her to boxing matches at the Westchester County Center in White Plains. Dad enjoyed these matches thoroughly, but Sandy could never warm up to the sound of leather boxing gloves hitting flesh. Sandy did enjoy the New York Rangers hockey team, and Dad got tickets for the Madison Square Garden events. Not wanting to make a second trip into New York City, Dad would always get an additional ticket for a family friend to escort Sandy to and from the Garden.

Although not into team competition, Sandy was a gifted dancer. Mom oversaw this phase of her development, ensuring that, among other modes of dance, she excel in Scottish dances, including the Highland Fling and other reels. This demand to excel in this form of dancing was to recognize and celebrate our Scottish heritage on my father's side of the family. This declaration by my parents of dedicating Sandy's proficiency in dancing Scottish reels, provides a positive link to our roots originating in Scotland.

With regard to the war years, Sandy also reminded me of the role Dad played as the Captain of the Area Air Raid Blackout Team. He would go out and make sure there were not any houses with lights on that could be seen from the outside; he would then receive reports from team members indicating that their areas of responsibility were under control. With red face and a feeling of shame, I have to acknowledge that even in those perilous times, a buddy of mine, Willie Voltz, and I would go around setting dead Christmas trees on fire just to see how responsive these Blackout teams were. There was a certain amount of "hell raising" in my makeup that I couldn't seem to subdue. The results would have been catastrophic if I would have ever admitted these transgressions to my father. During this period of time, my father offered his services to the Federal Government, in any capacity, at an annual price of one dollar. At age sixty-seven, his offer was not accepted, but it was just another demonstration of his love for his country.

My father, ever the teacher, introduced Sandy to the game Mah Jong and taught her how to play both two-handed and four-handed bridge. The latter was most important especially in light of the fact that playing bridge on the train between Scarsdale and New York City was a common "time killer:" When a fourth was missing, Dad would throw Sandy into the gap on those occasions she was with him after having started attending school in the City.

Dad also taught Sandy's husband, Jim, to play the ukulele. This discovery of my father's musical talent should not have come as a surprise in that he had been a member of the Banjo and Guitar Club for all four years while at Bowdoin College; however, the only memory I have of his musical appreciation was, when in an uproarious mood, he would burst into song such as:

> Oh, I itch, I itch like a son-of-a-bitch,
> I'm not poor and I'm not rich.
> My back is sore, and my tail is wet,
> With forty miles to paddle yet.

And, yes, the love of poetry:

> A wonderful bird is the Pelican,
> His mouth can hold more than his belly can.
> He takes in his beak food enough for a week,
> But I don't see how the hell-he-can.

Sandy and Dad were close friends, and in my and Joe's absence, became even closer. Joe, too, had a treasured relationship with Dad. Words left behind for Sandy to live by were: "If you can't say something good about someone, don't say anything at all." To Joe, the credo, by which he has always tried to live, was: "Be honest with yourself, and the rest will take care of itself." A ritual that was initiated by Dad and remained with us well into our teens was that each night, before going to bed, we would separately hug our father, and with our head resting on his shoulder, would say our evening prayers. These prayers would always start by asking God's blessing on our mother, and would include, among other thoughts, blessings on the other members of the family, and would end by asking blessings for our grandmother. It is amazing how a simple ritual like this can hold a family together within the embrace of God's love.

As one looks back to incidents and activities that occurred between fifty and some seventy years ago, they don't lend themselves to a coherent flow of that which transpired within our family of five. Instead I perceive these series of thoughts and recollections as a collage of a growing, vibrant family. Each element of the collage is likened to a Christmas tree decoration that in isolation is recognizable for what it is; however, it is only when they are all brought together and placed on the tree can one truly see the interrelationship between the individual elements. These are the ties that have bound us together, and in turn, provided the foundation for the building of our own families. It is a direct reflection of a mother and father who cared.

AS I discuss my father as my friend, I realize that he was a close friend to each member of the family. As I sense that, of all the children, I was Dad's favorite, I realize that each of us was his favorite. My father had love and friendship in abundance, enough to share with many.

My earliest recollection of my father in action was an incident that took place at Nauset Lighthouse in Eastham on Cape Cod.

I believe I was either three or four years old. It was in the early evening, we were visiting the lighthouse, and the lighthouse keeper allowed us to climb the steps into the room containing the light. A window leading to the parapet circumventing the light housing was partially open. Seeing the opening, I went for it and was almost out on the parapet when a pair of hands grabbed and pulled me back in. The emotions I remember from my father were joy for saving me from a long fall, and anger at the stunt I had just pulled. That incident seemed to define the relationship I had with my father. He was either trying to pull me back from getting into trouble, or giving me the confidence and push to get me back into the game of life. By and large he was extremely supportive of all that I tried to do. When I failed, he was the first one to pick me up, brush me off, and get me back on track. He was my mentor, a wise and trusted counselor. I was stubborn, impetuous and impatient. Without realizing it, I needed the self-control, instruction and guidance that only he could provide. He knew that disappointments would come, but he refused to allow me to become discouraged, always making me look at what had been accomplished. Failures became only stepping stones in the quest for greater achievement.

First and foremost, he taught me that there was one God the Father Almighty who guided and oversaw all that I did. This was not achieved through Bible instruction or church attendance, but, rather, through examples of the way he lived his life and the great wisdoms he imparted to me. Over time, as I matured, I started to realize how great was my father's love for me; knowing this, only then did I became aware of how much greater the love of Jesus Christ was for me. To this day this love still remains the anchor of my faith and my life. I can only remember my mother and father being in church at our family weddings; however, Sunday school attendance was mandatory for the three children.

Next, Dad taught me the importance of a value system consisting of integrity, morality and ethics. Although I have adopted them as my own, I have not always allowed them to guide me; however, when I have deviated from them, I have been painfully aware of that which I have done or not done. These missteps have always left me with the feeling of having betrayed a trust. Thank God for forgiveness

The instruction Dad provided for me covered a broad range of subjects, from inter-personal relationships to technical knowledge. With respect to inter-personal activities, it was through witnessing his interaction with others as much as the wisdom imparted through words that made its impact on me. When Dad met others, it was always with a firm handshake and a hand on the shoulder, while looking straight into the eyes of the individual. He had an open-mindedness and a genuineness about his greetings that was totally disarming and one that immediately reflected warmth, friendliness, self-confidence and integrity on his part. To my father, a handshake signifying an agreement was more binding than a written contract. Although these observations may seem frivolous, they gave definition to the type of person my father was. They also set the stage for the many pearls of wisdom he shared with me about human nature. Examples abound: "A promise made is a debt unpaid." "If you cannot be honest with yourself, you cannot be honest with anyone." "If you cannot live by yourself, you cannot live with anyone." "Be true to yourself, believe in yourself, do not fear any man." These thoughts just tumble out, truly words to live by.

My father taught me how to handle pain and how to shoulder loss. As shared earlier, just prior to a critical business meeting in New York City, Dad received word that his beloved younger brother Phil had died. I witnessed the impact of this tragedy had on him, yet, without hesitation, he went ahead with his business obligations. As Dad grew older, the forces of age continued to creep up on him. His knees were in bad shape necessitating the need for knee braces and the use of a cane. One was not aware of the pain he was in. He refused to let it change his zest for life, his love for his fellow man, and his sense of humor. He always had a positive attitude.

The lessons shared, the lessons witnessed gave me the courage to continue to march when my four-year-old son died in my arms. They gave me the courage to continue to fight following nine separate major and sub-major surgeries. They gave me the desire to cherish life and to live life fully, as well as the ability to love and to be loved.

With proper perspective, it is amazing how relatively trivial problems can be brought into focus. Yes, money was a commodity in short supply within our household for as far back as I can remember. A low point in finances came about when the mortgage on our Scarsdale home was foreclosed. I can remember celebrating Mom's birthday with a single piece of pastry holding a single candle and no presents. However, I can also remember Dad selling a story, apparently, one of his several novels. This good fortune seemed like an opportune time to retire several outstanding bills and mortgage payments. On the contrary, Mom and Dad pulled us out of school after the beginning of the January term, purchased tickets to go aboard the Monarch of Bermuda in New York Harbor. The end result was that we spent anywhere from ten days to two weeks in Bermuda. I have no idea what bills remained unpaid, but I do know we had a tremendous time together with memories that still linger to this day.

When school was out for the summer and, for one reason or another, we were not able to go to Cape Cod, there was no pressure on Joe or me to find summer work, although we did earn pocket money cutting lawns and doing other odd jobs. Our parents realized we had pushed ourselves hard during the school year, they wanted to keep us focused on our educational pursuits, and they did not want us chasing dollars. That would come soon enough. Lack of money never deterred the goals Mom and Dad had for us. The attitude was that God would provide, that the children were to keep their noses to the grindstone, and that things would work out. The lessons were well received. Years later, as a Marine Private First Class on a monthly salary of, I believe, fifty-one dollars, I would send five dollars a week home to Mom and Dad. How fortunate we were for the guidance we received, how grateful for values realized in times of stress. Early on in life the allure of making money lost its luster for Dad. As he shared with me, it is what you do, not what remuneration is involved, that truly counts.

Clearly I can remember walking the beaches of Cape Cod and sharing our thoughts. Dad would regal me with stories about the schooner he once owned and how he would sail into harbors under full sail, heeling the boat over so that he could pass over reefs too shallow for passage because of the tides. Using a cedar shingle as a learning tool he taught me how to sail. He introduced me to the terminology of tacking, coming about, running before the wind, running close hauled, reefing of the sails, and a myriad of other nautical terms and techniques. The art of rowing and sculling were also salt-water-related activities Dad shared with me. From there we ventured into the joys of fresh-water boating including the proper techniques for effective paddling. Dad was totally dependent upon the winds and brawn for movement on the water. Rivers and lakes soon turned into discussions about living in the wilderness. How one blazed a trail, dependency upon moss on trees for establishing compass points, sun and stars for finding one's bearings, and how to shave without a mirror were all elements of these lessons. The joy and beauty of nature, the feelings of loneliness, and the need to be at peace with oneself were items of discussion. And, then, we would shift to sports, athletics, competition and conditioning. I remember telling Dad I wanted to get into weight lifting, an activity that was just starting to be explored as a part of a conditioning program. Much to my chagrin he dissuaded me from getting involved saying that I would get "muscle bound." In retrospect, I feel that Dad's natural agility and ability with athletics were such that having above normal strength was unnecessary for successful participation. In vain, he tried to school me in the art of fencing. Much to his disappointment, I was not a very apt or enthusiastic student; however, in later years, as I looked back on a missed opportunity, it was with sorrow.

As a youngster, it had always been my dream to attend the United States Naval Academy in Annapolis, Maryland. In 1944, as a high school senior, the Dean of Students told me that, in his opinion, "I was too damned dumb to go on to college." For some reason, I was not fazed by his conclusion, nor did I accept the truth of his pronouncement. Already, during the course of the year, I had failed a qualifying examination for a congressional appointment to the Academy. The Dean's observation knocked me out of contention for a commissioning program, one of the opportunities embraced by my classmates as an opportunity to receive post-secondary education. This was at a time when World War II was in full sway, casualties were mounting, and I had a desire to get involved. The obvious solution, contrary to current wisdom, was to enlist. Two obstacles existed. The first was that I was too tall. Not too tall to get a commission, but too tall to enlist—the argument being that the uniforms would not fit. The second obstacle was that I was too young. I had graduated from high school at age sixteen, immediately turned seventeen, and, unless I had parental permission, could not enlist until age eighteen. Of course Dad had been terribly supportive of me after the high school dean had evaluated my academic talents; but now he held the trump card about giving me his permission, and he just didn't feel I was mature enough to get shot at. His permission was denied. I was not to be dissuaded, so I started to explore the different services to find out which ones would be willing to look beyond my excessive height. Because of my knowledge of the Coast Guard from Cape Cod, that branch of service became my first choice. Their response was negative, as was the response from the Navy. My last opportunity was with the Marine Corps, and they wouldn't let me get beyond the first desk in the Recruiting Office. At that moment, for some inexplicable reason, the Marine Corps became my challenge. Now I put the pressure on Dad, and when he saw that his arguments against my joining up with a bunch of "glory hounds" was having no impact on me, finally he relented. At the Marine Corps recruiting station the sergeant-in-charge, who had already rejected me three times, made the mistake of not being at his desk when the doors first opened that morning. Once inside the inner sanctum, an accommodating Navy doctor listed my height at the appropriate level, and I was on my way. Seventy-seven days after being sworn in I was home from boot training at Parris Island, South Carolina, met by my father who was now the greatest booster the Marine Corps could have ever had. I could not have had a more proud father.

But the story doesn't end there. Among other duties the Marine Corps gave me was the opportunity to fail the Naval Academy entrance examinations a second time. After some intensive schooling at the Naval Academy Preparatory School at the Naval Station, Bainbridge, Maryland, I passed the entrance examinations convincingly and was awarded a Marine Corps Fleet Appointment to the Academy. For me, it was a dream come true, a goal reached.

Four years later, in June 1951, I graduated with honors as a second lieutenant in the United States Marine Corps. Mom and Dad came to the graduation ceremony. My father could not understand why my name was not listed with my Brigade company classmates until it was pointed out to him that I was included with the group of graduates cited for academic achievement. When Dad shared with me the dilemma he had had, the only thing I could say was: "Thank you Dad. This honor is yours. If it had not been for your unwavering confidence in me as well as your support for what I was trying to do, I could never have done it. This is the only way I could have said thank you for all that you mean to me."

Yes, my father and I were very close friends. Because of the military obligations, our ability to be together over the next fourteen months was limited. In spite of the separations, we retained contact with each other by letter. When assigned to a Marine unit in Korea during the second year of that three-year Forgotten War, we exchanged letters on a regular basis. For the most part, the content of the letters concerned what news was taking place at home and in Korea. We were just two friends keeping tabs on each other; however, the underlying theme from my father's letters was a deep concern for my health and well-being. Still, they were positive upbeat and brimming with confidence.

Actually, the letter writing was not confined to correspondence between my father and me. Rather, it was a network that involved letters to and from my wife Nancy, letters to and from my mother and father, and frequent letters from my mother who would, on occasion, add post-scripts to my father's letters. Nancy would visit my mother and father on a regular basis, each time bringing all of my current letters with her so that she could share them with my parents. Reading these letters, more than half-a-century later, it is amazing how refreshingly current they seem and how quickly the years in between dissolve—so much so that 1952 seems like yesterday. Excerpts from three letters were revealing.

The first letter, my father's final letter to me written on July 27, 1952, alludes to a problem I was confronting and had shared with him. I have no recollection of what that problem was. "I judge from what Nan says of your letter that you are going through a somewhat similar atmosphere to what I experienced when things were uncertain, tempers were strained and everyone seemed to be trying to show the worst in them or at least to take it out on others. The natural response is to fight it, but that isn't politic—the thing to do is to keep your eye on what you want to accomplish and what concerns you most. And doing that, you are able to laugh off and evade all the disagreeabilities others seem anxious to put on you. Nothing is so easy as to get fouled up with someone ranking a bit higher, and that is the last thing you should do, for it only defeats what one really wants best.

"Mom says I have told you at least twenty times the experience to which I refer, so I won't give it again. You have a wonderful way with all people. Just keep in mind that all you want is to complete your job, whatever it may be, and come back."

In that same letter, my father gave an appraisal of the Cape Cod cottage. By now it had been wired for electricity and the dependence upon water from a hand pump at the bottom of the hill no longer existed. The hand pump had been replaced with a deep-well electric pump, the icebox had been replaced with a refrigerator, the kerosene stove had been replaced with a propane gas stove. Dad's response to this modernization program was what I had anticipated: "I often wonder what the push-button design of modern living is doing to the nation. People rarely walk or do any of the laborious things. Perhaps compulsory universal athletic training might offset it." How prophetic his words were.

Unfortunately, my premonition, sensed in January 1952, about our never again being together in this world, was a correct assessment. On August 1, 1952, Dad died while at work in New York City. His death was unexpected by all of us. Fortunately, my brother, living in Scarsdale, was able to be with Mom. My sister and her husband, a close friend and fellow Academy classmate, immediately came east from their duty station in Texas. Their presence brought comfort to Mom, who, ever the source of strength, handled Dad's loss with grace and equanimity. I, of course, was not able to be with her.

The second of the three letters was from brother, Joe: "I don't know where to start or what to tell you. I imagine that Nancy and Mom have told you a great deal already. Mom and Sandra are wonderful and perfectly okay. I think Mom's main concern is for you. So all you have to do is to get home safely which I know you will. I think that it is wonderful that Nancy is going to live with Mom. More than anything else I want Mom to hang on to the house, because it is home to Mom and I believe that she wants so much to have a place that you and Nancy and Sandra can come to and where you can spend some time without everyone having to sleep on cots or something. I think that is important for Mom at Xmas, etc.

"Mom has been great. She hasn't broken down and I don't think that she will. She has no regrets and neither should any of us. She has always done everything for Dad and Mom knows and realizes that, as do the rest of us. Likewise, Dad had no regrets—in every sense of the meaning he had made peace with the world and had had a full life. Believe me when I say all this, we have lost something, but at the same time Dad is with us and he always will be."

And, then, are the excerpts the third letter from my mother dated August 8, 1952: "It was wonderful to have you call me (a call placed by me on an international line from Pusan, Korea to Scarsdale, New York). Be happy for Dad. As he was getting on in years it had to happen someday, and if he had been sick or restricted at home to inactivity while I was knocking myself out working at that bank he would have been miserable. He was well and happy, he didn't know what hit him. There was no premonition that morning. He beat his opponents at bridge, and he was just as alert as a man twenty years younger. He was fooling around with the elevator man going back from lunch when he just slumped over, and that was the end.

"You would be proud of Joe and Sandy, also of Jim, Helen and Nancy. They did all for me they could do. In as much as I dreaded the idea of ever losing Dad, we never approached the subject of death. Consequently, we had no plans or anything. Joe went out and arranged everything. Everybody is doing all they can for me. There were no tears on anyone's part throughout the whole procedure. We thought we owed it to each other. Now that I have gotten this far, comes the problem of what next. Tomorrow I'm going to Cape Cod for a week, with Sandy and her family. When I come back Nancy and Brucie are coming to live with me.

"I have been living in fear, but I am not afraid of anything anymore. All that I was frightened of has happened, and I feel unhappy but calm. I want you to come home safe and sound. You have a wonderful wife and a wonderful son." And then Mom concluded this letter with an explanation of the new will she was going to have drawn, and what would happen to the remnants of a very limited estate so that the interests of her three children were properly protected. How typical of both Mom and Dad to be so dedicated to the lives of their children.

THUS ENDED the life of a remarkable man, a remarkable father, and a remarkable friend. Steadfastness gives definition to who he was and what he stood for. At age seventy-eight, he still had the firm handshake and mental alacrity of a man many years his junior. When, in a combat situation one had to turn to a single individual who would not fold regardless of how dire the circumstances, regardless of what the cost may be, Dad would be the one you would want covering your flank. In Dad's absence, the family did not disintegrate. We three children still feel the great love that our mother and father had for us. Our lives were their investment, and I cannot help but feel that this investment returned many, many joyous dividends.

My brother, Joe, is commended. He is the one who stayed close to Mom and Dad while my family and Sandy's family were moving from one duty station to another, none of them close to home. It was Joe who helped liquidate Dad's literary agency on a positive note after his death, and it was Joe who continued to physically touch base with Mom on a daily basis for the several years she remained in Scarsdale prior to retiring to Brewster on Cape Cod. My mother's bravery and courage matched our father's.

All of us have and continue to love deeply, all of us have grieved deeply, but the tears we have shed were tears of joy for the love embodied in the family built around our father. Thank God for family.

Made in the USA
Las Vegas, NV
02 July 2021